SURVIVING THE COMING WAR

T0273980

SURVIVING THE COMING WAR

A Guide to Wartime Survival for Civilians

James C. Jones

Skyhorse Publishing

Skyhorse Publishing books may be purchased in bulk at special discounts for sales promotion, corporate gifts, fund-raising, or educational purposes. Special editions can also be created to specifications. For details, contact the Special Sales Department, Skyhorse Publishing, 307 West 36th Street, 11th Floor, New York, NY 10018 or info@skyhorsepublishing.com.

Skyhorse® and Skyhorse Publishing® are registered trademarks of Skyhorse Publishing, Inc.®, a Delaware corporation.

Visit our website at www.skyhorsepublishing.com.

Please follow our publisher Tony Lyons on Instagram @tonylyonsisuncertain.

10 9 8 7 6 5 4 3 2 1

Library of Congress Cataloging-in-Publication Data

Names: Jones, James C., author.
Title: Surviving the coming war : a guide to wartime survival for civilians / James C. Jones.
Description: New York : Skyhorse Publishing, 2024. | Includes index. | Summary: "A practical guide for civilians to survive the next war"-- Provided by publisher.
Identifiers: LCCN 2024025749 (print) | LCCN 2024025750 (ebook) | ISBN 9781510780736 (trade paperback) | ISBN 9781510780743 (epub)
Subjects: LCSH: Survival--Handbooks, manuals, etc. | Survival and emergency equipment--Handbooks, manuals, etc.
Classification: LCC GF86 .J6587 2024 (print) | LCC GF86 (ebook) | DDC 613.6/9--dc23/eng/20240702
LC record available at https://lccn.loc.gov/2024025749
LC ebook record available at https://lccn.loc.gov/2024025750

Cover design by Kai Texel
Cover photograph by Getty Images

Print ISBN: 978-1-5107-8073-6
Ebook ISBN: 978-1-5107-8074-3

Printed in Canada

This book is dedicated to the Massachusetts Militia, who stood against tyranny on April 19, 1776, and brought forth a nation dedicated to democracy, freedom, and opportunity for all.

CONTENTS

ABOUT THIS BOOK

I never anticipated writing another book, but world events, combined with my personal experiences and research, provided strong motivation. While I was able to draw on material from my previous books for some chapters, it was still necessary to rewrite or modify text and illustrations to apply to war survival conditions. Basic disaster survival subjects such as water purification, first aid, and food storage had to include methods that would apply to war zones, while whole new chapters, such as armed self-defense, nuclear war survival and escape and evasion, needed to be included. The size of chapters varies from a few pages to over a dozen pages, depending on the subject. Some subjects required extensive illustration and I drew on a variety of government and military manuals, as well as my own creations, where needed. In covering multiple and overlapping subjects from different perspectives, some redundancy and even repetition was unavoidable. I left out such subjects as fire starting, CPR, edible plants, etc. that are not directly related to warfare survival conditions. These subjects are covered more extensively in my other books. I wanted each chapter to stand alone and immediately provide useful knowledge to the reader. As the work progressed, I found myself covering controversial and even dangerous topics. It is difficult to create a truly useful book about war survival without touching on issues such as military tactics, resistance, and weapons. In all such cases I tried to establish justification and historic examples. My goal here is to provide the unprepared citizen with motivation and basic knowledge, while also delivering useful information and direction to preparedness practitioners as they move from disaster preparedness and self-reliance to various war survival capabilities. Throughout this book I found myself using the terms *wartime, war zone,* and *combat zone* to describe various war environments. For the purposes of this book, the following definitions apply.

- **War time:** applies to conditions during a large-scale or world war that is not directly damaging life and property withing the United States, but is affecting the economy, society, and liberty of citizens. This is comparable to the conditions during World War II, between late 1941 and late 1945, when rationing, blackouts, and air raid drills

were common in the United States even though the war was being
fought in Europe.

- **War zone:** refers to areas that are not invaded or occupied but suffer from the effects of missiles, drones, sabotage, raids, and foreign
  instigated insurgencies. Israel and the Western Ukraine are examples
  of war zones. The survival challenges to civilians in war zones require
  skill, determination, and sacrifice.
- **Combat zone:** as the name implies, refers to areas that are being con-
  tested by military forces. In addition to missiles, drones and air strikes,
  artillery, grenades, and small arms fire combine to make these areas
  extremely dangerous. This is life or death for civilians caught in the
  crossfire. The civilian must do what is necessary to escape or survive.

The first three chapters are intended to provide reason and incentive for
war preparedness. By the time this book is published, I am sure that world
events will provide further motivation for the reader. While the current major
sources of aggression and war are China, Russia, and Iran, this is not to be
interpreted as an anti-Chinese, anti-Russian, or anti-Iranian book. The people of these nations are victims of corruption and oppression. This book is
certainly not pro-war but recognizes the precursors of war and is intended
to save innocent lives and reduce injuries and destruction resulting from a
variety of war scenarios. Preparedness is the duty of every citizen, and a self-
reliant people is the foundation of a free society.

INTRODUCTION AND IMPERATIVE

The invasion of the Ukraine is merely an intermediate stage in a larger European conflict.
　　　　　—Russian General Andrey Mordvichev, September 2023

As I write this book, the federal government is initiating the first full-scale test of the emergency alert system since the Cold War. Back in those days, an alert consisted of radio messages and sirens. Today's alerts would consist of messages to wired phones and cell phones, as well as radio and television. This reminds me of 1941, the year I was born. My mother told me that the hospitals were painting white crosses on the roofs in case somehow bombers reached Chicago. At that time, events in Europe were beginning to concern Americans and by December of that year, we were plunged into a full-scale world war. The world conditions and events today closely mimic those preceding World War II. Of course, atomic weapons, hypersonic missiles, and advanced technology make the coming war far more dangerous and widespread. It is with some regret that I am forced to create a book with such an alarming title, but current events and ongoing trends obligate me to face the real potential of total war.

My previous books have focused on the application of preparedness and survival skills related to various natural and manmade disasters and emergency situations. Today, citizens face an increasing number of hazards such as uncontrolled crime, a failing economy, civil unrest, climate instability, and a variety of natural disasters that increase in frequency and severity. These also are often precursors of war. War is the ultimate disaster, consuming lives, destroying cities, and forever altering society in unpredictable ways. Survival under war time scenarios necessitates inclusion of some controversial subjects and tactics that must be addressed to aid the civilian caught in the extreme and potentially violent circumstances of war in the twenty-first century. In the creation of this book, I have established four goals that I hope will be of significant value to the reader.

1. Dispel the existing denial and complacency regarding the potential for large-scale war and provide an imperative for immediate and effective preparedness.
2. Provide comparative analysis and historical examples of how civilians have coped with wartime challenges, including overseas conflicts,

ongoing low intensity asymmetrical warfare, and the potential for actual combat in the towns and streets of America.

3. Offer predictions and recommendations for surviving a wide variety of war scenarios ranging from tough times to nuclear war on the high-tech battlefield of the twenty-first century.

4. Teach practical skills, methods, and tactics for preparedness and survival under the extreme and even violent conditions created by war.

War is the ultimate disaster and generates virtually every known form of catastrophe including severe injury, epidemics, bombings, uncontrolled fires, famine, chaos, misery, and death. I have adapted some of the material from previous books related to preparedness, first aid, sanitation, and evacuations to war time applications for this volume. While disasters such as earthquakes, and tornadoes do create war zone–like damages and injuries, such as building collapse, flying blast debris, and injuries of all kinds, these hazards would be far more severe and widespread in a bombing target or combat zone, so more extensive information has been included. The coming war may or may not escalate into conventional or nuclear drone and missile strikes against American cities, but it is necessary to prove survival information for these worst-case situations. While the mention of "resistance" or "combat skill" is often enough to invite censure and condemnation, these subjects must be included in any authentic war survival text. It must be recognized that military-like tactics and weapons may be applicable when civilians are caught in combat zones and must defend their lives and the lives of family members. In addition to self-defense tactics, I have included chapters on escape and evasion, combat movement, and camouflage techniques that might aid the civilian survivor. When applicable, I have borrowed liberally from non-copyrighted government publications, such as Cold War nuclear survival manuals, FEMA/CERT, community emergency response training manuals, and US Army survival and combat manuals.

Americans have not experienced wartime conditions since 1945 and have not seen war on this continent since 1865. Unlike the citizens of Europe and most of Asia who can remember, or whose close relatives experienced war, Americans have difficulty conceiving such an event at home. Decade after decade of comfort, security, and dependence have left us complacent, and unprepared for even a remote and low intensity world war. Much like Rome before being sacked by the Visigoths in 410 CE, we remain naïve and vulnerable as the war clouds gather and the barbarians are at the gates. It is my hope that this book in some small way can help good and responsible citizens survive whatever form the coming conflict may take and help them to remain safe and free.

CHAPTER 1

THE COMING STORM

There is no avoiding war, it can only be postponed to the advantage of others.

—Prince Niccolò Machiavelli (1469–1527)

As a longtime student of history, I can assure the reader that war, not peace, is the natural state of humanity. I was born in 1941 and have never experienced a time when multiple wars were not in progress somewhere in the world. Big wars do not end, they just split into multiple small wars, and small wars eventually coalesce into big wars again. The preconditions that lead to both World War I and World War II are manifesting once again with accelerating frequency. Unlike the past wars, the coming war will not be an external event. This war will be, and already is, a battle in our towns, streets, and homes. While Americas might and two oceans have spared the American people the horrors of battle in our own cities and fields, that protection is no longer relevant in today's world. We are no longer the strong, united, and economically mighty nation that saved the world in 1941. America has been under siege for decades, our jobs and industrial base have been savaged just as effectively as bombers did in Europe in World War II, leaving cities in ruins. Fentanyl and other drugs manufactured and pushed into our cities by foreign powers kill millions each year. Cyberattacks and scams rob our business and citizens with impunity, while taking billions from our economy. Massive enemy (China, Russia) social media operations and their paid influencers pump lies, confusion, disinformation, and division into our homes and communities. These are the ways that the war has already begun. American citizens face a constantly declining standard of living, growing trends of crime and violence, and exactly the conditions that inevitably led to wars in the past. The current war in Ukraine is a precursor of what every American will face within the next ten years or fewer. While Europeans and Asians have some level of understanding and psychological preparedness for war at home, the majority of Americans have never experienced true war, given that the last true war fought on American soil was the Civil War of 1861 to 1865. The concept of a total war with enemy bombs and even enemy raids or guerrilla warfare in our cities and towns seems unthinkable, yet such events are not only possible but probable. It is difficult to predict exactly how a twenty-first century total war will manifest itself, but it will be a war of national and ideological survival between the totalitarian collectivism of China and Russia and the democratic freedom-loving nations of Europe, Southeast Asia, and America. Technology, space, and artificial intelligence will add new dimensions and new horrors to the battles to come. The war will be total, but it may be limited or unlimited in some ways. Regardless of geographic factors, it will bring challenges, hardship, and violence to every American. Although it may seem to be a conflict in terms, the war will be "total" in terms of methods and tactics, but it may or may not be limited in the application of force and weaponry.

LIMITED TOTAL WAR

> *Fear is a reaction; courage is a decision.*
> —*Winston Churchill (1874–1965)*

A limited total war would involve all aspects of traditional and asymmetric warfare without actual invasion, or massive bombing and destruction. In fact, China and Russia have been waging asymmetric warfare against America and Americans for decades. While symmetric or traditional war involves one nation's military force fighting the other nation's military force, asymmetric warfare involves one nation's military force waging war against the other's non-military, domestic, and economic institutions, and civilian morale. The Chinese have decimated or industrial capacity, ruined our economy, and sown division and confusion in our society. They have used drugs including fentanyl to kill millions of our citizens, and massive social media campaigns to divide and demoralize our society. They have manipulated the American mind into focusing on the past and petty differences, while they grow stronger every year. While America was hailed as "the arsenal of democracy" in 1941, China is now the arsenal of despotism for the twenty first century. The asymmetric warfare attacks below are already in progress, or soon will be, as hostilities grow in intensity.

- **Economic warfare**: China has reduced America to a third-rate industrial power through underhand dealings and currency manipulation. They have put us deeply in debt while using our money to build the world's largest navy and army. While we fought a long war in Afghanistan, China simply bribed the Afghan military leaders that we trained to surrender once we left.

- **Psychological warfare**: China, Russia, and other enemies of freedom use the internet, social media, and front organizations to foster hate, confusion, and division in our society. They have succeeded in making patriotism, pride, and hope for the future a rarity.
- **Cyber warfare**: Both China and Russia have devoted huge resources to cyber warfare operations, including creating millions of false social media sources, data mining our civilian, military, and government organizations, and establishing potential control of the electric grid, water supply, medical facilities, transportation network, and other critical infrastructure.
- **Chemical and biological warfare**: Much of the drugs coming into our streets through South America are sourced in China. Fentanyl is a Chinese product. While COVID-19 may have been an accident, it still helped China. China now owns a considerable number of American food processing companies and agricultural corporations.
- **Guerillas in our midst**: While the inevitable military combat may take place in foreign lands, on the seas, and in space, we can expect raids, drone attacks, sabotage, and the use of domestic based guerillas and civil disorder in our streets as hostilities spread.

If the above methods continue unopposed and succeed, America will be relegated to a third-world nation (the signs are already here) beholden to dominant foreign authoritarian states. There will be no safe, free place for American "refugees" to go.

UNLIMITED TOTAL WAR

War is hell, you cannot refine it.
—General William Tecumseh Sherman (1820–91)

While foreign invasion is improbable in the US, it is possible that foreign manipulation could create guerilla warfare forces or even well supplied rebel armies on America soil. These could then "invite" foreign troops or mercenaries to support them. This could even bring the "Red Dawn"* scenario to our hometowns and fields. While large numbers of uniformed foreign troops would probably unify resistance, the use of collaborators and domestic

---

*   *Red Dawn* was a movie featuring Patrick Swayze made in 1984. The film portrayed a communist invasion launched from South America and a resistance group called the Wolverines. Live Free USA conducted several training events based on this scenario that include a group of fully uniformed mock Russian troops. A remake was released in 2012.

mercenaries to create civil war is a real possibility. In any conflict, the possibility of massive conventional warfare or even a nuclear attack cannot be ignored. The events in Ukraine should serve as a warning. Modern drones and hypersonic missiles can strike anywhere at any time. Back in the 1970s and 1980s, survival groups focused on training for nuclear survival and Red Dawn-style civilian combat and resistance. These were popular and accepted survival education necessities that need to be revived and upgraded promptly.

SURVIVING WAR

Wherefore the citizens ought to practice war not in time of war, but rather while they are at peace. And every city which has any sense should take the field at least one day in every month having no regard for winter cold or summer heat and they should go out in masses, including their wives and their children . . . and they should have tournaments imitating in as lively a manner as they can, real battles.

—Plato, 360 BCE

Ultimately there are just three methods of surviving in war: run, hide, or fight (or a combination of these). If the war comes to American streets there is no place to run to, and with modern methods of surveillance hiding cannot last indefinitely. You should be able to run for a while and hide for a while, but eventually you are going to have to surrender, die, or fight. A limited overseas war like World War II will involve severe shortages, rationing, curfews, mass evacuations, and possibly martial law. Since most of us couldn't even handle a few rules and inconveniences during the COVID-19 pandemic, it is difficult to image these procedures not degenerating into civil disorder and chaos. In 1941 Americans turned *to* each other in the face of aggression, but now we seem more likely to turn *on* each other. If so, this will guarantee defeat and oppression. Surviving a war is the "gravest extreme" scenario requiring the highest levels of preparedness, training, organization, and dedication.

- Training for war survival must include all the basic survival subjects such as first aid, water purification, foraging, self-defense, firefighting, navigation, and shelter building, but more emphasis must be placed on combat, tactics, evasion and escape, communications, and advanced medical skills.
- Preparedness must include planning for escape, evasion, evacuation, and combat under war conditions. Even greater amounts of food, medical supplies, weapons, camouflage, and ammunition will be

necessary. Remote and well-hidden supply caches will be a essential, as will be places to hide valuables.

- Ultimately, resistance and survival organizations will develop, as will criminal and depraved gangs. Being part of a well-prepared and organized group of responsible citizens before the winds of war envelop your community will give you, and your family, a fighting chance to stay safe and free through these extremely dangerous times.

PREPAREDNESS AND SURVIVAL

Si vis Pacem fac bellum. (If you want peace prepare for war).
—Roman General Publius Flavius, 4th century AD

Your humble author would suggest that you will get a war anyway, but if you prepare for it, you are far more likely to survive it. While disaster preparedness has driven the survival self-reliance movement in recent years, war preparedness must be the driving priority whether it is fought primarily overseas or on home ground. Surviving the war will require survival preparations and skill greater than those needed for any other form of disaster. As we see in Ukraine, this war could grind on for years or decades and no one and no place will be free of damage, violence, and struggle. "Anticipate" is the first principle of survival. Denial is the first step towards disaster.

"This solidifies that we have entered a new era of authoritarian aggression."
—Alaska Senator Dan Sullivan responding to a joint Russian-Chinese eleven-ship taskforce off the coast of Alaska in July 2023

CHAPTER 2

THE WAR THAT'S HERE AND NOW

War is cruelty. There is no use trying to refine it. You might as well appeal against the thunderstorm as against these terrible hardships of war.
—General William Tecumseh Sherman (1820–91)

The title of this book may be misleading. The war is not coming, it is already here. It started with a click on a computer keyboard or maybe multiple clicks decades ago in China or Russia. China has 50,000 to 100,000 hackers managed by the Ministry of State Security and the Ministry of Public Security dedicated to penetrating every US government and private corporations' data bases and operating systems. Russian Unit 74455 is dedicated to attacking Americas infrastructure and planting malware. Russian Unit 54777 operates as part of the "Special Service Center" of the GRU's psychological operations to plant disinformation and divisiveness on social media. Unit 26165 is devoted to attacking American government and political organizations. Even Iran's "Immortals" and APT33 group engage in continuous cyber warfare attacks on America. In addition, these hostile countries host and sponsor hundreds of "private" proxy hacker organizations that engage in internet scams, date theft, malware distribution, and ransomware attacks against American hospitals, towns, business, and individuals. These acts of war drain hundreds of billions from the American budget that could be used to build our military, feed and house our homeless, and repair our infrastructure.

ASYMMETRIC WARFARE

Cyber warfare is just one element of the ongoing assault on our economy, our freedom, and ultimately on our capacity to survive. While most Americans think that we are at peace, we have been the target of asymmetric warfare for several decades. The term "asymmetric warfare" has become common in the post–Cold War era. It refers to warfare where the opposing sides use completely different tactics and weapons. Until recently, most warfare was mainly symmetrical. For example, during World War II, it was the Japanese Navy vs the US Navy and the German Army vs. the Allied Armies. In modern asymmetrical warfare, the opposing forces use non-opposing tactics and weapons. For example, The North Vietnams Army lost the battles against the US military but won the war by undermining America's will through media manipulation and street demonstrations staged by front organizations. Russia and China (among others) have been using various asymmetrical methods against the American economy, political system, and military strength for decades. In most cases, it's a war against our civilians and our society. The enemy cannot match our military forces, but they can drag down our economy, divide our population, and create chaos in our cities and towns. While America focuses on social issues, the next election and quarterly profit margins, our enemies engage in long-term operations to destroy America and institute world domination of collectivist totalitarianism.

The first of my Ten Principles of Survival is "Anticipate," and the second one is "Be Aware," so if you hope to survive in the twenty-first century and make preparations based on accurate information, you have to *anticipate* that your life and freedom will be constantly assaulted from every direction and *be aware* of the sources of disinformation, misinformation, and covert assault coming from the enemies of self-reliance and liberty. Everything you see, buy, think, or do can and is being used as a weapon to mislead, confuse, divide, and create chaos in the free world, by Russia, China, and other hostile states and organizations. In addition to cyberattacks, and social media disinformation, we now see food, fuel, international law, and economic weapons applied by both sides. While China has wisely chosen to pretend neutrality, it has eagerly deployed over 170 false social media "influencers" personas to spread pro-Russian disinformation and muddy the waters in support of Russian aggression.

Military War: While traditional army-against-army wars are still happening, they are (as Russia is learning) very dangerous and costly operations. Russia was able to gain control of the Crimea and some parts of the Don River valley through the use of proxies and mercenaries. Mercenary organizations have become big business. The US used Blackwater and several other private security organizations in Iraq and in Afghanistan, but Russia and China have used such organizations without acknowledging their connections. Russia created the Wagner Group and has utilized them extensively in Africa and the Ukraine. Paid assassins have been utilized by North Korea and Russia. So, what may seem to be a local terrorist or insurgent action is frequently a paid military action by a foreign power.

Surrogate Warfare: Back in the Cold War days, the Communist Party of the United States was the primary tool of the Soviet Union, but today the internet and social media are used to generate and support front groups and highjack social movements to generate hate and conflict in free world nations. So-called peace groups, and "social activists" are often (not always) funded and led by those seeking to prevent resistance to foreign aggression and oppression or to just weaken society.

Cyber Warfare: Hostile nations have huge departments devoted to developing and utilizing the internet to insert malware into our vital infrastructure. Recently Russia attempted to shut down the Ukrainian electrical grid but was thwarted by American cyber defense efforts. While Russia disavowed involvement in the recent oil pipeline shutdown, it was traced to a criminal hacking group in Russia. In many cases malware has probably already been inserted into critical systems such as power, gas, communications, and transportation systems, just waiting to be activated by an enemy state. The US, China, and Russia all have their own GPS satellite system. GPS is used to direct ships, planes, missiles, drones, and virtually all commercial transportation. These satellites can be disabled electronically or physically destroyed in orbit. While the military may have some redundance and backup systems, most civilian organizations do not. Many of us may be back to map and compass, dead reckoning, and radio direction. If war goes into space, the impact on everything on the ground will likely be catastrophic. It is difficult to determine how extensive this cyber sabotage network is, but the wise would-be survivor should not depend on any part of the grid, or emergency response systems functioning, if a true cyber war develops.

Narrative Warfare: Wars can be won by simply controlling the narrative of what the war is about. During the Vietnam War, the communists managed to sell the idea that America was the aggressor and was committing atrocities. The media ignored the stories of the communists massacring civilians, and of American acts of courage and compassion. The so-called Tet Offensive was sold as a defeat when in fact the US Army crushed the Vietcong, routed the North Vietnamese and at no time did the South Vietnamese people rise up against the current régime in favor of the communists, yet we withdrew because the narrative was inverted. This kind of thing is happening today as well. Well-crafted narratives can make friends into enemies and victories into defeats. The urban crime problem is portrayed as a gun issue instead of a drug cartel and gang issue. The border problems are made to be a racial migration issue instead of a South American political and crime issue. Any criticism of what China does is turned into a racial issue when it is really an issue of Chinese Communist Party–initiated oppression and aggression.

Economic Warfare: The Russian invasion of the Ukraine exposed the full-scale economic warfare that has been simmering for decades. While the United States remains in a good position to wage this kind of war against Russia, but like any kind of war, it will still cause casualties at home. If China elects to invade Taiwan and/or assert control over the South China Sea, the United States has no way to wage economic war in response. In fact, China could bring down the US economy due to our massive debt and dependence on China for just about everything we use. In addition, China has achieved equality, if not superiority, in naval and air power in the Pacific. In war, the biggest economy always wins.

Social Media: Social media is (in my view) the biggest threat to life and freedom since the atomic bomb. It has caused thousands of deaths due to disinformation, and promoted hate, crime, and division throughout the free world. So-called "social influencers" get paid more for spreading lies and controversy than for being logical and helpful. A recent study shows that a falsehood is spread through Facebook and Twitter fifteen times faster than a fact. Not only have China and Russia created thousands of artificial personae and influencers, but their bots pick up hateful and divisive posts and repost them thousands of times. A recent internet symposium in Europe started by showing a video of what looked like Hillary Clinton having sex with Vladimir Putin to demonstrate how "deepfake" videos can be created and used on social media. Believe none of what you hear and little of what you see, or better yet just stay off social media.

Lobbyist and Influencers: While lobbyists have always been a problem in Washington, foreign powers are able to influence our legislators in ways that damage our national economy, national security, and individual liberties. Foreign lobbyists are required to register as such, but since China has infiltrated so many American businesses, they can control how these lobbyists act as well. Your government representative may not be representing you at all.

Business Food, Fuel, and Trade: China has bought into many of America's essential economic institutions, including vast amounts of cropland, farms, food processing, shipping, technology, medical care, education, and even security. They can reach out and intimidate corporations and local government offering loans and "free" stuff or threatening to withdraw funding if cooperation is not forthcoming. They even forced Disney to modify various films by threatening to ban them from the vast Chinese market. China has bought into every facet of the American economy, including partial or controlling interest in General Electric, General Motors, Ford, Uber, Hilton,

Fisher-Price, Motorola, Craftsman tools, Black and Decker, F&G Life, John Hancock Life, Campbell's Soup and hundreds more. War with China will be the supply chain nightmare on steroids and an economic catastrophe for every American. The Ukraine has one of the world's largest supplies of uranium and is the source of about 30 percent of the world's grain. The war has already guaranteed that thousands in the third world will starve, and food prices will skyrocket, but if their Black Sea ports (Odessa and Mariupol) are cut off, millions may starve. Russia is using fuel as a weapon to intimidate Europe and there is no doubt that many will experience hardships. As Americans experience higher and higher prices and a lower quality of life, they are casualties of the ongoing war The whole world economy is at a tipping point.

Criminal Gangs: Crime and drug cartels are now interwoven into international political warfare. The CIA has often been implicated in using Mafia connections to do dirty work (often referred to as "wet work") in foreign nations. The Russian Mafia and various Chinese crime syndicates work with their government security agencies to spread drugs, counterfeit goods, and counterfeit money in free world countries in exchange for being ignored or even protected. Massive internet phishing scams, hacking, data theft, and ransomware operations that siphon billions from free world citizens and corporations are encouraged and protected by Chinese, Russian, and Iranian agencies. Drug cartels importing drugs into the United States from China and the Middle East use inner-city youth as non-state soldiers in their war on freedom. Much of the drug related crime, poverty, and deaths in the urban communities is a direct but deniable result of asymmetric warfare.

THE AGE OF TOTAL WAR

The wise prepper or survivalist should anticipate the impact of this age of total war, and be aware of how everything they see, hear, buy, or use is impacted by it. We all live in a combat zone, and you are both victim and combatant. While this stage of the war is less violent and obviously destructive as traditional, symmetrical warfare, it still destroys lives, creates misery, and inhibits progress and freedom. Moreover, there is no way to deescalate this conflict short of surrender and compliance with aggressive authoritarians. Escalation towards actual military combat is already underway and will accelerate. Whether this combat will spread to our streets and fields or even initiate nuclear conflicts remains to be seen. We can only prepare for the worst and hope for anything not the worst.

CHAPTER 3

HARD TIMES AND HAZARDS

Even if the coming war is confined to battles fought on foreign soil and at sea, the survival challenges for civilians in America will be unlike anything experienced by previous generations. The wars in Korea (1950–53) Vietnam (1954–75), or Afghanistan (2002–14) had little impact on civilian life in the US. Not to minimize the sacrifice and heroism of those involved, but these were minuscule events compared to the massive conflict that is developing throughout the world. The last time American civilians experienced the effects of a world war was from 1941 through 1945. In those times America was by far the greatest industrial power on earth with a massive economy, a huge skilled workforce, and great untapped resources. Throughout World War II we faced off against Germany, Italy, and Japan, all of which had far smaller populations, and productive capacities. America's geographic location prevented any significant kinetic assaults against our populations and our towns. While war raged and cities burned in Europe and Asia, Americans went about the business of manufacturing weapons for our military and our allies. While the Japanese attack on Pearl Harbor in December 1941 sank six battleships, American ship production by late 1942 could replace that tonnage in two days. Throughout the war, Americans supplied guns, ships, tanks, trucks, and aircraft for our forces, as well as for Great Britain, and the USSR. Today, China manufactures over 90 percent of the world steel, and the USA has fewer than six major shipyards and one tank factory. America has not won a war since 1945 and history tells us that the biggest, most productive economy always wins wars.

Past generations were tough. They had experienced the Great Depression, they or their parents came from the farms and frontiers, and most of them were accustomed to hard physical work and doing without most comforts that we take for granted. When war came, "the greatest generation" put aside their differences and united. Not only did virtually every family send loved ones to fight and die to defend our land and our freedom, but everyone also sacrificed and tolerated shortages and inconveniences to support the cause. The recent pandemic exposed the inability of today's population to tolerate even a few, short-term minor inconveniences. Instead of uniting and turning to each other for support, we protested, rioted, looted, and turned *on* each other. Our enemies have certainly noted this weakness and are encouraged to be more aggressive and use social media even more effectively in the war to come.

CHALLENGES ON THE HOME FRONT

World War II generated several challenges and hazards for civilians that will certainly be experienced again even if the actual fighting does not reach our streets.

Rationing

In order to meet the needs of the military and support our allies, the US government initiated rationing of certain war-critical materials starting in 1942. Among the rationed items were gasoline, tires, shoes, coffee, sugar, nylon, fuel oil, lard, meat, butter, coal, and batteries. Gasoline was limited to just three to four gallons per week. Considering the poor milage of automotive engines in those days, this greatly curtailed civilian self-transportation. Of course, trucks, buses, ambulances, and other essential services had much more generous allotments. Lending, trading, or transferring ration stamps was illegal, but cheating was prevalent, and regulations were difficult to enforce. Violations of rationing were so common that special courts had to be established. Rationing in the age of computers and the internet would be entirely different from what it was in the 1940s. Rationing would be much more pervasive and almost impossible to avoid. Detection of violation and enforcement would be facilitated by modern computer algorithms, artificial intelligence monitoring and anomalies in purchasing behavior. For example, not using credits to purchase certain items would trigger an investigation into potential black-market activities or hoarding. The ration stamps of the past would undoubtedly be replaced by a debit card of some kind. In fact, a debit card rationing system already exists for welfare recipients and could easily be expanded to the general population, perhaps replacing cash altogether and initiating total economic control.

Shortages

In 1941, America produced virtually all of our own vehicles, appliances, tools, clothing, and food. Shortages were not due to a lack of these items, but the need to divert production to weapons and war supplies. No civilian automobiles were available from 1942 through 1945. No refrigerators, vacuum cleaners, washing machines, or other major appliances were available

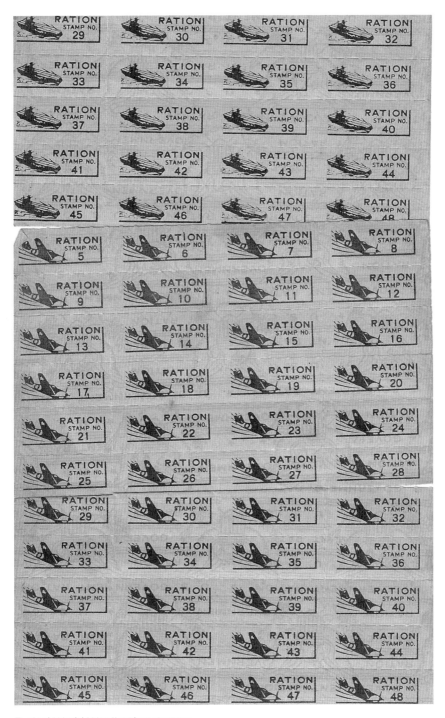

Typical World War II ration stamps.

throughout the war. Many things that were available were made with inferior materials. Toys were made with so-called "pot metal" or wood. Paper for school children was of such a low grade that you could actually find wood chips in it, and it would break if folded. Meat, sugar, alcohol, tires, gasoline, motor oil, and other essential supplies were either unavailable, unaffordable, or rationed. In today's global economy. many essential goods are produced overseas and much of what we need is created, controlled, and shipped by our potential enemies. The so-called supply chain on which we depend would simply disappear, and shortages of even domestic supplies would be exacerbated by cyberattacks, hijacking, and civil disorder. A considerable number of life critical medications are manufactured overseas and will be in short supply during wartime. Many of these are perishable and cannot be stored. Stock up on those that can keep. Be aware that the so-called "expiration dates" are arbitrary. Many medications can be stored and used for years if kept sealed, cool, and dry. If you don't have critical (food, medicine, fuel, etc.) supplies stocked away or you have not figured out alternative sources before the war develops, your very survival will be in jeopardy.

Hoarding and the Black Market

Shortages and rationing will inevitably lead to the creation of a thriving black market and hoarding of restricted goods. A so-called "grey market" already exists. The grey market refers to goods and services provided and traded outside of the regulated and taxed economy. Garden vegetables, haircuts, auto repair, daycare services, and a wide variety of "off the books" transactions go on daily. As the base economy continues to decline, this grey market will expand. Once severe regulation and shortages develop, a true black market will emerge. A black-market trade in stolen or smuggled goods and illegal services always involves criminals and intimidation. Inevitably the black market will attempt to suppress or control the grey market with violence and "protection" schemes. In a controlled economy, the black market becomes the dominant economy. Vladimir Putin's oligarchs are the direct successors of the black market that existed under the old communist USSR. Only a well-armed and organized underground economy will be able to provide needed goods and services without being subject to corruption, profiteering, and the criminal element. Stocking up on life critical supplies, acquiring tools and skills to provide goods and services to yourself and others, and preparing to survive in a black-market economy will be important survival skills.

Inflation

When the supply chain fails, and most goods become hard to get, runaway inflation will be inevitable. Without supplies from China, our massive debt will probably result in a complete economic collapse. This is already in progress. The dollar will be worth a few pennies, savings accounts, annuities, and retirement accounts will lose most or all their value and Social Security checks (if they are issued) will be hardly enough for a few loaves of bread. Gold, silver, and diamonds will retain some theoretical value, but who will part with food, medicine, or fuel for things that can't feed you or keep you warm? As one Russian woman put it during the siege of Leningrad in 1942: "Is good to have diamond necklace, is better to have toilet paper." Hard goods, such as food, fuel, medicine, tools, weapons, ammunition, etc. will be the currency of hard times.

Scrap Drives
Even though America had plenty of steel production capacity during World War Two there were scrap metal drives because steel can be manufactured faster from scrap metal than from iron ore. Boy Scouts and other organizations collected scrap metal, paper, and other critical materials throughout their communities to help the war effort. Sadly, America cannot manufacture enough steel for a sustained war. Scrap drives, and even forced confiscation of metals and other material may be expected. I remember that most automobiles had their bumpers removed for the valuable chromium.

Blackouts and Power Outages
Although neither Germany nor Japan had bombers that could reach the USA, blackouts were common throughout most of the war. Blackouts were more commonly enforced on the east coast because cargo ships would be silhouetted by city lights as targets for German U-boats. Blackout curtains or just blankets over windows reduced lighting. Automobile headlights had shades. Air raid wardens patrolled and enforced blackout rules. Modern missiles and satellites make trying to hide a city with deliberate blackouts pointless, but we still may find ourselves in the dark. Government regulations have rendered our power grid fragile and vulnerable. Heatwaves and cold snaps are already causing frequent grid failures, and a few well-placed bullets into transformers have demonstrated the ease with which terrorist can cause regional blackouts. Cyberattacks have already come close to not only causing blackouts but damaging generators and the power grid. It has been postulated that China and other enemies may have already planted malware in our power, fuel, and transportation systems, awaiting activation in the event of a war. Electromagnetic pulse weapons could knock out the grid and damage every electronic device not shielded. As we have seen in the Ukrainian war, power stations are high priority targets for air strikes, missiles, and drones. Power stations, solar farms, and wind farms are virtually indefensible against

terrorist, guerrilla, and any form of arial attack. Whatever you depend on electricity for, prepare to do without it, possibly for weeks or months. Once the lights go out, chaos will reign. It is estimated that up to 90 percent of urban populations would perish from primary or secondary effects of a prolonged loss of electrical power.

Censorship and Information Control

Of course, back during World War II we only had mail, the wired telephone, and newspapers. One cannot fault the military for heavily censoring information that, if revealed, would cost American lives. While the press back then was more patriotic and self-censored, some information leaks almost cost us the war. The fact is that Russia, China, Iran, and other despotic nations unapologetically control the press, social media, and all other sources of information while feeding disinformation to their own populations and to the citizens of nations where freedom of information is valued and unregulated. As the war develops, we can expect increasing efforts to regulate information by our own government and increasing efforts by hostile nations to feed lies, disinformation, and confusion into our digital and print media. At some point, military action or governmental initiatives may shut down social media entirely and severely restrict radio, television, and press communications. There is already an international war going on for control of many of our information sources. The wise citizen would do well to avoid dependency on social media or one source for guidance. Books, person-to-person communications, and the use of various amateur radio news may be better options. Neighborhood networks and even local newsletters may come back. Remember, as California Senator Hiram W. Johnson declared in 1917: "The first casualty when war comes is truth."

The Draft

Past wars were dependent on large numbers of available manpower. Massive armies supported by massive industrial production were necessary to compensate for massive casualties and massive destruction. Today the United States military depends entirely on voluntary enlistment, but this may not be adequate to cope with enemies whose whole populations are militarized. Decades of civilian complacency and government budget cuts have degraded the combat potential of every military service. Critical shortages of trained officers, technicians, and tactical personnel cannot be filled by reserves. While the draft-eligible citizens of past generations tended to be healthy, the majority of adults aged eighteen to thirty today will not be qualified to serve. Obesity, criminal records, poor health, drug addiction, and failure to meet the basic educational requirements would eliminate over 50 percent of potential draftees. While conscription for World War II started before the war reached America and the military continued to conscript, train, and field soldiers till the war ended, the coming war might well be over before a single draftee gets to camp. Still, it might be prudent to consider how a family might survive under wartime conditions if their key members are conscripted for service.

Civil Defense Drills

During World War II and the Cold War, schools, factories, and public buildings conducted "air raid drills," during which everyone would take cover in place (duck and cover) or go to a designated "bomb shelter" or later "fallout shelter." More intensive drills were limited to civil defense and emergency response organizations. Federally supported, volunteer Civilian Emergency Response Teams (CERTs) exist in some locations, but training is limited to natural disasters. More intensive and inclusive drills, and civilian training focusing on conventional and nuclear attack scenarios could be initiated but may come too late for today's fast-moving developments.

Such signs were common when Civil Defense focused on the potential for nuclear war.

Home Guards and Militias

In response to the impending invasion in 1939, the British government created the Home Guard. Great Britian's tradition of civilian disarmament and dependence on the state for protection resulted in a Home Guard armed with old shotguns and pitchforks. *The Home Guard Fieldcraft Manual* (I have a copy) focuses on camouflage, movement, observation, communication, and concealment rather than actual resistance and fighting, since few citizens had access to firearms. The book *Total Resistance* by Swiss Major H. von Dach Bern (Panther Publications, 1965)* was written for Switzerland's planned resistance to any invasion, and includes sabotage, ambushes, and other tactical operations. Twenty-three US states have legally authorized militias or more commonly called State Defense Forces that are outside of federal control. The broad definition of militia is an able-bodied resident between a certain age, eligible to be called forth in an

---

*   Panther Publications was a publishing house that specialized military and survival texts. It ceased operations in 2015.

emergency, but individuals have no legal right to activate themselves as a militia. In the event of an invasion, massive bombing, or the breakdown of order, states and even the federal government might choose to expand existing SDF/militias and/or recognize citizen militias to act to restore order, provide safety, and resist foreign and domestic military activity. Federal and state leadership and guidance will be important to avoid the proliferation of extremist and criminal militia gangs. In many states even military-like training is illegal, leaving America in much the same situation as, but better armed than, Britan in the 1940s. Militias could be either a great help or a great threat during the chaos of wartime, even if no actual foreign invasion or victory materializes.

Concentration Camps

There have been conspiracy theories and rumors about government plans to put various groups into camps for decades. While most, if not all these stories have been debunked, it is not out of the question that a paranoid or extremist government could enact some form of unconstitutional concentration camp or "relocation" program in the name of national security. Loyal Japanese citizens were carted off to such camps in the national paranoia of 1941, so the precedent exists. In tough times people who planned, hoarded supplies, or otherwise prepared better than their neighbors, are often seen as the enemy. Survivalists and the self-reliant can be seen or portrayed as uncooperative or even unpatriotic by a desperate and paranoid population. Confiscation and mass incarceration may not be as unlikely as some might think. In the Soviet Union and Germany, it was easier to round up unarmed and unorganized citizens than it would be in America. Of course, if a war is lost the victorious foreign power could demand that certain groups be rounded up in the name of public safety. Every freedom-loving American should remember Angela Davis's famous quote, "If they come for me in the morning, they will come for you in the night."

Forced Labor

Forced labor was initiated by many nations during World War II. In some cases, forced labor was disguised as labor or job creation programs. The citizens of conquered nations were simply carted off to the factories and fields to work for their conquerors. So, the difference during World War II was "work or go hungry" or "work or die." A prepared citizen with some level of self-reliance and skill may retain freedom of choice if democracy survives, and still have the ability to escape and resist in the gravest extreme if there is no alternative.

Martial Law and Restrictions

The dictionary definition of martial law is the replacement of civilian government by military rule and the suspension of civilian legal processes for military powers. Martial law can continue for a specified amount of time or indefinitely, and standard civil liberties may be suspended for as long as martial law continues. Martial law has been instituted in the United States only for limited times in specific regions. It was never initiated World War II and is unlikely to be initiated unless (1) a full nuclear exchange devastates major cities and infrastructure (2) a truly massive epidemic or cyberattack results in complete failure of the grid and/or civil order. It could happen. Any less obvious justification for such oppressive measures would result in resistance or more chaos from an armed population. Of course, martial law could very well be used in local or regional situations to protect property and maintain safety if looting or civil disorder develops during wartime.

Travel may also be restricted for various reasons. The old World War II phrase "Are your papers in order?" may be revisited on American roads. Trade and barter, and other self-reliance practices could very well be regulated or prohibited in a controlled economy. Radios were confiscated in occupied Europe during World War II. Radio Free Europe and the availability of Western video tapes and publications did much to bring down the Soviet Union. China and Russia strictly control all forms of communications within their borders. There is no doubt that "voluntary" and enforced censorship will be a part of life during war. Of course, if America loses the war, all of our information will be strictly controlled by the Orwellian edicts of authoritarians.

Raids and Infiltration

It is not at all beyond the realm of possibility that an enemy could insert military personnel into America cities to commit acts of sabotage or raids. Even a few such incidents would generate panic, paranoia, and terror. Our open borders and vast coastlines make it impossible to prevent such infiltrations. It is common practice even today for "special operations teams" from the US and other nations to conduct operations on foreign soil. These are, in fact, acts of war going on in a time of peace. China in particular uses "agents" to force Chinese-Americans to do their bidding through threats to harm relatives in China. Russia is notorious for planting so-called "sleeper agents" in American towns and cities. Who knows what mischief and mayhem these enemies in disguise may initiate once a war breaks out.

CHAPTER 4

COLLAPSE AND CHAOS

The coming war is not your grandfather's war. World War II and all of the regional conflicts and "police actions" have been fought with conventional weapons and tactics. These have been largely symmetrical wars where one opposing army, navy and air force fought the other army, navy and air force. Even in so-called guerrilla warfare or insurgency, the primary struggles involved military or paramilitary forces using guns and explosives. The term "asymmetric warfare" has become common in the post–Cold War era. It refers to warfare where the opposing sides use completely different tactics and weapons. Russia and China among other have been using various non-symmetrical methods against the American economy, political system, and military strength for decades. In most cases it's a war against our civilians and our society. At the beginning of World War II, America had the greatest production capacity and the most productive labor force in the world. At that time America was able to fight a ground war in Europe and a naval war in the Pacific while supplying England and the Soviet Union with millions of tanks, trucks, and planes. The outcome of this symmetrical conflict was preordained by our sheer economic power. The free world holds none of those advantages today. While our geographic distance and military power shielded our civilian population from the direct impact of World War II, today's global economy and technological entanglement will make World War III in any form a disaster of epic proportions for civilians. Our open society and technological dependency have permitted China to devastate our economy, infiltrate our institutions, and penetrate the systems that control our transportation, banking, communication, information, health, and emergency response systems. Even our survival and self-reliance equipment is usually made in China.

Free-world societies in the developed world have largely unregulated and poorly protected electrical, internet, cellular, and communications networks. Closed and oppressive societies such as China, Russia, and Iran employ whole agencies with thousands of employees to utilize these systems to infiltrate the minds and mislead the people of the free world while tightly regulating their own systems and isolating their populations from truth. Technologically speaking, the enemy is not at the gate, the enemy is in your living room. As hostilities increase and the stealthy asymmetrical war becomes a true symmetrical war both technologically and militarily, the technology that we have all come to depend on will be a target for open attack. During World War II the enemy could not turn off our telephones, shut down our radios, steal our bank accounts, misdirect our transportation, harm our health, or close our life critical establishments. As World War III develops, most or all the technology we now depend on will be attacked and rendered unreliable or completely nonfunctional. This could happen suddenly or gradually. Given that free societies and free economies are far more dependent and vulnerable than controlled and defended totalitarian regimes, those regimes may use the threat of economic or technological disablement to intimidate America or our allies into compliance with demands. Any modern surrender would include enemy access to our surveillance systems, government records, and citizens' information. Without a shot being fired civilians could experience a technological occupation far more effective than that of the Nazi SS or Soviet KGB. Even without a nuclear war or the application of electromagnetic pulse weapons, the weaponization and targeting of electronics and technology in the coming war will guarantee a period of total chaos and a collapse of critical systems.

Banking Accounts and Finances

China already has the capacity to cripple what's left of the American economy. We can expect them to start calling in our debts, intimidating our banks and businesses, and withholding all the production that we depend on. Since most of the world's wealth exists only in digital form, any kind of technological or military conflict could simply disappear your savings. The banking system is already weaponized. In wartime, banks could be closed, nationalized, or cyber-seized. This alone would probably result in massive civil unrest, and the initiation of martial law. Retirement accounts, pensions, IRAs, CDs, and all other financial products would be unavailable or drastically devalued. Any impending conflict could generate a run on the banks as people attempt to get their cash out while they can. The effect on the value of cash-in-hand by a war is difficult to predict, but certainly better than nothing on hand. While keeping large amounts of cash at home is not advisable, a few thousand dollars' worth of cash in small bills is advised by most preparedness advocates. The less cash-dependent you are, the better. Hard goods, tradable skills, and alternative trade goods will help survive in a disaster economy.

Credit Cards and Purchasing

During World War II the government instituted strict rationing of critical goods. Campaigns to sell "war bonds" and encourage thrift were universal and spending was considered unpatriotic. In modern wartimes, the government can simply outlaw the use of cash and control everyone's credit card. Through this method they can easily regulate how much and what you buy. Of course, a hostile state could infiltrate or cripple the banking system and disable all credit cards. As war approaches, don't depend on your credit limit as available funds to stock up on supplies.

Online Business

During World War II the enemy had no means of affecting the citizens' day-to-day purchasing and business activities. The modern global economy renders most business dependent on foreign trade, foreign products, and even foreign investments to survive. Even many "American" brands are wholly or partially controlled by foreign and often hostile foreign entities. In addition, a major portion of the American business economy depends on online sales and delivery services, all of which are likely to be impacted or disabled as hostilities increase. Both vendors and customers must anticipate and prepare for a massive disruption in businesses.

Electronic Communications

Internet services, email systems, and social media all will be affected and vulnerable to infiltration, attack, and disablement as warfare develops. These communications are currently a primary source of intelligence gathering by hostile nations. Seemingly benign communications are culled, analyzed, and used by artificial intelligence to recognize patterns and predict actions. Social media is a primary weapon of China and Russia to wage war on America even now through false flag influencers. The internet as we know it may be subject to cyberattacks and disabled, or it may be left to serve as a battlefield. If it stays operational it will be because it's a useful weapon of war. The user should be aware of this and act accordingly.

Cellular Services

Cell phones have become ubiquitous in modern society, but this dependency creates a serious risk to personal security in wartime. China's president, Xi Jinping, has stated that "technology is the sharp sword of the modern state" and carrying a cellphone is required by law in order to track and control every citizen. Cell phone dependency and addiction have become a public health issue in America and have caused considerable harm to the younger population. There is little doubt that these systems will be the first targets of exploitation and probable disablement during any kind of war. While they are highly useful, peacetime appliances becoming dependent on them and not developing alternatives puts the individual, business, and society at risk.

GPS and Satellite Dependent Systems

Probably the first evolution from the current low-intensity war to open warfare will be in near- space, where opponents will target each other's communications and GPS satellites. China and the US have already tested anti-satellite weapons and probably have already positioned them in orbit. While military systems are protected and established with backup systems, most civilian systems will be disabled in the first hours of a conflict. The impact on transportation and economic operations could be catastrophic. How effective emergency systems would be is difficult to predict.

Insurance

Insurance is based on the principle of distributed risk. Thousands of people pay a reasonable amount, but only a few will need to claim benefits. As was demonstrated during recent large-scale disasters, these funds are unable to handle claims exceeding even 10 percent of the insured. Business damage and continuation insurance intended to cover local power outages, storms, etc. could not cover a nationwide shutdown for a pandemic. Insurance companies invest the money paid by customers in national and foreign banks and businesses that are all vulnerable to wartime disruptions. Home insurance, health insurance, income insurance, and other forms of insurance are usually a good idea, but don't depend on them if a worldwide war develops with massive damage, injuries, and loss of life.

Medical Care

In past wars, civilian medical care was outside the reach of hostile forces and hospital roofs were marked with white crosses to hopefully discourage bombing. In recent years it has become common for terrorists and rogue forces to use hospitals and schools as bases, command centers, and weapons storage facilities to avoid attacks. This practice has resulted in the necessary bombing of otherwise restricted targets. Modern medical care is highly dependent on computers and computer-controlled systems. For this reason, foreign hackers have consistently conducted so-called ransomware attacks threatening to shut down hospitals and publish medical records. During wartime your Medicare and medical insurance cards and records may be compromised or invalidated. The experiences of the recent pandemic, and the images from the Ukraine and Gaza are just a sample of what would be experienced during a conventional war, much less a nuclear war. It would be prudent to obtain hard copies of your medical records, stock up on antibiotics, update your vaccinations, practice good health and dental care, and stock up on your prescription medications where possible. Be aware that most prescription and over-the-counter medications last far past their so-called expiration dates.

Mass Media

Radio replaced the newspapers as the primary means of mass communications during World War II. Many credit radio as the primary means that Hitler used to mesmerize the population and rise to power in Germany. England's Winston Churchill, and America's Franklin D. Roosevelt made effective use of this mass media to rally the populations to fight the war. Radio was also used by both sides to rally resistance to occupation. Tokyo Rose broadcast American music interspersed with Japanese propaganda to American forces in the Pacific. Most revolutions and invasions began with seizure of the radio and television stations. As online, cable, and satellite systems become subject to attack, basic radio and reginal television broadcasts may be better able to survive but are also vulnerable to both electronic and physical attack.

Emergency Media

Emergency broadcast systems were first initiated by the old Civil Defense Department to provide warnings related to nuclear attacks. They were later modified and expanded to include warnings and instructions related to natural disasters as the FEMA Emergency Alert System. This system will interrupt all television and radio broadcasts to alert and inform citizens of an impending attack. These systems are hardened and would probably be able to resist cyberattacks, electromagnetic pulse attacks, and even conventional or nuclear arracks, so keeping a good AM/FM radio on at all times during any international crisis would be advisable. The National Oceanographic and Atmospheric Administration (NOAA) maintains what is known as the "WX' or "Weather Radio" system that broadcasts constant weather conditions and warnings. Solar, crank, and battery powered emergency radios that include AM/FM, WX, and even GMRS (General Mobile Radio Service) bands are available at reasonable cost and should be part of every home survival equipment.

Off the Grid

In a war that will be waged on and in the very technologies we have come to depend on, the ability to survive, communicate, and do business off the grid and through alternative systems will be critical to civilians' survival and recovery.

CHAPTER 5

WARTIME EVACUATION

*Men who had fought in several wars and many bloody battles told me that
no horrors of a field of battle can be compared to the awful spectacle of the
ceaseless exodus of a population.*
— Russian General Vasily Gurko (1864–1937)

Mass evacuations and migrations have been initiated by war for thousands of years, and certainly will be part of the coming war. During
World War II, the British evacuated children and nonessential adults from
London and other cities to escape the Blitz. Russians ran east to escape
the Nazi onslaught. Germans fled west as Soviet armies ravaged the Reich.
During the Cold War there were plans to evacuate whole cities in the event
of a nuclear war. Organized or spontaneous evacuations and migrations
have always been chaotic, destructive, and often violent events. Fear, hunger, exhaustion, and desperation leave a trail of death and destruction along
evacuation routes. The enemy may attack the civilian refugees as both the
Germans and the Soviets did in World War II. Friendly military forces may
be forced to push civilians off the road with force to reach the front or
retreat from the enemy. Criminal and opportunists may rape and pillage
unarmed civilians with impunity. Hunger, thirst, exposure, and disease are
inevitable companions of these desperate marches. While invading armies
may not drive Americans from their homes, conditions created by a true
world war could necessitate enforced or voluntary evacuations of major
populations. Unlike the limited and temporary evacuations necessitated by
hurricanes and wildfires, these massive and long-term evacuations would
have all the hazards of past wartime mass migrations. Massive civil disorder,
failure of critical grid systems such as water, food, and electricity, spreading communicable disease, uncontrolled fires, impending nuclear strikes,
or even panic spread through social media could result in the flight of massive portion of the population. Unless the evacuation is well organized and
managed over several days or weeks, roads would be immediately clogged,
gasoline would be unavailable, and millions of unprepared men, women,

and children would be spread out along the roads, exposed to the elements. Premature or unnecessary evacuation may be the classic frying-pan-into-the-fire decision. Over my forty-five years as a survivalist, I have worked with dozens of survival groups in developing both shelter in place, and last-resort evacuation plans. During the Cold War, evacuation was the only option for the urban population, while shelter in place was the best option for those outside the blast zones. Today's population faces a far more complex combination of disasters and degenerations that make the decision whether to stay home or evacuate more difficult. While staying home may be impossible in some situations, evacuation has considerable limitations and hazards that must be considered before taking to the road. Those living in urban and suburban environments and/or near to potential military or industrial targets must have the capacity to evacuate on short notice during a future war. Events that may necessitate an evacuation may develop in two ways:

- Constantly worsening conditions such as lawlessness, grid failures, spreading disease, or the general breakdown of society may force the depopulation of urban and suburban areas. Aware citizens will have the opportunity to secure their property and drive to alternative locations. They may even be able to move significant supplies to well established retreat locations in advance of a war-related disaster. In some cases, the time to start this process is now.
- Immediate and impending disaster such as bombings, massive civil disorder, uncontrolled fire, spreading epidemics, total failure of food, water, sanitation systems, or an impending nuclear attack require unhesitating flight away from the afflicted or target area. In such cases life safety is the only priority. Attempting to protect property, shelter in place, or carry too much gear and possessions may prove disastrous. Advanced preparations, careful planning, and having sufficient and efficient evacuation packs for all family members can save precious time and provide essential items under this worst-case situation.

PRE-EVACUATION PLANNING

When war seems imminent, move children, the elderly, and disabled family members to any remote location you can establish, such as a relative's rural home, small town hotel, cabin, or camp site. If you can move pets to a safer location, do this also. Efforts to move these vulnerable people under developing disaster conditions may result in fatal delays for all of you. While your evacuation plans should not be dependent on being able to drive to your evacuation destination, you should always keep your vehicle fully fueled. Consider keeping a vehicle, extra fuel, and survival supplies at a remote self-storage unit or friend's place away from the likely target zones. If you are forced to abandon your primary vehicle, you can hike to your backup cache. During World War II, many refugees buried valuables in their yards to save them from bombings, looting, and fires. Those who sought to carry bulky valuables usually had to abandon them as they became exhausted or were robbed along the route. Have a plan to secure your valuables to prevent them from being burned or looted if you must abandon your home. Take only essential documents, your survival supplies, and self-defense weapons as you take to the road.

War Refugee Evacuation Pack Contents

Every family member should have an evacuation pack and gear ready to use in the event that staying home becomes untenable. Each pack should be created based on the needs, health, and carrying capacity of the family member that will carry it. The tendency is to overestimate what you can carry for any distance. The roads used by refugees and armies on the march are often littered with discarded items. Detailed lists of suggested evacuation packs, caches, and equipment will be covered in a separate chapter, but items such as camouflage, weapons, binoculars, fallout protection, maps, and shovels will take a higher priority than for general disaster evacuation packs.

Planning for Wartime Evacuation

Exigencies of war are already developing and may continue over several years, or they may accelerate overnight into immediate calamity. If you have already prepared for sheltering in place as well as evacuation for natural and made-made disasters, you must continue these efforts and adjust for the more severe, complex, and long-lasting consequences of war. If you are just beginning your war preparedness efforts, you need to establish two plans, one for preparedness and one for emergency action.

War Survival Preparedness Plan

The first priority is to make a survival and escape plan based on what you have now and what you can do if wartime conditions or direct warfare initiates in the immediate weeks or months before you can complete your full preparedness plan. Your next action must be to establish a schedule and budget for building up your capacity to survive hazards and threats ranging from hard times, and deprivation, to bombing, and combat in the streets. Start with basic disaster survival preparations such as storing water, non-perishable foods, first aid supplies, fire extinguishers, self-defense weapons, flashlights and lanterns, emergency radios, camp stoves, and sleeping bags. While evacuation is usually the last resort, war scenarios increase the likelihood that cities and towns may become untenable for civilians. For this reason, the preparation of your survival packs must be immediate. No matter how unprepared you are, get out of denial and get started. Having a basic plan, some basic supplies, and some kind of evacuation pack this week puts you on the path to safety and responsibility.

War Survival Action Plan

Every action plan must include a trigger. A trigger is a well-defined set of conditions that will justify implementation of the evacuation plan. A war survival action plan will necessitate drastic and consequential actions such as taking shelter, abandoning your home, fleeing into the weather and wilderness, or establishing isolation and fortification. Once initiated, it will have irreversible economic, social, and even legal consequences that cannot be taken lightly. Being panicked by sensationalist social media influencers or "panic of the month" survival supply marketers must be avoided. Establish certain events and trends that will trigger your action plan. Obviously, an outright attack, declaration of war, or sirens going off will be a trigger for action, but by then it may be too late. Patterns of multiple events such as foreign and Allied troop movements, military alert levels, invasions in Europe or Asia, or unexplained shifts in government resources and personnel may be the triggers for sheltering or evacuation. Trigger sources should be reliable and verifiable in this day of AI generated data and images. The military implements stages of readiness as DEFCON 1, DECON 2, etc. to define defense conditions. Civilians should establish a tiered system for survival preparedness and survival action as well. The SURCON table below adapts the US military to civilian preparedness scenarios.

Civilian Survival Conditions (SURCON)

Readiness/Action Condition	Trigger Condition	Civilian Actions
SURCON 1	Invasions of allied territories, threats, or limited use of tactical nuclear weapons. Initiation of drastic security and economic regulations.	Dig in or bugout? Fight or flight? Bomb shelter, fallout shelter, combat position, emergency aid, self-rescue, survival camp, self-reliance, help your neighbors. Do what is necessary.
SURCON 2	Relocation of key government personnel and equipment. Testing of warning systems. Drill for civilian emergency agencies.	Based on your location and developing conditions, establish final shelter in place or evacuation plans. Check evacuation routes and alternatives. Be prepared to take shelter, defend your home, protect against fallout, administer first aid, and carry your evacuation pack to a preestablished retreat or camp.
SURCON 3	Conflicts directly involving American and hostile forces. Indications of increased mobilization and readiness by military and civil defense agencies.	Move children, elderly, and disabled out of potential danger zones. Move extra supplies and valuables to remote areas or caches. Secure valuables. Fortify home for defense and isolation. Have vehicles and survival packs ready to go. Monitor emergency channels 24/7.
SURCON 4	Increased international tensions, incidents, and threats.	Review survival and evacuation plans with all family and group members. Inventory and improve supplies. Closely monitor news sources and emergency channels.
SURCON 5	Basic international relations with limited foreign conflicts.	Continue preparedness program. Build up supplies, adjust plans, establish escape routes.

Military DEFCON Readiness Scale

Although the military may keep its alert levels secret, it is probable that this information will leak to the public. Obviously what DEFCON level is in place would be a trigger for the equivalent civilian/personal SURCON action.

Readiness Condition	Term	Description	State
DEFCON 1	Cocked Pistol	Nuclear war is imminent	Maximum readiness
DEFCON 2	Fast Pace	Next step to war	Forces ready to engage in less than six hours
DEFCON 3	Round House	Increased force readiness beyond normal state	Air force ready to mobilize within fifteen minutes
DEFCON 4	Double Take	Increased intelligence and security above normal requirements	Above normal readiness
DEFCON 5	Fadeout	Low state of readiness	Normal readiness

EVACUATION ROUTES AND METHODS

Government mandated and managed evacuations will establish routes, schedules, and priorities, but these efforts may degenerate into chaos or just not be compatible with the best interests of individuals and families. Being able to initiate your evacuation without waiting for instruction and having established alternative plans and routes will be critical to escaping high threat locations in wartime scenarios. The would-be survivor should have plans and alternative plans based on "what if" scenarios.

- **Phase One, Escape:** The priority of any evacuation plan is to get clear of the immediate hazard as quickly and safely as possible. While it may be convenient to be moving towards your destination, that is not always safe. Escaping from a potential nuclear target, combat zone, civil disorder site, fallout pattern, or uncontrolled fire may dictate moving perpendicular or in the opposite direction from your intended destination. So, your planned escape route must take you out of harm's way, without going through or towards other hazards. You should be familiar with the roads, alleys, trails, obstacles, and bridges to navigate this part of your plan. Once you have established your primary waypoint, you can then establish multiple routes from there to your destination.

- **Phase Two, Travel**: Use maps and satellite images to plan routes from your escape waypoint to your destination. If possible, travel through these areas by car, bike or on foot in advance. Have good topographical maps, and print out satellite images of critical areas. Remember that GPS and cellular service may not be available. Depending on the distances necessary to reach your destination, you may need to establish sheltered rest stops and campsites along the route. Keep in mind that campgrounds, motels, and towns will probably be overwhelmed with desperate evacuees and possibly paranoid locals. Use satellite views to identify alternative shelters and camp sites.

- **Phase Three, Approach:** Ultimately you will need to stop running and establish some kind of retreat, or survival camp. This must be a place that offers shelter and the potential for sustained access to water, food, and security. It must be far enough away from hazards, but near enough to reach on foot while surviving off what you can carry in your evacuation pack. Most civilians cannot afford a survival cabin in Idaho or Montana. Most rural communities will not welcome unprepared and unskilled strangers straining their limited resources. Establishing relations and prepositioning supplies in an outlying area, or with a friend or relative living in a small town or rural location is most desirable. Organized survival groups can pool resources to establish cabins, trailers, or campsites in advance. Those with critical survival skills and the willingness to participate in community defense will be welcomed in many communities. Regardless of prior experiences or relationships, you should approach any retreat destination with extreme caution. If you picked this spot, others may have selected it also. The conditions on the ground and the attitudes of the local inhabitants may change once the reality of war has developed. Observe, approach with caution. Be prepared to find alternatives.

URBAN ESCAPE

The further into the urban area you live, the harder it is to escape. The gauntlet of blocked streets, bridges, overpasses, shooters, civil disorder, fires, and other hazards multiplies with every mile between you and open country. Areas on the fringes of the city or in the true suburbs are far easier to escape from or even hold out in. Consider this when relocating, but jobs and family obligations may dictate where you must live.

The sooner you move to evacuate the better. Once even a small part of the general population starts to evacuate, your chances of automotive movement with a significant amount of survival goods is about zero. As anyone who lives in the city knows, even a slight increase in traffic or disruption of flow brings everything to a halt. A 10 to 20 percent increase in outgoing traffic combined with the inevitable accidents and breakdowns will stop everything. This will be followed by panic, road rage, and chaos on the highways. Unless you head for the hills every time there is bad news, you probably will not beat the crowd. If driving your vehicle filled with survival and camping supplies is viable, you should definitely try it. To this end you should have supplies in tote bins ready to just be put into your vehicle and go. Of course, you should never let your fuel tank get below half full and if the conditions indicate that you may need to evacuate soon, keep the tank full. Every mile you can get by vehicle is one less that you will need to walk. Most people will head for the expressways and main roads that will jam up quickly. Now is the time to use topographic road maps found at truck stops, study Google Earth, and just drive around to locate backroads, side roads, alleys, and other drivable surfaces that may offer clear routes. Rivers, railroad tracks, and other features that cross your escape path will have only limited crossing points at bridges, underpasses, and tunnels. Try to get past these before they are closed off. Once these choke points are closed and the roads are blocked, you will have to abandon your vehicle and walk. You must be prepared for this eventuality. All your main survival supplies must be in backpacks and/or wheeled carriers. Be sure to include sturdy hiking boots and all-weather clothing in your supply bins. If water obstacles are anticipated, consider adding a canoe or inflatable raft to your equipment. You may want to carry a large bolt cutter in your vehicle for opening gates to service roads and shortcuts. There are going to be a lot of less prepared and more desperate people out there, so being well armed will be an absolute necessity. Getting through an urban area requires a close-range volume of fire more than long-range accuracy. You need to quickly disable and/or suppress hostile fire while escaping the danger zone. Large caliber, large capacity handguns; short-barreled shotguns; and carbines are all effective. I also recommend carrying lots of smoke grenades to facilitate screening of movement. These are available at paintball supply outlets.

URBAN ESCAPE ROUTES

Escape routes can make use of any unobstructed pathway that leads to a safer location. Out of the box thinking is good thinking for escape planning. Each city has a number of pathways cutting through the mass of built-up and populated terrain that can be used as escape routes. Refugees in the past have often used sewers, drainage systems, and even rooftops as escape routes. Anyone living in an area of closely packed homes and apartment buildings must have a ready knowledge of routes.

- Railroad tracks and abandoned rights-of-way offer unobstructed paths out of the city. Walking down tracks is not as easy as you may think, you have to focus on your footing and of course be alert for trains. Also, raised rail embankments make you a silhouette for shooters, but trying to walk on the slanted side of the embankment is almost impossible. Still, they lead straight out of town and often have necessary bridges over obstacles.
- River and stream edges can offer routes, but they are often obstructed with vegetation that may make walking difficult. If you have or can find a boat or raft, they are a great way out of town.
- Power line paths are usually kept clear of obstructions and often have unpaved service roads underneath the wires, but they seldom include ways for you to cross streams, rivers, and other obstacles.
- Bike paths and hiking trails and parkways are becoming more common in urban areas. Many of these are networked into systems that reach well outside of the city. The survivor would be well advised to become thoroughly familiar with these and consider a bicycle as a primary or secondary evacuation system. Bikes are faster and can carry more gear than walking with a pack. Consider that a lot of others are going to use these obvious escape routes, so don't depend on them alone.
- Alleys are the preferred routes through built-up urban areas. Fences, trash containers and garages offer plenty of cover and concealment while blocking you from the view of many windows. Crossing streets from alley to alley is faster than at street corners and less likely to be blocked or watched. Walking down the street or sidewalk is just not a good idea for survival evacuation if it can be avoided.
- Industrial areas will be pretty much abandoned in a general collapse. People don't live there, and looters will focus on shopping centers. So, routing through such areas may be much safer than residential and commercial zones.

BIVOUACS AND HIDEOUTS

In the jammed traffic of an evacuation, you may make five to eight miles per hour driving before stopping completely. The average person walks at about four miles per hour, but with your pack, zigzagging down paths and alleys you will be lucky to cover one or two miles per hour. It may take you several days to get out of the urban environment, so you need to consider safe places to hide and rest. Abandoned buildings, garages, and wooded areas may work for you. Underpasses and viaducts will probably attract too many others. Select locations that are of the main routes and paths that offer shelter without being too obvious.

BINOCULARS AND NIGHT VISION GEAR

Two items that can give you a clear advantage in an urban escape are binoculars and night vision equipment. A good pair of binoculars can let you see dangerous conditions and hostile individuals before you encounter them. Being prepared to deal with or avoid a problem ahead of time is a tremendous advantage. Night vision gear gives you the option to move at night and still see hazards ahead of you before they see you. Night movement with this ability can be much safer than day-time movement. In bivouac you can see who's coming before they are close enough to see you. These items are a must investment if urban escape is a necessary part of your survival plan.

EVACUATION AND ESCAPE VEHICLES

What kind of vehicle you will have to facilitate your escape will depend on where you are escaping from, what kind of terrain and environment you will be moving through, and your budget. Unless you have an unlimited budget and can have one vehicle for everyday use and one for escape, you will probably need to make some compromises. Sedans and small SUVs are the worst choices. Larger SUVs with four-wheel drive and good ground clearance can be your everyday and your doomsday vehicle. A Jeep or similar vehicle with lots of interior room, auxiliary fuel tanks, extra lights, and a cable winch would be ideal. Ordinary vehicles, even those with four-wheel drive, cannot negotiate cross-country terrain. Ultimately you will need to knock down barriers, pull down fences, and negotiate deep gullies and steep hills. Of course, if you have that kind of vehicle and things get desperate, you will have to be prepared to defend it from those who don't. Most of us must be prepared to use our feet as the ultimate cross-country vehicle. Two- and three-wheel bicycles can be an affordable option if you will have ready access to trails and backroads. Stick with pedal power bikes, as gasoline and electrical recharging will not be available in a crisis. Be sure to have tire repair kits and a hand pump attached to the bike. You can also add a small trailer that will give you considerable advantage over backpacking.

Fully equipped evacuation bicycle with trailer. Note the rifle rack on the trailer.

A Jeep like this one should be able to get off the road and cut across country. Note the large tires, high ground clearance, and cable winch that can be used to pull down obstructions and drag the vehicle out of almost any situation.

CHAPTER 6

BOMBS, MISSILES, AND DRONES

It has become appallingly obvious that our technology has exceeded our humanity.

—Attributed to Albert Einstein

During World War II, both sides engaged in massive carpet-bombing and fire-bombing campaigns. These operations were not aimed at military or industrial targets. They were intended to kill, disable, and demoralize civilians. For example: one air raid on Hamburg, Germany, killed 42,000 people in one night. Fire-bomb raids over Tokyo, Japan, destroyed sixteen square miles of the city and killed over 100,000 civilians. While these actions affected productivity by literally killing the workers, it did not significantly reduce civilian morale or resistance. Short of nuclear weapons, it is difficult to imagine such massive destruction and loss of life delivered by conventional explosives today. Modern hypersonic cruise missiles, ballistic missiles, and drones will deliver conventional explosives and will be used to target military bases, industrial centers, and critical infrastructure. Those working in or residing near to such a target will suffer as potential collateral damage. Strikes on nuclear power plants, chemical storage facilities, and transportation hubs will result in massive secondary casualties. Drones are smart, cheap, and accurate. They can be launched from ships, planes, or even smuggled in and launched within our borders. While they may not flatten or wipe out populations, drones can sow terror and chaos in American towns and cities. Ballistic missiles and cruise missiles armed with non-nuclear warheads may also be used against American cities in the next war. These weapons are expensive and would probably be reserved for high priority targets. In the Ukraine combination drone, cruise and ballistic missile attacks aimed at both military and civilian targets have become the norm. The nature of our potential adversaries indicates that these tactics would be extended to our homeland in any future conflict. Unlike Europeans and Asians, Americans have never experienced what the British called "The Blitz." Air raid sirens generally mean either nuclear obliteration or just another drill. Those in Ukraine, Syria, and

Israel hear the wail of these sirens and take cover and then emerge to assess damage and death. At some point the warning "incoming" may be a frequent expression.

BALLISTIC MISSILES

Ballistic missiles have been in use since the V2s of World War II. Until recently, they have been large rockets lofted into near-space and then descending on a ballistic course to deliver a single nuclear payload to a single target. In the late twentieth century, these missiles were equipped with multiple independently targeted and maneuverable warheads, making them exponentially more lethal and difficult to intercept. A single ballistic missile submarine can have twenty-four ballast missiles carrying multiple nuclear warheads or a combination of nuclear and non-nuclear ballistic and cruise missiles. Advance artificial intelligence and new hypersonic designs make previous defensive systems ineffective. Modern ballistic missiles can deliver a variety of non-nuclear weapons such as electromagnetic pulse generators, incendiaries, and explosives that are much more effective than those used during World War II. They can easily reach civilian targets and are often used in combination with cruise missiles and drones to overwhelm military and civil defense systems. The Chinese military is developing very large lifters that can carry scores of conventional warheads into orbit and then send them towards multiple targets at six times the speed of sound. Israel is using AI to select targets, regardless of potential civilian casualties.

CRUISE MISSILES

The first cruise missiles to be used in war were the German V1, "Buzz Bombs." These were simply unmanned aircraft flying in a straight line to deliver a single 1,870-pound warhead. Until recently these weapons were slow and vulnerable to anti-aircraft missiles and guns. Today cruise missiles have surpassed ballistic missiles in their ability to evade detection, penetrate defenses, and perform multiple tasks. Modern cruise missiles can be launched from offshore submarines or aircraft and use stealth, intelligent maneuverability, and hypersonic speed to deliver single or multiple warheads, or cluster bombs. During the Iraq war they were seen flying down urban streets following their preprogramed directions to target. Large and small cruise missiles will certainly be used in combat zones, but could also be directed at civilian facilities, and infrastructure if the war escalates or battles move closer to the continental United States or coastal areas.

DRONES

Nothing has impacted modern civil defense and survival more than the rise of intelligent drones in warfare. Relatively low-cost Ukrainian drones penetrated the defenses of Moscow. One struck the Kremlin itself while other drones crossed the entire country to hit targets near the Baltic Sea. Drones have brought a whole new dimension to warfare and a whole new threat of targeted and random bombing to military and civilian targets. The war in the Ukraine has escalated the development of war drones and demonstrated their ability to penetrate defenses and deliver explosives to specific targets. At the start of the war a few hundred relatively low-cost drones annihilated an entire column of Russian tanks, armored personnel carriers, and supply trucks, killing hundreds of Russian troops without any Ukrainian casualties. A $20,000 drone can kill a 1-million-dollar tank. Large reconnaissance drones such as Americas' MQ-9 Reaper can perform long-rang reconnaissance and launch missiles. China, Russia, and Iran, among others, have similar drones in their inventory. Smaller cheaper suicide drones are a more recent development. Turky has been providing the Ukraine with multi-purpose "Switchblade" drone systems since the start of the war. Over one hundred nations now produce some kind of military drone. Australia is selling cardboard drones that can carry an eleven-pound warhead out to seventy-five miles for just over $3,000 each. Eleven pounds of modern explosives delivered directly to a specific target can do a lot of damage. Drones can be launched from trucks, ships, aircraft, and larger carrier drones. They can even be deployed from submerged submarines. The technology is rapidly advancing, but basic drones can be built and used by foreign and domestic terrorists on a limited budget. We have all seen drone lightshows where hundreds of small drones create shapes in the sky. Drone swarms can and will be employed to overwhelm defenses and attack specified targets including individuals. This is existing technology. Unlike incoming ballistic and cruise missiles, drones can seldom be detected in advance. Lethal autonomous weapon systems known as LAWS are drones and other devices that can be programmed to seek and destroy a target or seek and kill a person without any human oversight or control. Such weapons can make decisions and strike much faster than human-controlled weapons. As Sun Tzu said, "speed is the essence of war." Drone attacks or combined drone and missile attacks will be a part of any new war. Old-fashioned civil defense and bomb shelters may return to Europe, Asia, and even America. The phrase of the year could be "Incoming!"

TACTICAL NUCLEAR WEAPONS

The paradigms that have prevented the use of nuclear weapons during the Cold War no longer apply. The concept of mutually assured destruction (MAD) was valid for an exchange of large ballistic missiles with multi-megaton warheads. Today, so-called "tactical" nuclear weapons delivered by smaller missiles, cruise missiles, or drones make the previously "unthinkable" thinkable. Russia and China have both indicated that at least tactical nuclear weapons are now classified as "normal" battlefield options. Rogue nations have increasing access to nuclear weapons and delivery systems. Initial use of such weapons on remote battlefields might easily escalate to limited and then unlimited strikes against domestic targets. Even if civilians are not directly in blast zones, the effects of fallout, infrastructure damage, and economic chaos would be catastrophic. During the Cold War, the Civil Defense Department maintained blast and fallout shelters, conducted drills, and provided books, booklets, and newspaper articles on fallout protection. The shelters were abandoned in the 1990s and FEMA has focused on natural disaster preparedness. Radiation, blasts, flying debris, fires, and building collapses would be just the beginning of survival challenges for civilians if nuclear weapons are employed in the coming war. Unless you are caught in the immediate blast zone, nuclear war is survivable, but only if you are informed and prepared. T. F. Nieman's 1981 book *Better Read than Dead* and *Nuclear War Survival Skills* (1986) by Cresson H. Kearny are again relevant, but both of them are based on Cold War ballistic delivery system scenarios.

CHAPTER 7

BIOLOGICAL WARFARE
AND EPIDEMICS

Biological warfare and communicable diseases have been an element of war for thousands of years. During the Middle Ages, dead animals, infected corpses, and excrement were catapulted over the walls of castles and cities to spread bubonic plague to the besieged army and population. The British "gifted" smallpox-infected blankets to the Chief Pontiac for his tribe in 1763 with the intention of spreading the disease to end the Pontiac rebellion. Before and during World War II, Japan's Unit 731 experimented with various biological agents on Chinese prisoners. Russia, China, the United States, and many other nations continue to conduct covert biological weapons programs. While rogue nations and terrorist organizations may not be able afford massive armies or nuclear weapons, biological weapons are affordable and easy to deliver. The incidental spread of infectious diseases has also been associated with warfare since the first primitive armies of ancient times. Masses of men grouped closely together and marching through foreign lands are always vulnerable to the spread of ancient and newly encountered pathogens. Up until the introduction of vaccines and effective antibiotics, casualty rates from diseases often exceeded deaths from combat wounds. Deadly viruses and bacteria do not discriminate between combatants and noncombatants. The Mongol invaders of Europe in the thirteenth and fourteenth centuries deliberately or accidentally carried the black plague that killed up to 66 percent of the population of Europe. While the recent COVID pandemic may have been accidental, it may have been the result of experimental biological war agents. This comparatively mild pathogen shut down the world economy, engendered panic and violence throughout America, and significantly impacted military readiness. In addition to all of the other hazards and deprivations of wartime, civilians must be prepared to cope with the potential of the deliberate or incidental spread of a variety of diseases. In the event of actual bombing, sabotage, or combat on American soil, sanitation systems, water supplies, and medical facilities may be damaged or disabled. Radiation exposure, poor nutrition, and stress can also significantly impact the immune system.

BIOLOGICAL WARFARE AGENTS

Many of history's worst epidemics and pandemics have developed in the wake of wars, revolutions, and large-scale disasters. There are over thirty known pathogens suitable for weaponization, including anthrax, botulism, plague, smallpox, and Ebola. The objective of a deliberate biological warfare attack would be to kill and disable as many civilians as possible in order to shut down military and civilian resistance. The ideal biological warfare agent would have the following characteristics:

1. It would have a long period of communicability before symptoms appear. This would permit the pathogen to be disseminated through aerosol spray, contact, and person-to-person for days and weeks before the target population and medical services became aware of the attack.
2. It would have a long surface survival time that would facilitate continued spread and necessitate vigorous decontamination.
3. It would have a high morbidity rate and cause extended disability to create panic and incapacitate the population.
4. The aggressor would have developed effective vaccines, or protections for its troops and civilians prior to deployment of the weaponized pathogen. Terrorists may not adhere to this logical precaution.

COVID–19 had some of these characteristics and was developed in a Chinese laboratory. It would seem reasonable to assume that the laboratories of hostile and rogue nations and terrorist groups are actively developing such pathogens.

There are four ways that diseases can be transmitted to humans:

- **Contact transmission.** Direct contact transmission is from one infected person to another uninfected person through actual touching. Indirect contact transmission occurs when an infected person contaminates an inanimate object and then another person touches that object and acquires the pathogen. Once a deliberate or incidental pathogen is introduced into the environment, the potential for contact transmission exists. While some pathogens may remain infectious on surfaces for only a few hours others may remain infectious for days. Biological warfare agents may be designed to be sprayed on surfaces in major population centers such as rail stations, airports, or public transportation vehicles. If the potential for biological attack exists, citizens will need to avoid contact with surfaces in public places, use N95 respirators, or surgical masks, and latex or vinyl gloves in public spaces. All items brought from public areas, such as groceries and clothing, should be washed with soap and water and/or sprayed with disinfectant.

- **Airborne transmission.** As the name implies, airborne transmission is carried in the air from an infected person's coughs or sneezes. Droplets carry the pathogen through the air and are inhaled by others. During a war, airborne pathogens could be disseminated from aircraft, drones, or small aerosol devices in public spaces. Airborne transmitted pathogens are the fastest spreading and preferred method of weaponizing diseases. While natural or accidental airborne pandemics such as COVID–19 spread slowly from one (patient zero) source, biological warfare pathogens would be disseminated from multiple targets simultaneously and spread much faster to overwhelm containment efforts. Only immediate and total isolation combined with masks, gloves, and effective decontamination would be effective.
- **Vehicle transmission.** In this case, the pathogen is introduced into the body through contaminated food, water, fluids, or blood. Water and food born infections may be bacterial, viral, or parasitic, including E. coli, cholera, botulism, dysentery, and salmonella. Under wartime conditions, water and sanitation systems may be damaged or water may be deliberately infected. Having stored water, water purification systems, and bleach to disinfect water will be critical. Methods to burn, bury, or decontaminate waste may also be necessary.
- **Vector transmission.** Typical vector transmissions are from mosquito bites (i.e., malaria), ticks (i.e., Rocky Mountain spotted fever), and animal bites (i.e., rabies). Garbage, rats, standing water, and poor sanitation generate large insect populations. Insect spray and insect repellent must be included in survival supplies.

The chances of developing an infection from exposure to a communicable disease is dependent on three factors:

1. The amount (dose) of the organism present, how contaminated the environment is, and the source of the pathogen. Dosage can be reduced through the use of masks, gloves, and decontamination measures.
2. The extent to which the pathogen survives on surfaces when exposed to air and light. This is known as virulence. The virulence of pathogens differs greatly from a few hours to many days. Decontamination of potentially contaminated surfaces and items with a 10 percent bleach-to- water solution is recommended.

3. The individual's resistance to infection. People with weakened immune systems, poor nutrition, or preexisting conditions may become ill while healthier individuals may not.

The formula for determination of infection probability is:

Infection = Dose times multiplied by virulence, divided by resistance.

The best protection against airborne transmitted pathogens is the proper wearing of an N95 respirator whenever there is the potential for exposure. The best protection against contact transmission is the wearing and proper removal of latex or vinyl gloves. It is best to wear gloves, an N95 respirator, and eye or face protection to guard against contact, airborne, and vector (blood, sputum) borne pathogens when rendering aid to any patient. Cautions should be followed when exposed to those with a fever, diarrhea, draining wounds, or jaundice (yellow skin color) as these are definitive signs of many communicable diseases. Thorough handwashing and the careful disposal of contaminated gloves, use of respiratory protection, and decontamination of equipment and exposed surfaces is critical to avoiding infection. Two typical biological agents are anthrax and plague, but laboratory created, and naturally evolving viruses and bacteria are being created constantly.

Anthrax: Anthrax has been used as a biological weapon by military and terrorist organizations and may be used in any future conflict. There are four forms of this bacterium. Effects of the intestinal form include diarrhea that may be bloody, fever, abdominal pain, nausea, and vomiting. Morbidity rate for this form ranges from 25 to 75 percent if untreated. The skin form of the infection presents with a fever and the development of small blisters that become dark abscesses. The morbidity rate for untreated skin anthrax is 24 percent. Respiratory airborne anthrax is the most probable form of war time anthrax infection. Symptoms of anthrax lung infection include chest pain, fever, and increasing breathing difficulty. If left untreated, the morbidity rate for this version of anthrax is from 50 to 80 percent. The fourth form of anthrax is injected and unlikely to be encountered by civilians. There is a vaccine for anthrax that might be made available in the event of a war, and it can be effectively treated with antibiotics such as doxycycline if available.

Plague: Plague comes in three forms. Bubonic plague is the most common and well known. Often called "the black death," it killed an estimated 25 million people in twelfth-century Europe. Symptoms of this form include high fever, vomiting, shivering, joint pain, headache, apathy, and intolerance to light.

The main vector of infection is through flies and insect bites. Effective sanitation in most parts of the world has controlled this form. Systemic plague invades the bloodstream and can develop from other forms of infection. The symptoms include severe fatigue, fever, and internal bleeding. Pneumonic plague is the deadliest form of this disease, presenting with pneumonia, fever, weakness, and difficulty breathing. If untreated, death is almost certain within three to four days. Pneumonic plague is transmitted through airborne droplets and therefore could be used as an effective weapon. The efficacy of a plague vaccine has been found to be limited. Antibiotics such as Ciprofloxacin and Doxycycline may or may not be effective in all cases. Plague or an enhanced form of the disease could be weaponized by hostile nations as well as terrorists.

VITAMINS FOR PREVENTION AND TREATMENT

Research has shown that low levels of Vitamin D3 can result in increased vulnerability to cold and flu. A strong correlation has been found between those with TB, hepatitis C, and Vitamin D3 deficiencies. Vitamin D3 helps the body make an antibiotic protein called cathelicidin that is known to kill viruses, fungi, parasites, and bacteria. During flu season (or during an epidemic) it is recommended to take 50,000 IU (international units) daily for the first five days and then 5,000 to 10,000 daily thereafter. More than thirty clinical studies have confirmed the antiviral effects of Vitamin C against a wide range of flu viruses. Vitamin C inactivates the virus while strengthening the immune system's ability to resist the virus. The general recommendation is 1,000 mg orally daily, but some stronger viruses (like Corona) may require intravenous doses as high as 100,000 to 150,000 mg.* If IV vitamin C is not available, a gradual increase of oral Vitamin C up to 50,000 mg may be possible before bowel tolerance is reached.

ANTIBIOTICS FOR NON-VIRAL INFECTIONS

It is important to keep in mind that biological warfare and incidental epidemic pathogens may be viral or bacterial. Viral infections are not affected by antibiotics, but other non-viral pathogens such as streptococcus, salmonella, E. coli, tuberculosis, cholera, and bubonic plague may beset the virus infected victim

---

* Monika Olczak-Pruc, Damian Swieczkowski, Jerzy R. Ladny, Michal Pruc, Raul Juarez-Vela, Zubaid Rafique, Frank W. Peacock, and Lukasz Szarpak: "Vitamin C Supplementation for the Treatment of COVID-19: A Systematic Review and Meta-Analysis." NIH National Library of Medicine. https://www.ncbi.nlm.nih.gov/pmc/articles/PMC9570769/.

who may have a weakened immune system, be undernourished, or exposed to poor sanitation. For this reason, antibiotics should still be kept available. Antibiotics are available from pet supply stores, fish supply stores, and survival supply outlets. These are the same products as are prescribed for humans, but at a much lower price without any prescription required. It is advisable to maintain a supply of these, but they are not to be used for viral infections.

Self-prescribed and obtained antibiotics should be used only when no other alternative is available and serious infections and diseases are evident or imminent. Antibiotics are most effective against various types of plague pathogens that could be the primary source of an epidemic and against many secondary infections common in disasters. Dosages information can be obtained from the internet, the *Merck Manual* and are based on the type of disease and patient's weight. Yes, in some cases the survivor may be forced to guess and err on the side of more. Adult dosages of most antibiotics range from 250 mg to 500 mg every six to ten hours. Dosage decreases with child ages.

Penicillin is the first antibiotic that was developed in 1928. It is also the longest and most overused, so some bacteria have become resistant to it. Penicillin is generally effective against common staphylococcus and streptococcus infections as well as clostridium and listeria genera. These common bacterial infections would be anticipated in open wounds and bacteria would also be present in contaminated water and food during a long-running disaster. About 10 percent of the population may be allergic to penicillin.

Amoxicillin is effective in treating ear infections, strep throat, pneumonia, skin infections, urinary tract infections, and other types of bacterial infections. It also is used for some kinds of stomach infections. It has been used effectively for people exposed to anthrax. Its effectiveness against pneumonia and skin infections make it an essential survival medication since these infections are most common in disasters and nuclear events. Amoxicillin should not be given to those who are allergic to penicillin.

Cephalexin is effective against infections of the middle ear, bones, joints, skin, and urinary tract. It can also be used against certain kinds of pneumonia and strep throat. Cephalexin is not effective against methicillin-resistant staphylococcus known as MRSA.

Bottles of antibiotics can be purchased from veterinary, aquarium, or survival supply vendors. Each bottle contains 30 × 250 mg tablets. Hydration powders, wand sanitizers, bleach, and respiratory protection are also essential elements in surviving biological hazards.

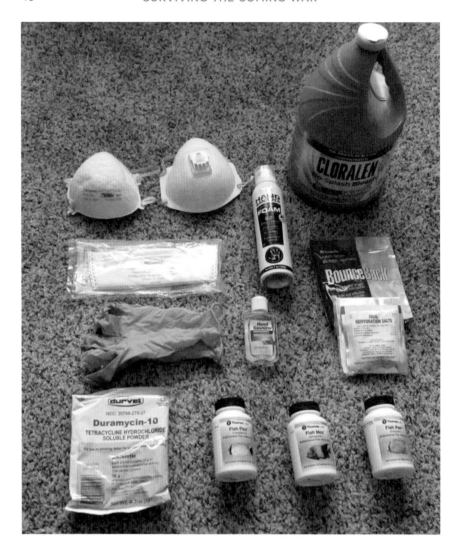

HERBAL REMEDIES

A variety of studies have shown that some herbal remedies are effective against some viruses.[*] Elderberries can be effective against influenza A and B. Astragals root has been shown to be effective against the Coxsackie B virus. Licorice root has been used to treat hepatitis C and HIV. Olive leaf has been proven effective in the treatment of flu, colds, hepatitis C, malaria,

---

[*]   Chilot Abiyu Demeke, Alem Endashaw Woldeyohanins, and Zemene Demelash Kifle: "Herbal Medicine Use for the Management of COVID-19: A Review Article. NIH National Library of Medicine. https://www.ncbi.nlm.nih.gov/pmc/articles/PMC8519661/.

gonorrhea, and tuberculosis. Other foods that may be effective in prevention and treatment of viral infections include wild blueberries, sprouts, cilantro, coconut oil, garlic, ginger, sweet potatoes, turmeric, kale, parsley, red clover, and elderberry. Herbal remedy books are a good addition to any survival library.

SURVIVING A CONTAGIOUS DISEASE EPIDEMIC

Although they are not always listed specifically, almost all communicable diseases can cause nausea, vomiting, loss of appetite, sweating, and diarrhea. These conditions lead directly to severe dehydration that in turn results in organ failure and death if not treated. Maintaining good oral hydration and electrolyte balance in the early stages of these diseases is critical. Once the patient can no longer tolerate oral fluids and/or is unconscious, oral fluids must be avoided and only IV and rectal (fluid enemas) are feasible. Maintaining hydration and the use of antibiotics where effective can greatly reduce mortality rates for most of these diseases.

INFECTION PREVENTION AND DEFENSE

The single most effective defense against being infected is the ability to restrict or eliminate all contact with the population and sources of contamination as soon as possible. Once symptoms are detected and the word or rumor of an epidemic is spreading, you must be able to instantly isolate yourself and your family and remain isolated until the epidemic has burned itself out. Being able to hole up in your home for four to eight weeks with enough food, water, medical supplies, fire extinguishers, defensive arms, and lighting and heating capacity is the only sure way to avoid becoming a victim of these deadly pathogens. The worst places to be are public transportation, grocery stores, hospitals, and disaster aid centers. If other potentially infected persons attempt to enter your home, you are justified in turning them away and using force if necessary to protect your own life and your family. In a "worst case" situation where you are forced to evacuate your home or are unable to get to your home, you will need to have survival packs and skills that allow you to survive for an extended time without aid or contact with others. Water filtration, respiratory protection, safe food, and defensive arms will be especially important to survival in the open. Anything and anyone coming into contact with you during a biological attack or natural epidemic must be considered dangerous. Wearing N95 respirators when you are away from home or while caring for afflicted family members is essential. All water, regardless of the source, should be boiled for five minutes or treated with bleach at one quarter teaspoon per gallon. Wear latex gloves when handling any potentially contaminated items and use a spray of ten percent bleach/water solution to decontaminate surfaces, canned goods, and any other potentially contaminated items from outside.

Most communities have plans for coping with a mass epidemic. There are stockpiles of antibiotics and medications ready for distribution, but civil disorder, infrastructure disruption, and other factors are sure to interfere with these efforts to some extent. Emergency volunteers and medical personnel will get these supplies first. How many of these people will be healthy, available, and ready to expose themselves and their families to a highly contagious and debilitating disease is difficult to estimate.

CHAPTER 8

CHEMICAL WARFARE SURVIVAL

C hemical agents were first used on the battlefields of World War I. While biological agents are far more effective at killing, and nuclear weapons are far more destructive, chemical weapons are effective at killing and disabling quickly in a designated area. Chemicals are most often used as a battlefield weapon but have been used by rogue states and terrorist organizations against specific civilian populations. Iraq used nerve agents against Iran throughout their war in 1984. Syria has made extensive use of chemical weapons against Kurdish civilian targets. In 1995, the Japanese religious movement Shinrikyo released the nerve agent Sarin into the Tokyo subway, killing thirteen and injuring five thousand people. Sarin is a complicated agent to produce, but this group managed to create and deliver it to a high-population target. In a war, chemical agents could be delivered by locally manufactured drones, by enemy agents or surrogate terrorist groups. Targets would include government facilities, commercial centers, and large gatherings such as sporting events or political demonstrations. Chemical agents could also be released on the ground or from the air from any kind of vehicle. Defense against such attacks would be difficult, expensive, and ineffective. Chemicals that are used in weapons are also used in many industrial applications and therefore are already deployed in or transported through most communities. Terrorists might just sabotage existing rail cars, trucks, and storage tanks to envelop towns in deadly clouds. An accidental release of methyl isocyanate in Bhopal, India, in December 1984 killed ten thousand people within days and over thirty-five thousand over time. These people lived downslope and downwind of the heavier than air vapors and were enveloped as they slept. In a total war, chemical, biological, kinetic (explosives) and even nuclear weapons could be used against civilian targets. If you are not located near to or downwind of stored or transported chemical agents, and do not live or work near government installations or high-density populated facilities, you probably will not encounter chemical warfare agents. If the potential for exposure to chemical warfare agent does exist, the information and recommendations to follow may save your life.

CHEMICAL AGENTS EFFECTS AND IDENTIFICATION

Chemical weapons fall into five categories: nerve agents, blister agents, choking agents, incapacitating agents, and toxins. Nerve agents are the most likely weapons to be used against military and civilian targets. Blister agents were commonly used during World War I and tend to remain on surfaces for long periods of time. Choking agents are usually battlefield weapons. Incapacitating agents are intended to temporarily disable victims to be arrested or dispersed. These might be used to round up potential resistors or disband looters under wartime conditions. Toxin agents are not immediately detectable and are easily dispersed, they might be used by terrorists or hostile nation agents to kill and disable targeted populations. The table below shows the most common chemical agents, but more advanced chemical weapons have been developed by Russia and many other potentially hostile nations and groups. Note that dosages depend on the route of infection.

Name/Type	Form	Smell	Effects & Symptoms	Primary Routes of Entry
Nerve Agents Tabin "GA" Sarin "GB" VX	Vapor Liquid Vapor	Fruity or odorless	Respiratory system. Salvatory and sweat glands, heart, and nervous system. Paralysis.	Skin contact, inhalation, digestion
Blister Agents Distilled Mustard Nitrogen Mustard	Liquid Vapor	Garlic, fish, or soap	Eyes, skin, lungs, internal tissues. Causes bronchopneumonia.	Skin contact and inhalation
Chocking Agents Phosgene	Colorless gas	Freshly mowed hay	Respiratory organs. Victims drown in their own mucus.	Inhalation
Incapacitating Agents "CN" "CS" "BZ"	Visible vapor Visible vapor Visible vapor	Apple blossoms Pepper Odorless	Eyes, skin, respiratory system, central nervous system. Can cause hallucinations and manic behavior.	Eye and skin contact, inhalation

Name/Type	Form	Smell	Effects & Symptoms	Primary Routes of Entry
Toxin Agents Botulin "X" "A" Saxitoxin "TZ" Enterotoxin "B"	All can be powder or liquid	? ? ?	Body tissues and nervous system Causes desiccation and paralysis. Can affect the digestive excretory system body tissue	Inhalation, ingestion, through wounds

These agents can be spread from drones, low-flying aircraft, or planted aerosol devices. Be alert for suspicious aircraft, vapor clouds, or odors. Avoid potential target areas and if necessary, carry charcoal-impregnated N95 respirators that would help reduce inhalation exposure while escaping the area.

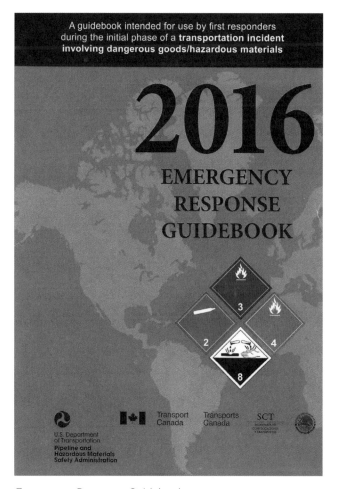

Emergency Response Guidebook cover.

Every fire engine and ambulance carries a copy of the *Emergency Response Guidebook*. The book is divided into five color-coded sections. White pages contain general information about various types of placards, rail cars, trailers, and containers. Yellow pages list content numerically by UN numbers. Blue pages list content alphabetically by chemical name. Orange pages contain guides for responding to each chemical, including hazards, health effects, protective clothing, evacuation requirements, fire extinguishing, spill control, and first aid for contact and exposure. The green pages contain special precautions and instructions related to spills. There is also information about evacuation and standoff distances for various improvised explosive devices, from suicide vests to truck bombs. This book could be helpful in the event of chemical weapons use or leakage from storage tanks or vehicles near you.[*]

PROTECTIVE SUITS AND MASKS

All the chemical agents pose threats to the respiratory system, ranging from immediate lung damage to the development of pneumonia and death. During wartime, the N95 respirators may be the most important everyday carry items in your pockets. Basic N95 respirators offer significant protection against toxic dust from explosions, radioactive fallout, and most biological hazards. They are not intended or rated for chemical agent protection but offer "better than nothing" protection that may buy time to escape. Charcoal-impregnated

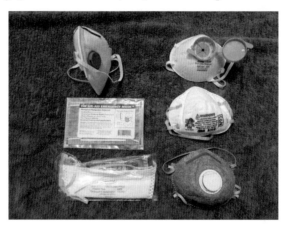

A variety of N95 dust/mist respirators are pictured here. The ones on the left are foldable and easy to carry in pockets. These are not true "gas masks" but offer some temporary protection against some of the chemical agents. The center left and lower right are impregnated with activated charcoal, and offer better protection from chemicals, but are still only for survival and escape use. Be sure to follow the instructions for proper fitting. In improperly fitted mask offers little or no protection.

---

[*]   Copies can be purchased from Amazon or at www.jjkeller.com.

masks can provide real but short-term protection against chemical agents. While full-face military surplus or industrial "chemical protective" gas masks provide far better protection than any kind of N95, they are bulky and less likely to be at hand when you need them.

Basic fit instruction for an N95 respirator.

Full Face Gas Masks

If your location or activities make exposure to chemical agents probable, investment in full face chemical protective masks may be justified. Military surplus gas masks and filters are available at survival supply and military surplus outlets. Older military mask such as the Russian GP-5 are cheap, but often offer limited visibility. The Polish MP-5 and the Chinese MF–11 provide good visibility and effective protection at a modest price. Masks with full face viewing, double filters, and speaking diagrams designed for first responders and industry are available for less than one hundred dollars.

Left to right: Vietnam-era US Army gas mask; commercial gas mask with improved visibility and alternative center or two side-mounted filters; Israeli civilian gas mask.

While professional first responder are trained and equipped to perform detailed decontamination procedures for chemical exposure, private citizens must rely on using copious amounts of soap and water, followed by multiple rinse cycles before removing masks and protective wear. Since the decontamination procedures will inevitably contaminate the area, it should be performed well away from habitats and shelter. Steps should start with a washdown with soap and water and brushes. If a second person is performing the decontamination, they must wear protective clothing and a respirator as well. The washed person then moves to a clean location for a thorough rinsing, then to a final rinse location before moving away to remove the mask and clothing. Contaminated water should be routed away from municipal drains and water sources.

TREATMENT

The primary treatment of chemical agent exposure must be to remove the patient from the contaminated area and removal and isolation of all contaminated clothing, followed by soap and water washing. Special attention must be

Citizens practice using a garden sprayer for decontamination. In reality, this procedure would be done multiple times outdoors.

given to protecting the eyes from further contact and brushing them with clean water for at least twenty minutes. Administer oxygen if available. If CPR is necessary, do not use mouth-to-mouth respirations. Apply sterile bandages to wounds and burns. Maintain hydration and oxygenation. In all cases, get the exposed person to professional decontamination and medical support as soon as possible.

CHAPTER 9

NUCLEAR WAR SURVIVAL

While the basic principles and techniques of nuclear war survival have not changed since the Cold War, the scenarios for the use of nuclear weapons have multiplied significantly. Russia still maintains over 6,800 nuclear warheads distributed in a variety of ballistic and cruise missile systems. China has at least 270 nuclear warheads and at least six ballistic missile submarines capable of launching nuclear warheads against the United States. Pakistan and India each have over one hundred nuclear bombs and missile warheads. North Korea's rogue dictator possesses at least twenty nuclear weapons and a few long-range missiles. The old single 10- to 25-megaton warheads have been replaced by far more accurate smaller, multiple-reentry warheads. Both ballistic and cruise missiles have acquired hypersonic speed and artificial intelligence evasion capabilities that make penetration and on-target detonation much more probable. The concept of selected tactical nuclear targeting has replaced the old mutual assured destruction (MAD) paradigm that prevented their use in past decades. Current technology dictates that he who shoots first, wins and he who hesitates is annihilated. Three different nuclear war scenarios exist:

1. A limited nuclear exchange may occur on battlefields in Europe, the Middle East, or Asia resulting in various levels of fallout over the United States. Unfortunately, the old Civil Defense fallout shelters and system of trained radiological monitors and supplies have been long neglected by FEMA.
2. A nuclear exchange limited to military targets such as missile bases, military installations, and naval facilities by highly accurate missiles could develop from an ongoing overseas conflict. While such a scenario might spare most major population centers, those living in proximity to military targets would be subject to immediate blast, radiation, and heat effects and significant fallout would blanket most major cities and towns.

3. Either of the above scenarios could easily degenerate into a tit-for-tat nuclear exchange against population centers or even a full-scale nuclear war. Certainly, civilians caught directly in the so-called ground zero blast zone of a nuclear detonation would not survive, but those in the outlying areas have a better chance of surviving the outgoing blast, heat, and radiation if they know what to do. Those living in more remote towns and rural areas would be subject to intensive radioactive fallout lasting for several weeks, and to secondary effects of grid failure, civil disorder, disease, and contamination. A recent Princeton University simulation estimated that there would be 45.3 million deaths within the first forty-five minutes of a full-scale nuclear change.[*]

BLAST ZONE SURVIVAL

If you are far enough away from ground zero to avoid immediate incineration, you will experience five immediate effects. The intensity of these will depend on your distance and location.

Flash: A flash of blinding white light will be the first indicator of a nuclear detonation. You may feel a tingling sensation from radiation. If caught out in the open, directly exposed to the flash and radiation, you will at least experience radiation sickness. As with lightning, there will be a delay before the next effect impacts you. The length of this delay depends on the distance you are from the center of the detonation.

Heat: The thermal wave will follow the flash and will range from immediately incinerating all humans and structures, to ignition of flammable structures and causing severe burns. Those outside the incineration zone and sheltered by walls, ditches or other obstacles may escape being burned.

Blast and Debris: The pressure wave from a nuclear detonation will radiate outward from the center and diminish in intensity with distance. This wave can travel at over 180 miles per hour, creating an overpressure of up to twelve pounds per square inch from three to five miles from the center of the blast. Flying glass, debris, and pressure will kill most unsheltered citizens. The speed and pressure of this wave will dissipate quickly, so there will be many injured and uninjured further away from the blast.

---

[*] "Simulating Nuclear War," Science & Global Security, Princeton University. https://sgs .princeton.edu/the-lab/simulating-nuclear-war.

Backblast: The outward movement of air will leave a partial vacuum at the blast site, and the rising heat of the fireball will pull air inward, causing an inward rush or backblast immediately after the blast wave has dissipated. This will not be as intense as the initial blast, but may still be tornadic and sustained, resulting in further damage and flying debris.

Fire Collapse and Chaos: The immediate aftereffects of a nuclear blast will depend on the distance from ground zero. Those just outside the area of destruction will be escaping burning and collapsing buildings and will be severely injured. Outside the blast destruction zone, most buildings will be damaged, and many uncontrolled fires will rage. Even many miles outside of the target area's damage, fires and chaos will result in injury and death to refugees. Those areas immediately downwind of a detonation will be subject to heavy granular fallout within hours of the detonation.

The standard texts of the original Cold War nuclear survival programs were based on the results of the nuclear testing conducted in Nevada in the 1960s. The two most popular nuclear survival books were *Better Read Than Dead* by T. F. Nieman and *Nuclear War Survival Skills* by Creston Kearny. The latter is back in print and available through Amazon and other book dealers. These old Cold War–era manuals assumed single detonations of from 1 to 10 megatons in power. Unfortunately, we can now anticipate larger warheads with up to 25 megatons or multiple smaller warhead dispersed around the target area. Scattered smaller warheads will create a much larger destruction zone. The population center of a city, major industrial and transportation centers, and military and government facilities will be the targets of warheads. Based on this and your distance from these potential targets you can use the illustration and table below to estimate severity of damage and the chances for survival where you live.

Megatons	Ground/ Air	Fireball Diameter	Total Destruction	Heavy Damage	Damage and Fire Spread
1	Ground	0.7 miles	1.70 miles	5 miles	7 miles
1	Air	0.7 miles	2.50 miles	8 miles	15 miles
5	Ground	1.4 miles	3 miles	8 miles	13 miles
5	Air	1.4 miles	5 miles	12 miles	16 miles
25	Ground	2.50 miles	5 miles	14 miles	22 miles
25	Air	2.50 miles	7 miles	18 miles	26 miles

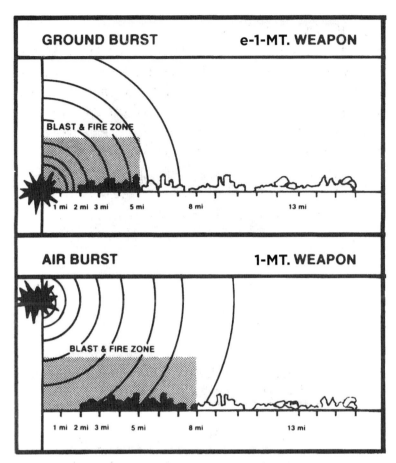

The illustration above shows the destruction ranges for a 1-megaton surface burst and air bursts. An air burst is much more likely and a blast of 10 or more megatons is also more probable today. Large cities would be targeted by four to six warheads.

WHAT CAN I DO TO SURVIVE?

If you cannot escape the target area, your only choice is to take cover in the strongest building or structure available. Put a wall between you and the probable source of the blast and lie flat. Get into a culvert, ditch, manhole, or other protection. If caught outside or in a building when the flash occurs, throw yourself flat under any available protection immediately. Yes, duck and cover works. If you are not too near the detonation, anything that obstructs the heatwave and flying glass and debris can save your life. You may still experience radiation sickness, which may be survivable, but radiation burns and being shredded by flying glass can be avoided.

- A house located about eight miles from a 5-megaton blast would be significantly damaged and possibly catch fire, but people sheltering in the basement would have some chance of survival. A 25-megaton blast would move this survivability zone out to about twelve miles.
- All structures within five miles of a 5-megaton blast would be heavily damaged and ignited. This level of destruction would be out to at least eight miles from a 25-megaton blast. Only those sheltering underground or in hardened structures could survive.
- Everything from the center of a 5-megaton blast out to three miles would be blasted and burned. This zone of total destruction would extend out to at least eight miles from the center of a 25-megaton blast. No one would survive the combination of over-pressure, blast, heat, and radiation within these zones.

If you are in the second or third situation, consider evacuation or finding stronger shelter than your house.

Evacuation

While survival fiction books often involve heroic families heading for well-developed bunkers or retreats in the mountains, most of us are not former Navy SEALs with flexible employment and hundreds of thousands to invest in bunkers. We are forced to live in or near our places of employment that are usually potential targets. You may have family responsibilities that prohibit moving to remote areas. For most, evacuation will have to be timely and fast. Having a plan and being just a bit ahead of the crowd may be the only hope you have.

Once the sirens go off or the flash is seen, your only hope is to run to the basement and cover your head before the blast and overpressure strikes. If no immediate protection is available, lie face down, facing away from the flash and cover your head as best you can.

Equipment

If you are sure that you have several hours or more to get away from the target area you can take your full survival bug-out bag, but if you have only minutes, take a handgun, a knife, respirators, and a reflective Space Blanket.™ Wear light-colored cotton clothing to protect against flash and burns, as it reflects rather than absorbs heat. Have plenty of N95 dust/mist respirators to avoid breathing in radioactive particles. A space blanket may help reflect the heat wave and of course provide some protection from radioactive fallout and rain. The need for a gun and knife should be obvious. Yes, you would want to have a lot of other stuff, but if you don't get far away fast enough to survive the blast, it won't do you much good. If you are sure that you are in the more survivable, light damage zones you can shelter in place or evacuate to an even safer place with your full pack after the initial blast effects subside. If you survive the initial blast, you will need to get out of the fallout zone and/or find a suitable fallout shelter. Immediately donning a dust mask, rain poncho, rain suit, or Tyvek™ painter's suit to keep fallout out of your lungs and off your skin until you reach uncontaminated shelter will significantly reduce overall radiation exposure.

Route and Method

If you live in a target area, you will need to make a detailed evacuation plan and select the safest routes in advance. If you have not gotten away before the panic, you are probably not going to drive. You may be limited to moving on foot or on a bicycle. While evacuation from other types of disasters such as civil disorder or epidemics would permit carrying evacuation packs, the priority here is speed and distance above all else. Let nothing slow you down. Run if you can. Every mile you go increases your odds of survival. Select routes such as railroad right-of-ways, trails, bike paths, etc. leading away from the most probable targets and out of population zones the fastest. Be sure to avoid moving towards other potential targets such as industrial centers or government installations if possible.

Here are six expedient blast shelters:

If caught outside, you will get a warning from the flash just seconds before the heat wave and blast occur. You must instantly get something between you and that detonation. The illustrations above offer a few options. As you evacuate or when you hear the sirens, you need to constantly be ready to jump into the best nearby shelter. If nothing is available, lie flat with your feet towards the probable target site. Many survivors of the Nagasaki and Hiroshima bombs were just in such places while those caught in the open were burned and/or torn to pieces by the blast wave.

Fallout Survival

Nuclear detonations will result in radioactive fallout. Fallout is simply radio-active particulates and fine dust thrown upwards by the blast. Since the heavier particles fall first, they start falling downwind closest and soonest after the blast. This makes these particles the most dangerous. The finer dust will fall further downwind over days and weeks following the initial blast. All radioactive fallout is subject to decay in radiation, so it is most dangerous within the first hours and days after it is created but continues to radiate at a declining rate for years and decades.

The chart below illustrates a typical fallout footprint. The size of the fall-out area footprint depends on the size and altitude of the initial dust plume and the strength and direction of the wind. If you know what happened and when, you can make a pretty good guess as to what direction to evacuate in. If radiation levels are going up, you are moving towards the source or into the downwind footprint. Lowering levels indicate the best way to go, but if you are moving downwind your exposure time will still be higher than if you move at right angles to the wind direction and get out of the footprint as fast as possible. If there are multiple detonations throughout the country, all areas will fall within a fallout footprint within a few days of the attack. So, you will need to escape the immediate fallout footprint area and still find shelter within twenty-four hours.

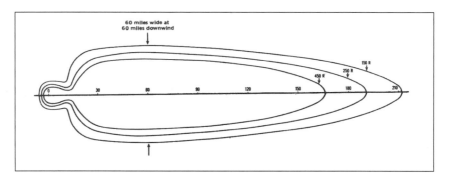

WHAT IS RADIATION?

There are three sources of radiation exposure from fallout:

- **Alpha particles** cannot penetrate unbroken skin, but if ingested on contaminated food or drinks or inhaled from fallout in the air, they can reach unprotected internal organs and can have serious effects.
- **Beta particles** can cause beta-burns if left on the unprotected skin and can cause more serious damage if ingested or inhaled.
- Both alpha and beta exposure hazards can be reduced by washing or dusting off particulates and wearing an effective dust mask.
- **Gamma rays** are like X-rays in that they can penetrate most materials with ease. These rays pass through the body, damaging cells and vital organs. The more intense the gamma radiation and the longer the time of exposure, the more severe the damage is. In addition to keeping particulates out of and off our body, you must act to get out of the contaminated area as quickly as possible and thoroughly decontaminate yourself once out of the area. All clothing and equipment exposed to fallout must be abandoned or decontaminated. It will probably be difficult to clean all fallout off clothing.

Fallout shelters use massive amounts of soil, concrete, and other materials to reduce the amount of gamma radiation from outside that penetrates the shelter. Additional filtering of air reduces the amount of gamma radiating material that enters the shelter. The more time you spend in such a shelter or even within a massive building or basement the less exposure you will receive. However: if the area of contamination is limited, such as downwind of a nuclear power plant incident, prompt evacuation and decontamination if practical would be far more effective than remaining in the contaminated area in any kind of shelter.

PERSONAL PROTECTION AND DECONTAMINATION

Unless you are in a fully stocked shelter with filtered air, you will be exposed to radioactive fallout dust to some degree. Your top priority is to keep alpha and beta particles off your skin and out of your lungs. Donning clean N95 dust/mist respirator is a must. You should have at least five to ten of these in a sealed plastic bag. As you travel and remove the mask to eat and drink the mask will get contaminated on the inside and must be replaced. Throw away the used mask. Even a simple plastic rain poncho will help protect you from fallout. A full rain suit, Tyvek™ suit with pants, or even plastic bags as shown below can keep you from being contaminated until you get out of the fallout zone or into a shelter. Be sure to have a head covering and gloves. Plastic booties can be purchased at painting supply stores. You don't want to be walking around in a contaminated boot or tracking fallout into a shelter. Once you have reached an uncontaminated area or are ready to enter a shelter, you must remove all your protective items mask last. If any source of water is available, wash or rinse the dust off the outer protection before removal. If not, dust, brush, or wipe away as much as you can prior to removal. In short: keep it out, keep it off, get it off, leave it off.

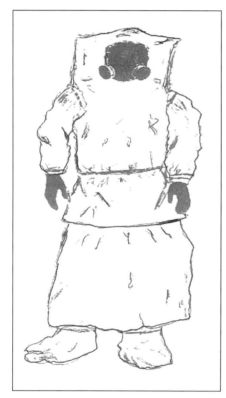

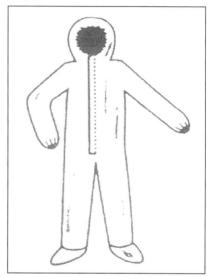

Bask Tyvek™ painter's suits are cheap, light, and available at hardware stores. Be sure to get the ones with a hood and get the attached or unattached booties as well. Don't forget disposable gloves.

This improvised fallout suit made from various sizes of plastic bags could be quite effective if nothing else is available.

FALLOUT SHELTER

The sooner you get to a shelter and the longer you stay there, the better your chances are. You will need to get into a place where you are safe from the mob and have enough water and food to stay for at least two weeks. If you have relatives, survival group members, or friends in semi-rural or rural locations, try to cache supplies at their location and make arrangements with them. If this is not an option, think about places that can be "occupied" and sources of supplies in advance. If you already live beyond the immediate destruction zone, preparing and fortifying your home as a fallout shelter may be your best option. The more mass and distance you can put between yourself and the fallout dust landing on the buildings and ground, the safer you are. The center of a basement offers some shielding. Covering the basement windows with soil, and piling heavy books, and furniture above the shelter area increases protection. Any kind of shelter that puts masses of soil, or bricks between you and the outside will help.

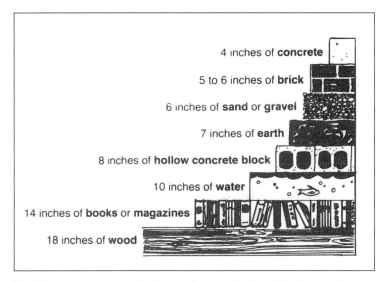

4 inches of **concrete**

5 to 6 inches of **brick**

6 inches of **sand** or **gravel**

7 inches of **earth**

8 inches of **hollow concrete block**

10 inches of **water**

14 inches of **books** or **magazines**

18 inches of **wood**

The illustration above indicates minimum effective shielding against radiation for various materials. Any combination of material between you and the radiation source is helpful and more is always better.

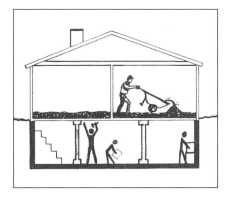

This illustration shows soil being added to reinforced floors to make a basement shelter. It is doubtful that one would have time to do this, but any amount of mass (furniture, books, etc., piled above the shelter point in the basement would help).

Here an improvised shelter is prepared using shelving, tables, and other available material in the corner of a basement. While you might not be able to stay in such an uncomfortable space all day, sleeping there and staying there as long as possible would reduce accumulated exposure.

RADIOACTIVITY EXPOSURE AND ITS EFFECTS

The table on the following page provides the estimated effects of radiation exposure. Note that even without the benefit of knowing the dosage in roentgen units, how soon the symptoms appear and how many people in the same area are affected is a good indication of developing disability and fatality rates. Be aware that disability and death rates may vary widely depending on the health and age of the exposed personnel. The lower exposures (50–120 roentgens) might be anticipated from distant events such as overseas nuclear exchanges or nuclear power plant accidents. Being close to or downwind of a nuclear detonation or power plant meltdown could result in exposures from 100 to 300 roentgens depending on distance and how long you spent in the contaminated area. Higher exposures would be limited to those directly in or near to a nuclear detonation or detonations. Of course, any exposure can increase your potential for cancer, leukemia, and a host of other medical issues in the future. It is particularly important to protect children and adolescents from any level of exposure because it is more likely to cause illness and birth defects years and decades later.

Expected Effects of Short-Term Gamma Radiation Exposure

Acute Dose (Roentgens)	Anticipated Effects of Radiation Exposure
0–50	No obvious symptoms. Possible minor blood changes.
60–120	Vomiting and nausea will affect about **5 to 10 percent** of exposed personnel within 24-hours of exposure. **Some fatigue may occur, but no disability or deaths anticipated.**
130–170	Vomiting and nausea will affect about **25 percent of exposed personnel** within about one day. This may be followed by other symptoms of radiation sickness, **but no deaths can be anticipated.**
180–220	Vomiting and nausea will affect about **50 percent of exposed personnel** within about one day. This will be followed with other symptoms of radiation sickness, but **no deaths can be anticipated.**
270–330	Vomiting and nausea will affect nearly **all exposed personnel on the first day.** This will be followed by other symptoms of radiation sickness, Prolonged recovery time and **20 percent deaths within 2–6 weeks** can be anticipated.
400–500	Vomiting and nausea will affect **all exposed personnel within the first day after exposure.** Severe symptoms of radiation sickness will last months, and **50 percent of exposed personnel will die.**
550–750	Vomiting and nausea will affect all exposed personnel **within 4 hours after exposure.** Severe symptoms of radiation sickness. **Few survivors** and prolonged convalescents time for those who survive.
1,000 >	Vomiting and nausea will affect all exposed personnel **within a few hours of exposure. Few or no survivors from radiation sickness.**
5,000 >	All exposed personnel **incapacitated almost immediately, 100 percent fatalities** within one week.

Rule of Thumb for Estimation of Total Dosage Accumulated:
D= Dosage in roentgens
I= Intensity of roentgens per hour
T= Time of exposure in hours
$D = I \times T$
For example: If the dosage rate is found to be 70 roentgens per hour and you have been exposed for three hours it is $70 \times 3 = 210$ roentgens accumulated dosage

SIGNS AND SYMPTOMS OF RADIATION SICKNESS

Radiation sickness results from the damage that gamma rays do to the cells and organs of the body. How soon the signs and symptoms appear and how severe they are is a good indication of exposure rates and potential mortality. Initial symptoms include nausea, irritability, vomiting, diarrhea, and general fatigue. These symptoms may disappear after a few days but reappear within one to two weeks with more serious symptoms of hair loss, hemorrhaging, and bleeding under the skin. Compromised immune systems will result in fever, infections, and disability. Vomiting, diarrhea, and internal hemorrhaging result in severe dehydration. The sooner these symptoms appear after exposure, the lower the survival rate will be. Radiation sickness is not contagious. Exposed but decontaminated victims cannot "infect" family members or caregivers.

What to do if you know or think you are being exposed to radioactive fallout:

- Get out of the contaminated area as fast as you can to reduce total exposure rates.
- Put on a dust mask or improvise a respirator from dampened cloth immediately to keep particles out of the body.
- Dust off any contamination on your clothing.
- If possible, don a rain poncho, rain suit, plastic bags, or other waterproof and dust proof clothing. Be sure to have your head covered to keep particles out of your hair.
- Once out of the contaminated area, carefully remove contaminated outer garments. Dust and wash (spray or shower) skin, hair, feet/shoes, etc. as thoroughly as possible. Remove the dust mask last. Leave contaminated clothing and material well away from shelter.
- Decontaminate any food cans, utensils, and equipment before use.
- If available, take potassium iodide pills or liquid per dosage instructions. Note: overdosing on potassium iodide can be harmful, so follow instructions.

TREATING RADIATION POISONING

In addition to preventive use of potassium iodine tablets, there are other measures you can take to improve your survival chances and shorten recovery time:

- Maintain hydration with vitamin and electrolyte fortified water. When and if oral hydration cannot be tolerated, the use of intravenous fluids or fluid enemas may be necessary.

- Strong iron supplements should be given to combat severe anemia and weakness.
- Antibiotics should be given at the first signs of fever or infection, as the immune system may not be able to fend off even minor illness or wound infections.
- Burns and wounds must be treated with special care to avoid any kind of contamination.
- Since internal bleeding often occurs in radiation poisoning, aspirin should be avoided.
- Milk of magnesia or Pepto-Bismol may be used to reduce diarrhea and vomiting.

RADIOACTIVE DECAY AND THE RULE OF SEVENS

Although heavily radiated areas such as those near Chernobyl can be unsafe for decades or even centuries, most contaminated areas will become safer and safer as time passes. This is because of radioactive decay. All radioactivity declines by a factor of ten for every sevenfold increase in time after the initial event. This is known as the "rule of sevens." So, after seven hours, the residual fission radioactivity declines 90 percent, to one-tenth its level of one hour. After 7 × 7 hours (49 hours, approx. two days), the level drops again by 90 percent. So now it's just 1 percent of the dosage it was after one hour. After 7 × 2 days (two weeks) it drops a further 90 percent, and so on. After fourteen weeks the rate drops even faster.

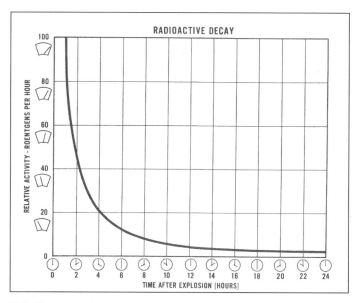

This illustration from a Civil Defense publication illustrates radioactive decay.

RADIATION DETECTION INSTRUMENTS

Back in the 1960s through the 1980s the Civil Defense Department (now FEMA) trained a lot of citizens (including the author) in radiological monitoring. There were a lot of CDS V-742 and 750 dosimeters and CD V-700 survey meters. There were complicated nomograms to calculate how long one could be outside, and trainees had to search buildings for hidden radiation sources planted for us by the instructors. The Nuclear Regulatory Commission has long since retrieved these low-level radiation sources. There are a lot of reasonably priced older dosimeters and survey meters on sale at preparedness shows and on the internet. Uncalibrated radiation detectors sell for about twenty dollars because the calibration radiation sources used for this procedure are so strictly regulated, but there are sources to have them calibrated. Calibrated survey meters sell for about $80 and new ones sell for about $150. There are also more modern nuclear radiation detectors and monitors on the market. These range in price from $180 to over $300. Regardless of calibration, any detected exposure levels ranges or area radiation above normal is cause for concern and precautions.

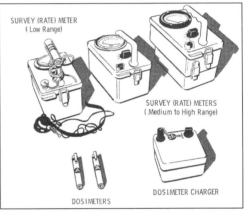

SURVEY (RATE) METER
(Low Range)

SURVEY (RATE) METERS
(Medium to High Range)

DOSIMETER CHARGER

DOSIMETERS

Surplus civil defense survey meters such as the CV-700, 751, 720 etc. can be purchased at preparedness shows and on the internet at reasonable costs. Some are calibrated and others are not, but calibration services are also available. These CD V-742 pocket dosimeters and CD-V750 chargers are also still available. These are used to register personal exposure rather than area radiation.

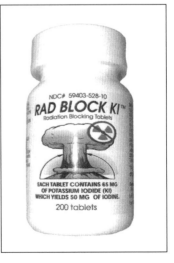

NDC# 59403-528-10

RAD BLOCK KI™
Radiation Blocking Tablets

EACH TABLET CONTAINS 65 MG
OF POTASSIUM IODIDE (KI)
WHICH YIELDS 50 MG OF IODINE.
200 tablets

Potassium iodide is a specific blocker of thyroid radio-iodine uptake. Taking potassium iodide effectively prevents the thyroid gland from being saturated with harmful radio-iodide from fallout contamination that can lead to cancer. A bottle of fourteen 130 mg.

potassium iodide pills sells for about twenty-five dollars. The government has stockpiles of these pills for distribution, but having your own supply is highly advisable.

FALLOUT SHELTER SUPPLIES

No amount of sheltering will be effective unless you have adequate supplies of food, water, sanitation, and medical supplies to remain in the shelter for up to two weeks. These supply requirements apply to surviving other types of disaster such as grid failure, epidemics, and civil unrest. The illustrations below are from Civil Defense's Cold War training materials.

Basic Fallout Shelter Water Requirements

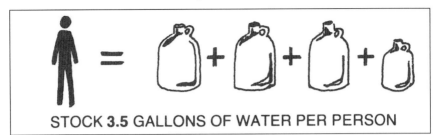

STOCK **3.5** GALLONS OF WATER PER PERSON

Sanitation Supplies and Methods

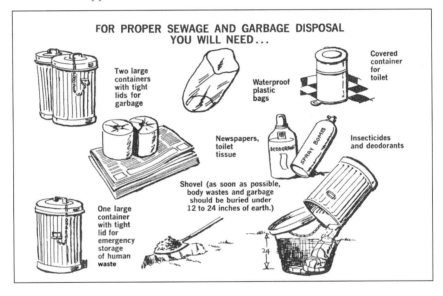

FOR PROPER SEWAGE AND GARBAGE DISPOSAL YOU WILL NEED...

Two large containers with tight lids for garbage

Waterproof plastic bags

Covered container for toilet

Newspapers, toilet tissue

Insecticides and deodorants

One large container with tight lid for emergency storage of human waste

Shovel (as soon as possible, body wastes and garbage should be buried under 12 to 24 inches of earth.)

CHAPTER 10

WAR ZONE SEARCH AND RESCUE

Images of rescuers digging through the rubble of collapsed buildings are now a daily part of the news cycle. Previously, the most common source of such tragedies was earthquakes, but war has increasingly become the leading cause of massive building fires and building collapses. Anyone who has watched events in the Ukraine, Gaza, and Israel can appreciate the horror and desperation of citizens frantically searching and digging for loved ones among the massive destruction of bombs and missiles. All of these disasters may seem remote to Americans, but the world has changed, and we are no longer immune to conventional and even nuclear bombings. Drones, hypersonic missiles, and terrorist actions can and probably will impact cities and towns throughout the United States. Remember 9/11. While trained first responders and rescue teams can effectively conduct operations for isolated disasters, wartime attacks will be widespread and beyond the capacity of these agencies to respond to multiple situations. Individual citizens and neighbors will be the first responders in many cases. Prompt rescue and effective access to first aid will save many lives, including your family members and fellow citizens. The following instructions are derived from first responder and fire department training, and from Community Emergency Response Team (CERT) training materials.

SEARCH AND RESCUE EQUIPMENT

The volunteer citizen rescuer may not have access to all the items listed below, but most home workshops and garages will have some of these items. Rescue tools should be kept apart from buildings that may catch fire or collapse and make the tools unavailable. However, some items may be stored in a shelter to facilitate self-rescue if you are trapped.

Search and Rescue Safety Gear

The following safety items are issued to civilian first responders in the CERT program and should be acquired by prepared citizens:

- Safety hard hat helmet
- Heavy-duty work gloves
- Knee pads
- Safety goggles
- Multiple N95 dust respirators
- High intensity, heavy-duty flashlight
- Chemical lights

Typical rescue safety gear issued to volunteer first responders.

The tools listed below may help facilitate rescue from fallen debris and collapsed structures:

- Adjustable wrenches for turning off gas and water valves.
- Various sizes of crowbars and prybars
- Small and large sledgehammers
- Shovels
- Cable/ratchet come along or block and tackle

- Various auto and utility jacks
- Lumber two-by-fours and four-by-fours for bracing and shoring

Assorted crowbars, sledgehammers, an axe, a shovel, and two hydraulic jacks rated to lift several tons. The Cable and Ratchet Come Along on the left is rated to pull one thousand pounds.

SEARCH AND RESCUE SAFETY

Searching through damaged and unstable structures and attempting to free people from fallen debris and wreckage is a dangerous activity. The rescuer can become another casualty or even further endanger the person or persons they are trying to help. If professional rescuers are anticipated and the trapped person is in no immediate danger, maintain contact at a safe distance, render immediate first aid if practical and wait for help.

- Do not enter a burning or obviously unstable structure.
- Turn off the gas and electricity to all damaged structures before attempting rescue.
- If you must enter any damaged structure do so only if someone else remains outside to get help if you get into trouble.
- Be alert for exposed nails, broken glass, and other sharp hazards.
- Be alert for unstable footings and overhead hazards.
- Before removal of debris be sure that doing so will not cause further injury to the victim, and that it will not destabilize other debris or the whole structure.

- Unless the victim is in immediate danger from collapse, fire, or hazardous materials stop severe bleeding, splint fractures and stabilize the cervical (neck) spine before movement.
- Know your limitations. If you cannot safely extricate a victim, go for help. When possible, leave someone to care for and comfort the victim until help arrives. If you must leave a victim to get help, use the standard markings to let other rescuers know that a live victim is in the structure.

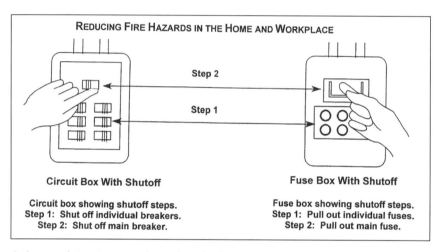

REDUCING FIRE HAZARDS IN THE HOME AND WORKPLACE

Step 2

Step 1

Circuit Box With Shutoff

Circuit box showing shutoff steps.
Step 1: Shut off individual breakers.
Step 2: Shut off main breaker.

Fuse Box With Shutoff

Fuse box showing shutoff steps.
Step 1: Pull out individual fuses.
Step 2: Pull out main fuse.

A damaged structure may have detached wires and exposed electrical lines creating the hazard of electrocution and fire. If you can safely access the circuit breaker box, follow the instructions above to cut the power.

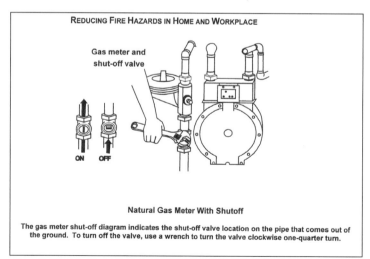

REDUCING FIRE HAZARDS IN HOME AND WORKPLACE

Gas meter and
shut-off valve

ON   OFF

Natural Gas Meter With Shutoff

The gas meter shut-off diagram indicates the shut-off valve location on the pipe that comes out of the ground. To turn off the valve, use a wrench to turn the valve clockwise one-quarter turn.

Gas lines are frequently broken when a building is damaged. Always find the main gas valve and shut off the supply prior to entering any smell gas. Do not enter until the gas is off and any odor of gas has dissipated.

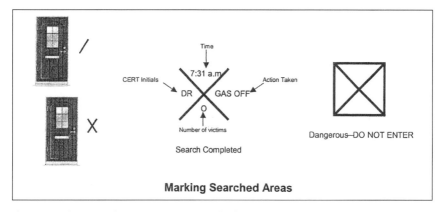

Marking Searched Areas

If you see these markings on or near to the building's entrance, it has been searched by first responders and you do not need to enter. You can use these markings with spray paint or markers and put you initials in place of the "DR" shown above.

CONDUCTING A SEARCH

Any search should be conducted slowly, methodically, and thoroughly. A sloppy search can result in overlooking a live victim and leaving them alone to die. Victims may be unconscious or unable to speak. Victims may be hidden under rubble and dust. Victims may be small children, fearful and hard to find. Rescuers should frequently call out "Hello!" or "Rescue, does anyone need help?" and then stop and listen for any movement or reply. Search room by room, void by void, corner by corner, floor by floor. Different types of structural collapse in different ways. The illustration below indicates three types of collapse patterns. Note that the safest place for blast, earthquake, or tornado survivors is next to a basement wall. This is the most likely location for survivors to be found, but searching for structures that have collapsed to this point can be extremely hazardous.

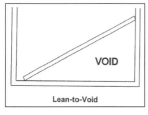

Lean-to-Void

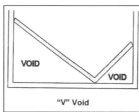

"V" Void

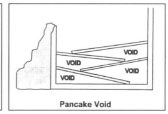

Pancake Void

RESCUE VICTIM MOVEMENT

Once the victim or victims are located, they must be removed to a safer location for further evaluation and care.

- If there is no immediate hazard, it is best to splint fractured limbs and stabilize the neck and head before moving the victim.
- If additional help is available, a two-person carry if safer for both the rescuer and the victim.
- Plan your route to safety and remove hazards and obstacles to assure smooth and fast extrication.
- Doors and other items can be used as improvised stretchers.

A few basic carry techniques are illustrated below.

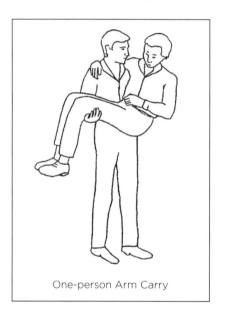

One-person Arm Carry

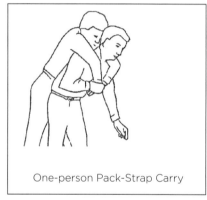

One-person Pack-Strap Carry

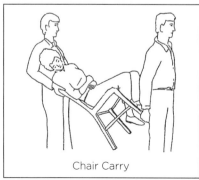

Chair Carry

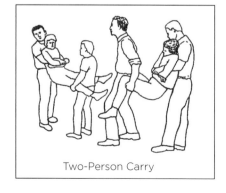

Two-Person Carry

If you are unable to carry the victim, the drag techniques below may be your only option. Use extreme care to protect the neck and head.

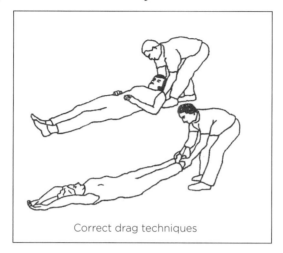

Correct drag techniques

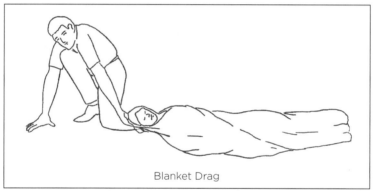

Blanket Drag

For longer moves improvised stretchers will be more practical and safer for all.

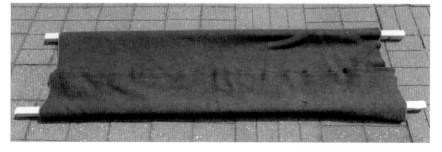

This stretcher is improvised using two seven-foot-long poles and an army blanket.

An improvised stretcher using two poles and two strong shirts. Three shirts would be preferable, and the victims' heads would need to be supported throughout the move.

In the gravest extreme untrained citizens may be the only hope of rescue during the kind of massive disasters created in wartime. It is highly recommended that responsible citizens seek training from local disaster response organizations and encourage local governments to sponsor citizen preparedness education.

CHAPTER 11

WARTIME ESCAPE AND EVASION

The further backward you look, the further forward you can see.
—Winston Churchill, 1874–1965

Escape and evasion techniques have been part of military training throughout history. Soldiers and airmen caught behind enemy lines would need to be skilled in survival, evasion, camouflage, first aid, and unarmed combat in order to avoid capture and return to friendly locations. In recent years, the clear lines between friendly and hostile territory have blurred. Israeli and Ukrainian citizens have been massacred, tortured, or take prisoner by invading forces. Terrorist raids have been conducted solely for the purpose of killing or capturing civilians. Governments have been overthrown or turned on their own citizens. Even if rescue efforts are initiated, they often come too late. While a variety of "night vision" and infrared detection gear has become available it is in limited supply and not as effective as the movies portray. Good evasion, concealment, and camouflage techniques can still prevent detection and assault. While most of the material related to escape and evasion is derived from military training, it is all applicable to civilian threat situations. Most of the clothing and equipment can be purchased through surplus outlets or improvised. There may be a good reason why camouflage has become a popular style in twenty-first century America. A few decades ago, a person could "disappear" and establish a new identity with relative ease. Modern technology makes it almost impossible to disappear for any length of time. Artificial intelligence (AI) and quantum computing have built up a "profile" on every citizen including education, travel, family, friends, political affiliations, finances, skills, hobbies, habits, and medical records. More importantly, AI can create a psychological profile to predict what you will do, where you will hide and how you will react under high threat conditions. If you have practiced escape and evasion while you had your cell phone or used your GPS-equipped vehicle, or passed through any cameras or plate readers, your escape routes are compromised. However, wartime conditions, and massive disruption of political and social system may overwhelm and disable technology. The ability to remain unseen and to move with stealth can keep you safe from military, paramilitary, and rouge civilian threats.

CAMOUFLAGE

Camouflage is not just a pattern on clothing. Camouflage is whatever one does to avoid notice or detection. It is a combination of appearance and action that reduces the distinction between the person and the environment. The person wearing woodland camouflage clothing in the city is not camouflaged while the guy wearing jeans and a Gap sweatshirt is well camouflaged. In survival, there are two classes of camouflage. There is "passive camouflage" that is used to avoid being noticed or avoid standing out from others. And there is "active camouflage" that is used to avoid being seen by those actively looking for you.

Passive camouflage should be used in everyday life. You can look like an outdoor person without looking like a survivalist. In urban areas, gray and tans are good camouflage without looking like camouflage. In areas where hunting and fishing are common, actual camouflage (e.g., woodland, tree bark,) may be okay. In many cases, jeans and T-shirt or slacks and sweater may be true camouflage. While you may like to wear "Don't Tread on Me" shirts or full camouflage pattern clothes at gun shows or survival group meetings, it is not advised for street attire.

Active camouflage is an important part of military survival training and is also practiced by hunters and to some extent by law enforcement. In survival situations camouflage can be used to evade detection by criminals and looters. It can aid in hunting game for food, and it gives the survivor the choice of when and if he or she becomes visible to others. While modern infrared and night vision technology can limit the effectiveness of camouflage, they have limitations and may not be in use by those you are trying to evade. So, knowing the principles of camouflage will remain an important survival skill. There are five key elements to good camouflage listed below.

Shape: The human form is distinctive from most surroundings. A round head peering over a rock will be noticed. A straight rifle barrel stands out from bent and forked branches. Use branches or camouflage netting to break up your shape and that of your equipment.

Shining: Cover, enclose, or wrap up anything you have that will reflect light. This includes jewelry, watches, glasses, buttons, belt buckles, and binoculars. One glint of light off of these items, day or night, can undo all your camouflage work.

Silhouette: This is your shape against the background. Is the sun or moon or town lights silhouetting you? A white gravel road or a snowy field or white smoke in the background can make you stand out as a target. If you are casting a shadow, you are casting a silhouette. Be aware.

Any of the above errors can put you at risk under escape and evasion conditions.

Shadow: You may be well hidden from direct view, but your shadow may give you away. If you have successfully broken up your shape it will help. Keeping low will also reduce your shadow. You must be aware of your shadow and use the shadows of trees and rocks to cover your shadow when possible. Shadows are especially distinct against flat surfaces like buildings, roads, and snowy fields. Near perfect winter camouflage to blend into the snow and the pines will still produce a clear black-on-white shadow profile of you on a sunny day.

Shading: the colors and the shade (dark or light) of the camouflage is the most essential element. It must match the environment as closely as possible in pattern and color. As you move from one location (e.g. dry grass) to another (e.g. green forest) the effectiveness of your camouflage may be lost and require changing. Ghillie suits and netting are good for staying in one location, but tend to snag, pull, and tear in movement. Fortunately, there is a wide selection of camouflage clothing for just about every location and season. If you're moving from civilization (I'm just a hiker) to escape and for evasion, you may have to use basic dark and earth tone clothing enhanced by foliage and face paint when needed. Apply camouflage paint in patches or stripes across the face based on the patterns of light and shadow in the environment. The eye sockets, cheeks, and below the chin are shaded and therefore should get most of the lighter green and tan colors while the more exposed nose, ears, and forehead get the darker green and black tones. Do not forget the neck and the back of the hands. If you do not have camouflage paint, dirt, and charcoal can be used. Carrying camouflage gloves and a face net or mask is handy if you don't have time for painting.

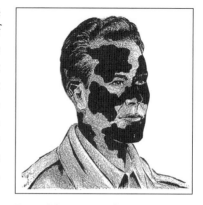

Typical face camouflage breaks up the pattern of the face.

Movement: Movement attracts the eye. Slow movement is often missed even if camouflage is poor. Ninjas were masters of camouflage and stealth and very, very slow movement. When you must move through a location where observation is likely, move slowly and stay low.

AVOID SWISHING—
LIFT KNEES HIGH

PUT TOE DOWN FIRST

This military illustration shows how to walk quietly. No foot dragging or shuffling.

Secondary motion: As you move, you may move branches and tall grass or stir up dust. This may give away your presents and location.

Sight level: Whenever you stop moving or are observing, do it while crouching or lying down. People naturally look at eye level. The lower you are, the more you blend into the ground and are overlooked.

The importance of staying below sight level is well illustrated above.

Noise discipline: Your equipment must not bang, squeak, or rattle. Water canteens must not gurgle. NO TALKING! Use hand signals or low volume, in-your-ear whispers.

Light discipline: No flashlights or matches or cell phones at night. When necessary, red lens lights can be used under a tarp or low in bushes just long enough to read a map, fix a weapon, or render first aid.

Time selection: If you can do so, select a time to move through an area that will be best for you. Maybe there is more noise to cover your movement at a certain time. Maybe it is foggy in the morning. Is there a full moon? How will the sun's location affect your visibility? Night or day?

Route selection: Route selection makes the best use of all available concealment, including low areas in the ground, foliage, background, lighting, and of course the location of the hostile observers. Moving through thick woods may give good concealment but make a great deal of noise. Gravel roads are noisy. Look at the map below to see how routes would differ from day to night.

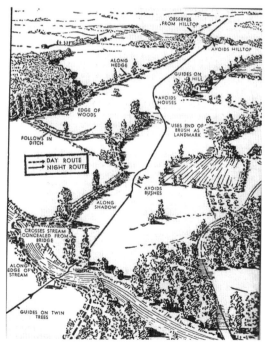

The map above illustrates the difference between a good daytime route and a good night route. A full moon or bright ambient light may affect route selection.

THE IMPORTANCE OF OPTICS

The importance of a good pair of binoculars or at least a monocular in escape and evasion situations cannot be overstated. You should always carry a pair of binoculars in your vehicle and have a small pair of binoculars or a monocular in your evacuation pack. The ultimate in stealth and camouflage is to literally not be there. If you can see a threat or potential hostile individual before you enter the danger zone, it can be avoided, or you can use your camouflage more effectively to get past it. You can select your route well before moving and constantly make observations as you move. Your knowledge of the camouflage and stealth techniques covered in this chapter should help you in knowing what to watch for such as shadows, patterns, silhouettes, and shapes that are not natural. If you can acquire any kind of night vision optics, you will have a huge advantage, but remember that this only gives you day-like vision. Night vision gear has come a long way since the large, expensive, and clumsy units of the 1970s, and small night vision binoculars are available for less than one hundred dollars. A basic night vision monocular can be had for less than twenty dollars. Of course, truly professional grade night vision gear still costs north of ten thousand dollars. Regardless of the quality of the gear, good camouflage works against light enhancing optics as well as it does in daylight. It is important to keep in mind that any hostile person or group may be using optics as well. Just because there is no immediate threat does not mean that potentially dangerous people are not watching you from a distance. Keeping a low profile and following basic stealth and camouflage rules should never be ignored.

When making observations with or without optics never look out the window while standing close the window. Stay back in the shadows. If it's brighter inside than outside they can see you. You do not want to draw attention, or attack while making observation.

CHAPTER 12

WAR ZONE FIRE PREVENTION AND SUPPRESSION

Long before there were nuclear weapons, fire was the primary destroyer of towns and cities. The great Chicago fire in 1871 destroyed seventeen thousand buildings, displaced one hundred thousand people, and killed three hundred citizens. A single fire raid in March of 1945 on Tokyo killed 124,711 people and leveled sixteen square miles. The glow from the firestorm could be seen 150 miles away. The German city of Dresden was virtually wiped out with over one hundred thousand dead from one night of firebombing during World War II. By comparison, the atomic bomb dropped on Hiroshima killed thirty-five thousand to fifty thousand people. Historically, accidental and arson fires have devastated Rome (27 AD), London (1666), Chicago (1871), and Boston (1872). The massive fire that followed Hurricane Sandy in New Jersey illustrates what happens when the fire department is not available. More recently, fire killed eighty-five residents of Paradise, California, in 2018 and ninety-seven residents of Maui, Hawaii, in 2023. Only effective fire departments prevent the spread of fires through densely populated cities and towns. Hostile agents, terrorists, and incendiary drones could easily start multiple fires that could overwhelm any municipal fire department. Fire is also a major component of any nuclear detonation. Civil unrest and looting almost always results in fires that the fire department cannot get to. Any wartime emergency, epidemic, or level of economic chaos could impede or paralyze fire department operations. On a more basic level, any home fire that occurs when no fire department response is available will be catastrophic unless the citizen is able to extinguish it in its very early phases. Fire doubles about every one to two minutes, and with your home goes your shelter, food, and survival supplies. Under worst-case war-survival conditions, rescue, aid, and insurance may not be available. Having effective fire prevention and extinguishing equipment as well as plans to protect and evacuate critical supplies and valuables must be part of wartime survival preparedness. There are five essential priorities for fire survival:

1. Prevent fires from starting in your home.

2. Prevent fires from spreading to your home.
3. Extinguish incipient fire that start in or come from outside your home.
4. Evacuate your home and your area if fires cannot be extinguished.
5. Minimize losses and survive if fire devastates your community.

INTERIOR FIRE PREVENTION

A home fire is a disaster. Fires caused by arsonists, nuclear blast heat, or uncontrolled brush and building fire raging through your community may prove to be overwhelming. Fires that start inside your home are preventable. Under emergency conditions, citizens may need to use candles, lanterns, camp stoves, and portable heaters that pose serious fire risks. If local fire departments are inoperable only the care and vigilance of the homeowner can prevent disaster.

Home Fire Prevention Safety
1. Store fuels and refill lanterns, stoves, etc. outside and well away from your home.
2. Keep combustible and flammable material away from furnaces, stoves, and other ignition sources.
3. Use extreme care with candles, gas lanterns, oil lanterns, and camp stoves.
4. Have fire extinguishers immediately available when using any kind of flame or heat device.
5. Never leave heaters, lanterns, candles, or stoves unattended.
6. Do a regular home fire hazard inspection looking for potential ignition sources, fuel sources, and combustible items.
7. Keep blankets, bedding, and clothing clear of ignition sources.
8. Think "what if?" If it can happen it will happen unless you prevent it.

EXTERIOR FIRE PROTECTION

Fire can come into your home from outside sources. Radiated heat from nearby buildings or forest fires can ignite your home. Heat from a nuclear blast miles away can set fire to thousands of structures instantly and then spread to areas well beyond the blast area. Civil disorder, deliberate arson, and so-called Molotov cocktail firebombs may all be elements of a wartime worst-case.

Home Exterior Protection Actions
1. Remove flammable and combustible materials from the areas around the exterior of your home.

2. Replace flammable curtains and shades with less flammable blinds over windows.
3. Move more flammable furniture away from the front room windows.
4. If water is available, activate the sprinkler and wet down exterior walls, porches etc.
5. Remove fences, shades, and other combustible attachments that may carry the fire to your main building.
6. If possible, replace asphalt shingles with metal roofing.

EXTINGUISHING FIRES

Under wartime conditions, fire department services may be impacted by shortages in personnel and equipment. In the event of any kind of direct attack by conventional or nuclear weapons, fires will be out of control and citizens alone may be tasked with saving their lives and property. It is therefore essential that citizens have adequate fire extinguishers, available water, and the knowledge to make wise decisions and take effective action should fire threaten their life

It is far better to have too many extinguishers than not enough. The garden sprayer on the left is great for small class A fires only. All the other extinguishers can be used for A, B, and C fires, but the small ones on the far right are only intended for small incipient kitchen fires.

and property. Fire extinguishers come in a wide variety of sizes and classes. The most common types are A, B, and C. Class A extinguishes combustibles such as paper, wood, and cloth. Class B will safely extinguish flammable liquid fires such as gasoline, oil, or kerosene. Class C extinguishers are usable for electrical fires such as motors or circuit boxes. A, B, and C extinguishers are usually dry chemical or CO_2 and can be used for all three. Never use a water A-only extinguisher on a B flammable liquid fire as it will only spread the fire and using water on C electrical fire can result in your electrocution. However, since the majority exterior source fires would be Class A: brush, wood, siding, curtains, etc. Having plenty of water and a method of spraying it would be advisable. Having at least two large A, B, C extinguishers, several water-filled garden sprayers, and several smaller extinguishers is recommended. If you can have a pool or pond and a utility pump rigged to a hose, you may be able to prevent heat ignition and hot embers from setting your home on fire, but this will not be enough to put out a structural fire once it is initiated.

The mnemonic PASS covers the four steps in fire extinguisher operation:

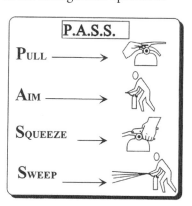

Pull out the pin that retains the extinguisher valve handle.

Aim the extinguisher nozzle or hose nozzle at the front edge of the fire.

Squeeze the valve handle firmly.

Sweep the extinguishing agent (powder, CO-2, water) back and forth over the fire, moving the stream further back until the fire is extinguished.

EXTINGUISHER USE SAFETY

1. Call the fire department first or send someone to call them before attempting to put out anything but a very small fire.
2. Never enter a space fully engulfed in fire or completely filled with smoke.
3. Never use water on burning liquids or electrical fires.
4. Never let the fire get between you and an escape route.
5. Always have a second extinguisher and preferably a second person with an extinguisher available.
6. If the fire is out, continue to observe and have a second extinguisher ready in case it reignites.
7. Inspect the fire area for hidden sparks or heat transfer through wall ceiling etc.

If your extinguisher(s) fail to put out the fire, leave immediately.

FIRE ACTION FLOW CHART

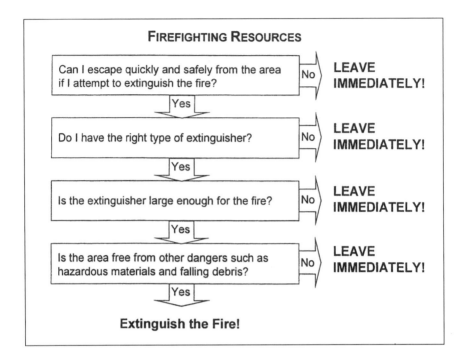

EVACUATION FROM AND THROUGH A FIRE

Regardless of your fire prevention efforts, your home and your whole community may be part of a general conflagration caused by natural or wartime occurrences. Fires from nearby civil disorders, or out-of-control accidental fires may spread to generate moving fire-fronts or firestorms that can move at incredible speed. The heat from any kind of nuclear blast will ignite entire communities and then generate a spreading fire that will only stop when there is nothing left to burn. If most of the buildings upwind of you or surrounding you are on fire, you will not be able to save your home. Do not hesitate to evacuate. A fire a mile away will be on you in just minutes. If adjoining homes are on fire, you have seconds to act. You should plan for this possibility.

- If you can use your vehicle to put any distance between you and the fires, do so but be prepared to abandon it if necessary.
- If you can, plan a route that will take you out of the fire's path and through less built-up and populated areas.
- Try to get out of the fire's path as it will move upwind, uphill, and through the densest supply of buildings and fuel.

- You should have a prepared survival evacuation pack for every family member and have a package of essential documents including birth certificates, insurance records, medical records, financial records, and property records in your pack. Copies of important documents can be kept with trusted people outside the danger zones.
- Identify some valuables that you will take with you, but do not try to carry items that will inhibit your movement and speed. Life is the top priority.
- During World War II, citizens of European cities often buried valuables including jewelry, furniture, and even machinery in their backyards to be unearthed after all else was gone. Creating such places in advance may be a good precaution.

FIRE SURVIVAL

Since fires may start and spread through populated areas at any time, it will be necessary to post a twenty-four-hour watch once emergency conditions develop. This will also guard against looters and arsonists. If you wake up to a smoke-filled room, do not sit up. The air just above you may be heated to several hundred degrees and filled with toxic gasses. Roll out of bed and crawl to the nearest exit. You have only seconds. A dust mask and a flashlight kept in a bedside drawer may save your life in the dark smoke-filled house. Once outside, never return to a burning building. You will not come out again! You should have trained every member of your family in escaping fire and have a meeting place outside. Doing drills where family members are blindfolded and must roll out of bed and crawl to the exit may be well worth the time spent.

Fire has always been a major factor related to civilian wartime survival. Being prepared to prevent, extinguish, or escape out-of-control fires will continue to be an essential responsibility of citizens under a variety of emergency scenarios.

CHAPTER 13

WAR ZONE FIRST AID

This chapter will focus on the types of first-aid skills covered in military first aid manuals with the focus on managing traumatic skeletal and soft tissue injuries that may result from projectiles, blasts, falling debris, and impacts. The objective of treatment is to quickly stabilize the patient, prevent further injury, and minimize pain, infection, disability, and death. All civilians should be certified in CPR, and basic first aid. In the worst case, where advanced medical care and long-term care may not be available, the civilian may need more advanced training or at least access to the necessary books, and instruments to perform minor surgery, suturing, and other skills. I recommend *Emergency War Surgery, Tactical Combat Casualty Care and Wound Treatment*, and the *Prepper's Medical Manual* from Skyhorse Publishing as additions to your medical care library. Even if actual military combat is not brought to America soil, the lawlessness, civil disorder, and violence we are already experiencing will only worsen during a period of war and the side-effects of wartime. Dependency on so-called "urgent care, or "rapid care" facilities has rendered most citizens with little or no first aid skills or home medical supplies. Conditions in the Ukraine, Gaza, and other war zones where hospitals are bombed and supplies are unavailable may be replicated in American towns during a future conflict. You may be on your own when you need it most.

WAR ZONE SOFT TISSUE INJURIES

Severe Bleeding

Severe arterial bleeding (hemorrhaging) can result in the death of a patient within one or two minutes unless stopped by the first aider's actions. Venous bleeding is dark red and flows steadily from a wound. This slow bleeding needs to be controlled, but the body can adapt to the loss for a while. Arterial bleeding is distinguishable from venous bleeding by its bright red color and spurting under pressure. The blood spurts out with every beat of the heart at such a rate that the body will be unable to compensate, and hemorrhagic shock and death will occur within minutes. The average adult has about six liters (1.56 gallons) of blood. The loss of 10 percent (600 ml) or more of this blood volume is very dangerous. Along with airway clearing and CPR, the ability to quickly control arterial bleeding is a primary and essential first aid skill.

The most effective methods of stopping severe external bleeding are the application of direct pressure over the wound site, elevation of the wounded extremity, and application of a tourniquet. While many older first aid manuals listed the application of pressure over arterial pressure points to reduce bleeding, these points are often difficult to locate, and do not fully stop bleeding because bleeding continues through other secondary veins and arteries. Earlier manuals and classes also limited the use of tourniquets to a "last resort" methodology because of the belief that the interruption of blood flow could result in the loss of the limb below the application point. It has been found that tourniquet application seldom results in limb damage if access to professional medical care is available within a short time. However, direct pressure and elevation remain the first step in bleeding control, and a tourniquet should only be used to supplement direct pressure if that method fails to stop the bleeding. Arterial bleeding is a serious medical emergency and 911 should be called immediately upon encountering this type of injury. Surgical intervention and blood transfusion will be required to save this patient.

As soon as spurting, bright red arterial bleeding is observed, the first aider must immediately apply direct pressure over the wound. Use the bare hand or any immediately available piece of cloth as a pressure dressing. There is no time to look for bandaging materials or a first aid kit. Once direct pressure is applied it should not be relaxed. If the blood soaks through the original compress, just pile on more material. Also raise the injured extremity to slow blood flow. Secure the pressure dressing in place with a tight bandage secured with the knot directly over the wound.

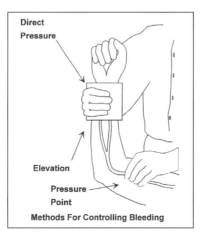

Direct pressure on the wound followed by application of a pressure dressing is usually sufficient to control severe bleeding distal to the elbow or knee.

Direct pressure and elevation are often sufficient to stop even arterial bleeding, but if these steps fail to stop the blood flow, a tourniquet should be applied about two inches above the wound site. While it is desirable to use a purpose made tourniquet device, a cloth bandana, cravat bandage, or other cloth material can be used.

Tourniquet Application Procedures

1. Fold the bandaging material so that it is approximately three to four inches wide, and a few layers thick.
2. Wrap this bandage around the extremity twice, a few inches above the wound.
3. Tie a knot in the bandage, place a stick about six inches long on top of the knot, then tie a knot over the stick.
4. Using the stick as a lever, turn it to tighten the tourniquet until the bleeding stops.
5. Use another piece of cloth or cordage to secure the stick so that it cannot unwind.

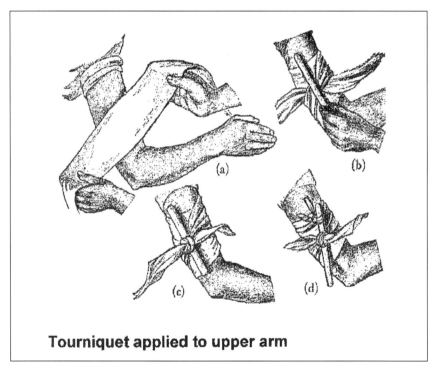

Tourniquet applied to upper arm

The illustration above shows how a tourniquet can be made from a bandana or other pieces of cloth to terminate severe bleeding to the arm.

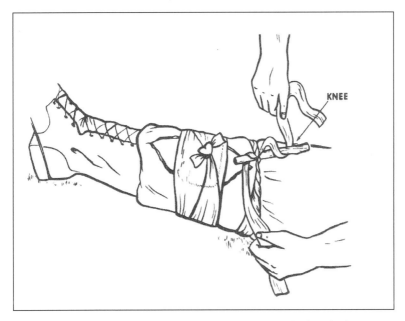

This illustration shows the same kind of tourniquet applied to the leg.

Tourniquet Application Precautions

- Never use wire or narrow material for a tourniquet, as it will cut into the skin.
- Once a tourniquet is applied, do not loosen it. This must be done in an ER where surgical repair and intravenous blood and plasma transfusions are available.
- Never cover a tourniquet with bandaging, splinting, or clothing. It must be in full view.
- Always write "TK" and the time that you applied the tourniquet on a piece of tape or directly onto the patient's forehead. This is important information for care providers.
- Never place a tourniquet below the elbow or below the knee. Bleeding in these locations seldom requires a tourniquet and application can damage nerves. Direct pressure should be adequate for these locations.

Once the bleeding is controlled, the first aider can proceed to examine for additional injuries and gather patient information. In all cases where arterial bleeding has occurred, the first aider must anticipate the onset of hemorrhagic shock and commence treatment of that development (see below). Splinting of the injured extremity is recommended to prevent movement and further bleeding.

Tourniquet Devices

After tourniquets were reaccepted as a method of bleeding control, a variety of specialized devices came on the market. Tourniquet devices range from the SWAT-T™ that is a simple elastic band, to the CAT™ combat application tourniquet that incorporates a lever and a locking device. Prices range from ten to thirty dollars. The CAT tourniquets are very effective, but a bit bulky for pocket carry. Police now carry the CAT tourniquet in a belt holster. Small tourniquets like the SWAT-T can be rolled up and kept in the pocket. One of the best all-around tourniquet/bandage devices is the Israeli battle dressing. This item can be adapted to almost every trauma situation. The basic dressing/compress is an effective bandage for most wounds, while the elastic bandaging can be used to secure splints or stabilize sprains. The device can also be applied as a tourniquet to stop severe bleeding. The ties are long enough to secure the compress over head wounds, abdominal wounds, and thoracic wounds.

Popular torniquet devices, left to right: TAC torniquet, Israeli bandage, SWAT-T™ tourniquet. Such devices are fast and effective and should be carried whenever the potential for injury is present.

Blood Stoppers and Packing

Hemostatic powders and impregnated gauzes can be used to effectively stop arterial and venous bleeding. Hemostatic dressings are impregnated with a substance that accelerates the clotting process while not sticking to the wound the way a normal bandage would. If available, hemostatic dressings can be the first pressure dressing applied, but do not delay application of direct pressure to get them. Hemostatic granules can be poured onto an open wound and will stop bleeding effectively. Large hemostatic dressings are especially effective on abdominal and hip injuries where a tourniquet cannot be applied. The two most established brands for hemostatic agents and dressing are Celox™, and Quik Clot™. Z-fold hemostatic gauzes are long strips of narrow (usually one inch) wide impregnated material that can be stuffed into an open wound to stop bleeding. Celox™ makes an application plunger device that is inserted into a deep puncture wound such as a gunshot wound, then the plunger is pushed to inject hemostatic granules that will seal the wound. Hemostatic powders can be poured onto or into any open wound.

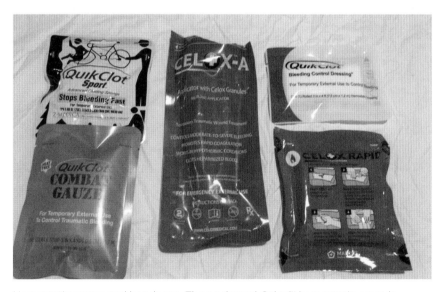

Hemostatic gauze and bandages. The packaged Celox™ hemostatic granule injection devices for bullet wounds is in the center.

Hypovolemic Shock

Hypovolemic shock, or hemorrhagic shock, usually results from significant blood loss due to severe external or internal bleeding. Low blood volume and hypovolemic shock can also develop because of severe thermal burns where plasma leaks from the circulatory system into the burned tissue, from dehydration. If the patient is dehydrated prior to the injury, shock may develop more rapidly from bleeding. When blood volume drops, circulation becomes inadequate to supply the vital organs and shock develops. Shock should be expected to develop in all cases of severe bleeding or violent trauma.

The following are the most common signs and symptoms of shock:

1. Restlessness and anxiety are often the first signs of impending shock.
2. A weak and rapid pulse that may be difficult to feel.
3. Cold, moist skin, often described as "cold and clammy."
4. Profuse sweating.
5. Pale skin color that may turn bluish (cyanosis).
6. Shallow, labored, and rapid breathing that may become irregular or gasping.
7. Dilated pupils and dull lusterless eyes.
8. Marked thirst.
9. Nausea and vomiting.
10. Slowly, but steadily falling, blood pressure. It is best to assume that anyone with a systolic blood pressure of 100mm Hg. or lower is developing shock.
11. Loss of consciousness in the late stages of severe shock.

Shock is a medical emergency and must be treated before further examination or first aid treatment can be performed. The following actions must be applied whenever the symptoms of shock are present:

1. Assure that the patient has an open airway and is breathing well.
2. Control bleeding with direct pressure and apply a tourniquet if necessary.
3. Place the patient in the prone position and elevate the lower extremities about 12–18 inches. Note: avoid raising the legs further as this may inhibit breathing.
4. Calm the patient and avoid rough handling.
5. Keep the patient warm by placing blankets over and under them but avoid overheating.
6. Splint fractures to reduce bleeding and minimize pain.
7. Do not give the patient anything to eat or drink.
8. Monitor the patient's level of consciousness, blood pressure, and other vital signs.
9. Get the patient to professional medical care as soon as possible.

Patients in or going into shock are placed in the shock position with legs elevated 12 to 18 inches and covered with a blanket as shown above. Do not elevate the legs more than 18 inches as this may interfere with breathing.

The objectives of open soft tissue wound treatment are to control bleeding, prevent further contamination, and immobilize the injured part. Bleeding can be controlled by application of a sterile dressing that covers the entire wound. If bleeding continues, the original dressing should be left in place and additional dressings placed over it. When the bleeding is controlled, roller bandaging can be used to secure the dressings in place. If the injury is extensive, the injured extremity should be splinted to reduce bleeding. All open wounds will be contaminated to some extent by the source of the injury and the contaminants on the skin and clothing. In most cases, the first aider should avoid trying to remove hair, clothing and dirt from the wound, as this may worsen bleeding and pain. Application of a sterile dressing will prevent further contamination until the patient reaches professional medical care where wound cleansing and debridement can be performed.

Bandaging Principles and Methods

While modern bandaging products are preferred, the first aider may need to improvise. Bandaging may be created by tearing cotton material into long strips, usually two inches wide and three to four feet long. These bandages can be sterilized by boiling and drying. They should be heated to 274 to 364 Fahrenheit (134 to 138 degrees Celsius) for five minutes or microwaved for no more than sixty seconds.

If no other bandaging material are available Saran™Wrap can be used, wrapped tightly around the entire extremity to cover the wound.

Modern self-adhesive and elastic bandages usually do not require additional methods to stay in place, but surgical tape may be necessary to secure cotton bandaging or gauze. If surgical tape is not available, electrical tape or duct tape can be used.

Securing cloth bandages

Combat bandages come with two strips to tie the bandage in place. The civilian may need to use available clean cloth to make a bandage. Tear the ends of the bandage lengthwise into two strips. Run one strip around the extremity in the direction of bandaging and the other back in the opposite direction and tie them together where they meet.

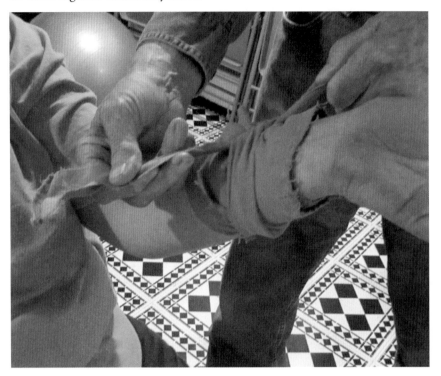

Tear the ends lengthwise long enough to go around the limb in opposite directions then bring them around and tie over the wound.

- Whenever practical have someone hold an extremity while you apply bandaging to prevent movement.
- When winding a bandage around an extremity always start at the narrower, distal end of the limb.
- If using non–self-adhesive bandaging it will be necessary to "lock" the starting end in place to prevent unwinding as you pull the bandage around the limb. The first time around, overlap a corner of the material and then wrap over the tab before continuing bandaging, then tightly wind over the tab and continue wrapping bandage.

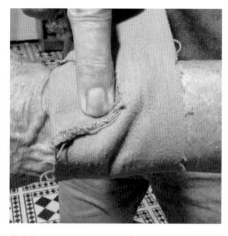

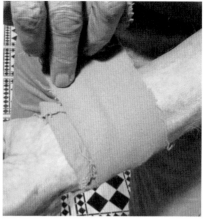

Folding over a corner of the material and hold in place while making the second wraparound.

Tightly wrap over the tab to lock the bandage and then continue wrapping as needed.

The techniques for bandaging various parts of the body using a cloth cravat are illustrated below.

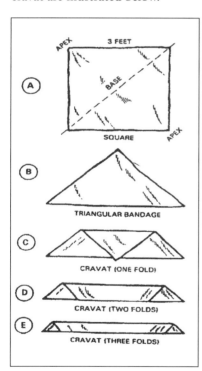

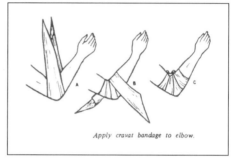

Cravat bandage applied to an elbow injury. The same technique could be used on a knee injury.

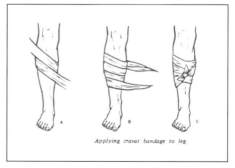

The basic three foot by three-foot cravat can be used as a sling, folded into a triangular bandage or a cravat as shown above.

Cravat bandage applied to the lower leg. This could apply to the forearm as well.

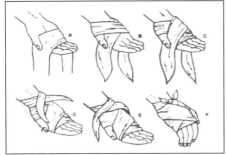

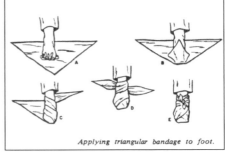

Applying *triangular bandage to foot.*

Cravat bandage applied to the palm of the hand.

Open cravat bandage applied to a foot injury.

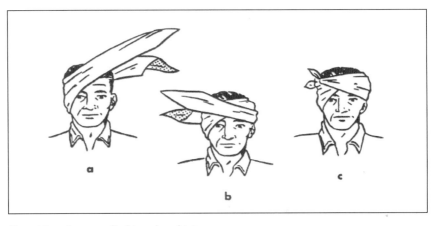

Cravat bandage applied to a head injury.

GUNSHOT WOUNDS

Under war zone conditions, gunshot wounds and other penetrating wounds are more likely. As any modern urban resident knows, you do not have to be a combatant to be the recipient of flying bullets. Explosions can also create fast flying debris that can penetrate any part of the body. Such wounds always contain foreign materials and debris that will cause infections unless the wound is cleaned and antibiotics are administered. Other than obvious graze wounds, there is no such thing as a minor bullet wound; any bullet wound must be considered life-threatening and requiring the fastest access to professional care.

Managing Gunshot Wounds

As with all soft tissue injuries, the priority is to control severe bleeding with direct pressure, hemostatic dressings and if necessary, application of a tourniquet. If the bullet has penetrated the thorax and created a sucking chest wound, the hole must be sealed to prevent the development of a pneumothorax. Packing the wound with sterile gauze or, better yet, hemostatic gauze, can be effective in control of bleeding. Be sure to check for an exit wound and seal both openings. If the wound is to an extremity (arm or leg), apply a splint to prevent further damage. Treat the patient for shock before symptoms appear. Transport the patient to professional medical care as soon as possible.

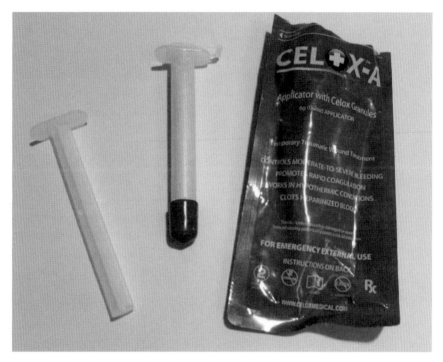

This hemostatic powder injector is specifically designed to seal bullet wounds and has saved lives. The injector is inserted to the depth of the wound and then slowly extracted while injecting the hemostatic material for the length of the wound.

Bullet Extraction

Bullet removal is far beyond first aid and any legal protection in a Good Samaritan situation and should only be attempted in the gravest extreme situations, when no professional medical care can be accessed or anticipated. No attempt to remove a bullet should be made for bullets that have entered the skull, thoracic cavity, or abdominal cavity. Bullets may be extracted if the bullet wound is shallow and the bullet is visible, the bullet has only penetrated the fatty, or muscle tissue, or the bullet is in an extremity. A bullet may have penetrated or nicked an artery and be the only thing preventing severe bleeding. Consider this possibility if the wound is in the thigh, shoulder, or upper arm.

Preparation

1. Any bullet extraction will be extremely painful to the patient. If pre-scription pain relievers are available, administer them, if not, a combination of two Tylenol™ and three Aleve tablets will have pain relief comparable to codeine.
2. Have at least one assistant to hold the patient down.
3. Clean the area around the wound with surgical wipes or soap with water.
4. Have plenty of sterile bandages on hand.
5. Boil all instruments to sterilize them. If not practical, use a flame.
6. Wear sterile surgical gloves and a surgical mask or equivalent.
7. Have a syringe or bulb syringe with sterile water available to flush the wound.
8. Be sure that the patient is not showing any sign of shock, as attempting this procedure will only worsen the condition.

Removal

1. If the bullet wound is shallow, palpate the skin to locate it.
2. If the bullet is not visible, flush the wound and use a flashlight to attempt to see it.
3. If it is too deep to visualize, slowly insert a sterile probe to determine how far in the bullet is located. Be sure you are contacting the bullet and not a bone or bone fragment.
4. Slowly insert a sterile pair of long tweezers, hemostat, or (if not available) needle-nose plyers.
5. Once the bullet is felt, open the device just enough to grip the bullet.
6. Firmly grip the bullet and slowly pull it from the wound.
7. If the bullet has deformed, mushroomed, or turned, it may catch on the skin at the wound site requiring some manipulation or even a small cut to free it.
8. Thoroughly flush the wound with sterile water or saline solution and bandage.
9. Use hemostatic dressings, hemostatic injectors, or tourniquets if severe bleeding results.
10. Treat the patient for shock.
11. Administer antibiotics if available.

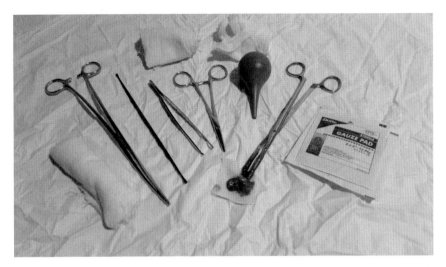

Bullet probe, various instruments, gauze, and a bulb-syringe to flush the wound. If antibiotics are available and the bullet has penetrated only muscle and fat tissue, bullets can be extracted, but when bullets have impacted organs and/or major blood vessels, prompt, professional, surgical intervention is the only effective option.

BURNS

Burns are a common injury in war zones. Explosions are often followed by fire, arson is a common military and terrorist weapon, and any kind of nuclear detonation will result in radiation burns.

First Aid for Thermal Burns

Preliminary first aid for burns is simple but must be initiated promptly to be effective.

1. Stop the burning process. In addition to putting out any remaining burning clothing or debris, the first aider must cool the skin with cold water or cool wet dressing to stop the ongoing burning damage to deeper tissue.
2. Cut away burned clothing but avoid touching the burned area. Do not try to remove burned material from the burned flesh.
3. Cover the burned area with dry sterile dressings to decrease the risk of infection.
4. Be alert for signs of shock, airway obstruction, hypothermia, and other complications.
5. Get the patient to medical care.

While ointments should not be applied to second- or third-degree burns, first-degree burns and surface chemical burns can be treated with Sulfadiazine

1 percent ointments. Sulfadiazine decreases the risk of bacteria causing blood infections. Prescription Sulfadiazine comes in 2-percent strength, but efficacy of the over-the-counter strength can be improved by covering the treated burn with plastic cling wrap.

Complications of Burns

Damage to the skin's capacity to protect the body from infection, retain bodily fluids, and regulate body temperature can result in severe, life-threatening complications. The first aider should be aware of the following:

1. Ointments and salves should never be used on any burns that exceed the "minor burn" classification.
2. While cooling with cold water can reduce the severity of a burn when immediately applied, it should not be sustained for more than ten minutes, to avoid over cooling.
3. Infection is the greatest danger for third-degree burns. Only clear water and sterile dressing should be used.
4. Extensive burns cause significant loss of fluids that can result in hypovolemic shock. Be prepared to treat the patient for shock.
5. Burned tissue is unable to regulate temperature, leading to the development of hypothermia. Keep the patient comfortably warm.
6. Burned tissues on fingers and toes should never be bandaged together. Soft, sterile dressing must be used to separate adjoining burned tissue to prevent them from healing together.
7. Any indication of burns to the face, or potential inhalation of hot or toxic smoke or fumes, creates the danger of respiratory compromise. Any patient with such indication, regardless of how minor the apparent burns may be, should be rushed to emergency care.
8. If professional care is not available, first aid for burns must be directed at preventing infection, reducing pain, and maintaining patient hydration.

WAR ZONE SKELETAL INJURIES

While penetrating injuries may be more common combat related injuries, fractured bones and dislocated joints are the most frequent injuries suffered by civilians. These injuries result from blasts, falls, and being struck by or crushed beneath falling debris and structures. Prompt and effective splinting will reduce pain and prevent further injury until professional aid can be reached.

Principles of Splinting

1. When in doubt about the nature of the injury (bruise, sprain, fracture, etc.) splint it.
2. If possible, remove clothing from the extremity to be splinted in order to inspect the injury and secure the splint properly.
3. Cover all open wounds with sterile dressing prior to splinting. Avoid covering up bandaged wounds with splinting.
4. Do not move the patient before splinting.
5. Assess the distal pulse, circulation, sensation, and ability to move before and after splinting. If these functions are lost after splinting, loosen the splint and gently reposition the limb to restore the functions before reattaching the splint.
6. Whenever possible, splint any dislocation or fracture in the position it is found.
7. If the limb is so extremely deformed that it cannot be splinted as found, apply gentle traction to realign bone ends enough to splint.
8. Pad splints to prevent chafing and discomfort to the patient.
9. If possible, have one person hold and support the injured limb, while another applies the spilt. This will prevent movement and pain for the patient.
10. For bone fractures, the splint must immobilize the joint above and below the injury.
11. For joint injuries, the splint must extend to the bones on both sides of the injury.
12. A complete field realignment of a fractured bone can only be justified if no access to medical facilities can be anticipated for an extended length of time. This requires at least two people. One person is required to apply (pull) firm, but gentle traction to the limb, while the other holds the limb and assesses the alignment. Ideally, a third person should be holding the patient in place to prevent dragging. Once alignment is achieved, a ridged splint is applied and secured above and below the fracture before traction is removed.

Splinting Methods

While following the above principles, all splinting is performed the same way, regardless of the type of musculoskeletal injury involved. The objective is to immobilize the injury. While purpose made splinting such as Sam Splints™ or inflatable splints are effective, the first aider can use wood, rolled newspapers, cardboard, blankets, pillows, or even an adjoining body part (chest, opposite leg, etc.) to immobilize the injury. Cloth, tape, or other wide, strong material can be used to secure the splints in place. It doesn't have to be pretty; it just has to work. The following are some examples of splinting techniques.

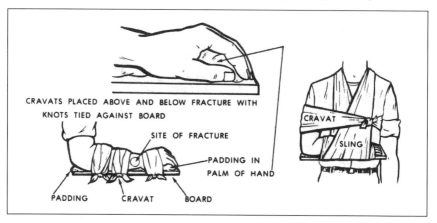

A fractured wrist needs to be splinted to immobilize the hand and forearm.

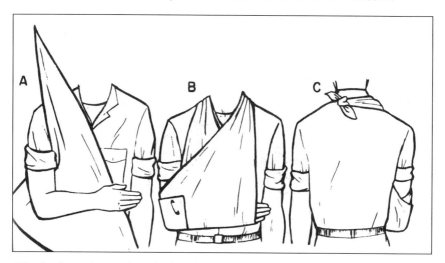

A basic sling using a triangular bandage is shown above, but anything that can support and immobilize the arm, including the shirttail or a belt, can be used.

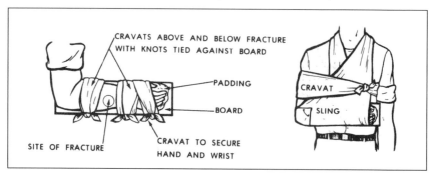

This illustration shows how to splint a fracture of the lower arm and use a cravat or other device to secure the sling to the chest.

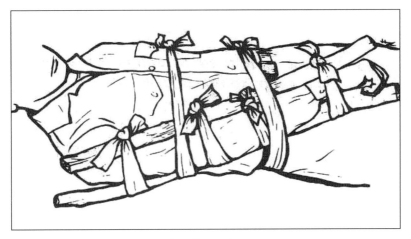

Upper arm splinted and secured to the body.

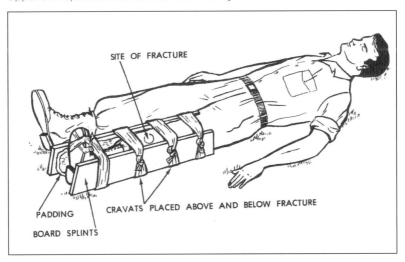

SITE OF FRACTURE

CRAVATS PLACED ABOVE AND BELOW FRACTURE

PADDING

BOARD SPLINTS

Splintering for lower leg.

Dislocated knee splinted as found. The same technique would apply to an elbow joint.

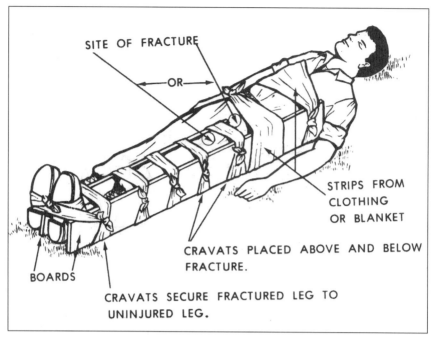

Upper leg or hip fracture splint using padded poles.

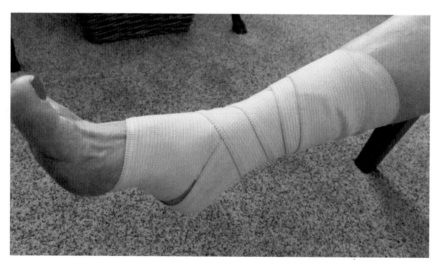

Ankle bandaged for sprain. Bandaging starts at the bottom of the foot and crisscrosses upward. Elastic bandages are best for this. The same technique can be used for a sprained wrist starting in the palm of the hand.

THORACIC INJURIES

Penetrating and impact injuries to the chest include hemothorax, pneumo-thorax, flail chest, tension pneumothorax, and paracardial tamponade. The serious first aider should become familiar with the recognition and responses to all these conditions. We will cover the essentials for the two most common chest injuries here.

Sucking Chest Wounds

An open pneumothorax or sucking chest wound results from a penetration of the chest wall by a sharp object such as a knife, bullet, or piece of flying debris. As the patient breathes and the chest expands and contracts, air will pass through the wound into the chest cavity instead of the lung. The lung will collapse further and further and the patient's ability to breathe will deteri-orate unless the hole is sealed with an airtight dressing such as aluminum foil, plastic, Vaseline, gauze, or a purpose-made chest seal device. The seal should be large enough to assure that it is not sucked into the wound and should be secured to the chest with tape. The patient's breathing must be monitored constantly. In some cases, a tension pneumothorax may develop after sealing the wound, if the patient begins to show signs of increasing difficulty breath-ing, remove the seal immediately.

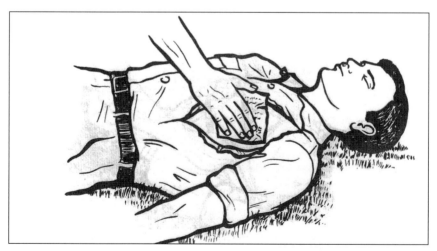

The hole in the chest is sealed with plastic, foil, or occlusive dressing. Use an Ashman™ chest seal or other chest seal device if available.

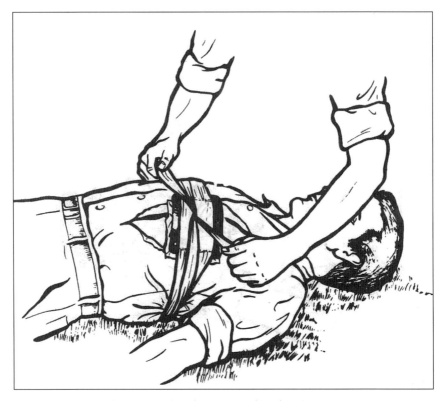

Secure the seal in place with a bandage or combat dressing.

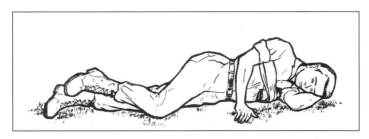

Once the chest is sealed, place the patient on the injured side to
allow the uninjured lung to work properly.

In a sucking chest wound, air from the outside enters the chest cavity and
compresses the lungs with each breath. Closing the hole will usually prevent
further collapse. Vented chest seals will allow some decompression.

*Note: The Ashman™ chest seal device has a one-way valve to vent excess air
out of the chest, preventing the development of a tension pneumothorax. A variety
of chest seal devices are available and at least one should be included in every
trauma kit.*

Flail Chest

Flail chest can result from blunt force or impact trauma to the rib cage. Flail chest develops when two or more ribs are fractured in two or more places. When this happens, the chest wall at that location becomes a free-floating segment that moves independently of the rest of the chest. The segment will collapse inward slightly when the chest expands and protrude upward slightly when the chest contracts. This condition is called paradoxical motion, or flail chest. This is a serious injury and is also very painful. The force required to create a flail chest will always injure the lung tissue beneath the flail segment, resulting in swelling and bleeding into the lung and associated loss of lung function. This is a serious, life-threatening injury. The flail segment can be splinted by application of a pillow or similar material held firm over the segment, either held in place by the patient or secured with bandaging. The patient should be transported lying on the injured side so as to facilitate breathing by the uninjured lung.

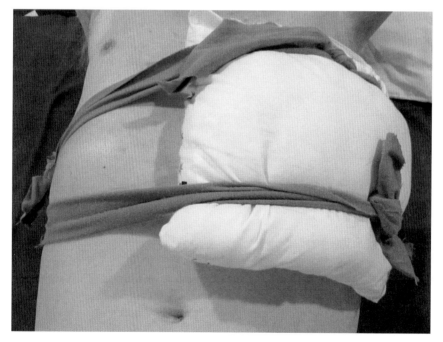

A small pillow or large soft dressing can be used to stabilize a flail chest segment.

ABDOMINAL INJURIES

Abdominal injuries can result from exposure to blast pressure impact from debris, or penetration by flying fragments. The abdomen contains the stomach, intestines, liver, kidneys, bladder, gallbladder, and spleen. The aorta and inferior vena cava run through this space as well. Blunt and penetrating injuries to the abdomen can damage vital organs resulting in severe bleeding and life-threatening complications. The abdominal cavity can hold enough blood to cause shock and death without any sign of external bleeding. A rupture of hollow organs will result in spilling the contents of the stomach and bladder into the abdominal cavity causing peritonitis, a severe inflammation of the peritoneum resulting in intense pain, muscular rigidity, and abdominal distention.

Evaluation of Abdominal Injuries

Permit the patient to lie prone or with the knees flexed and supported for comfort while conducting the examination for these signs. Most patients with severe abdominal injury or illness will prefer to lie still with their knees drawn up.

Signs and symptoms of abdominal injury:

1. Local or general abdominal tenderness.
2. Abdominal bruising.
3. Resistance to movement due to pain.
4. Obvious wounds. Penetrating wounds such as gunshot wounds may have a small entrance wound and a much larger exit wound. Be sure to check for exit wounds.
5. Evisceration of internal organs through the abdominal wall.
6. Altered vital signs such as rapid shallow respirations, declining blood pressure, and rapid pulse, and other signs of shock.
7. Distention of the abdomen. Pulsing of the abdomen may indicate sever internal bleeding.
8. Nausea and vomiting as a result of damaged or ruptured internal organs.

Treatment of Blunt Abdominal Wounds

Blunt force to the abdomen may cause severe injuries to vital organs and ruptured or torn major arteries or veins, and intra-abdominal hemorrhaging. Be especially alert for signs of shock such as sweating, paleness, rapid pulse, and falling blood pressure. The patient should be positioned on one side with the head turned downward and to one side to prevent aspiration of vomit. Keep the patient's mouth free of vomit and maintain a clear airway. Gain access to professional medical care without delay.

Treatment of Open Abdominal Wounds

Unless the wound is obviously superficial, the first aider should assume that the penetration has injured internal organs and major blood vessels, even if the signs and symptoms have not yet been presented. If the penetrating object is still in place, it should be left in place and stabilized with bulky dressings. Be sure to inspect thoroughly for exit wounds opposite the entry point. Dry, sterile dressing should be applied to all open abdominal wounds.

Treatment of Eviscerated Abdominal Wounds

When the abdominal wall is lacerated, abdominal organs may protrude through the wound. In some cases, a significant amount of the intestines may spill from the wound. The first aider should not attempt to push or replace the organs into the wound. The protruding organs must be kept moist and warm. Cover the organs with a moist, preferably sterile dressing. Keep the dressing moist with sterile water as needed. Aluminum foil securely taped over the wound can retain moisture and heat. Transport an evisceration patient prone to prevent shifting of the organs.

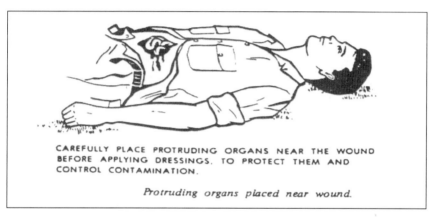

CAREFULLY PLACE PROTRUDING ORGANS NEAR THE WOUND BEFORE APPLYING DRESSINGS, TO PROTECT THEM AND CONTROL CONTAMINATION.

Protruding organs placed near wound.

A laceration to the abdomen can result in the intestines spilling out. Many more intestines than shown here may spill out.

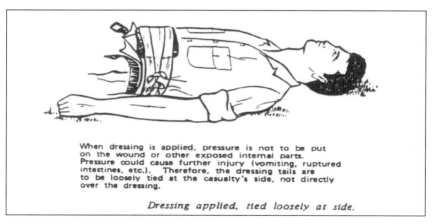

When dressing is applied, pressure is not to be put on the wound or other exposed internal parts. Pressure could cause further injury (vomiting, ruptured intestines, etc.). Therefore, the dressing tails are to be loosely tied at the casualty's side, not directly over the dressing.

Dressing applied, tied loosely at side.

All intestines must be placed on the abdomen and covered with a soft, moist dressing. The dressing must be kept moist to prevent the intestines from drying out.

CHAPTER 14

WAR SURVIVAL PLANNING AND TRAINING

No battle plan ever survives first contact with the enemy.
—German General Heinz Guderian (1888–1954)

To paraphrase General Guderian's famous quote: "No emergency plan survives first contact with reality," but you still need to have one. Throughout this book I have enumerated the threats and challenges to life and freedom generated by wartime and war zone conditions. I have also tried to provide solid "what to do" and "how to do it" information to meet these challenges. Here, we will establish some guidelines for creating individual and family war emergency plans and training priorities. While these concepts apply to general emergency and disaster-planning paradigms, they become more critical and immediate when applied to the massive and sustained nature of war. While national and regional agencies have detailed emergency plans in place, they have proven inadequate to cope with many recent natural disasters and are hardly adequate to address the complex disaster scenarios generated by a conventional or nuclear war. The responsible citizen and family would be well advised to make their own emergency plans for those situations that may endanger their lives and property. Having the right emergency equipment and skills is important but having a plan for their effective and timely use is a key element survival response. Emergency planning is a process of identifying potential threat scenarios and answering the challenges they created before they occur.

THREAT IDENTIFICATION

While natural disasters such as storms, earthquakes, and floods deserve preparedness planning, as do home fires, criminal assaults, and home invasion, we will focus on war-generated and war-related threats here. Of course, natural disasters do not pause for war so such events may occur concurrently with war. Primary war threats include nuclear and conventional bombing, military action conducted by surrogate or infiltrated forces, sabotage or cyberattacks on infrastructure, and biological warfare. Secondary effects will include shortages of food and critical goods, civil unrest, economic instability, and deteriorated fire, police, and medical services. All these situations may occur periodically or immediately. It is unlikely that World War III will be declared, it will just be. While no one will be safe from the ravages of war, what specific effects will impact any person or family will be dependent on their location, profession, family situation, and level of preparedness. A short list of probable war related challenges that would require having a plan includes:

- **Nuclear warfare:** Planning would require shelter in place, rapid evacuation, and fallout protection, depending on your location.
- **Conventional warfare:** Planning would include home defense, evacuation under war zone conditions, application of combat skills, and advanced first aid.
- **Biological warfare:** Planning would need to include isolation, home defense, respiratory protection, sanitation, and medical care.
- **Grid failure:** Planning would include methods of water purification, food acquisition, shelter enhancement, fire protection, self-defense, and general self-reliance.
- **Civil disorder or insurrection:** Planning would include the application of significant defensive methods as well as fire suppression and first aid.
- **Economic instability or collapse:** Planning would include asset protection, fund security, alternative financial methods, and establishment of long-term self-reliance.

ANSWERING THE QUESTIONS

Once you have a short list of potential emergencies, the process of planning for each one can begin. Emergency planning is the process of answering questions before the emergency requires the answer. Some questions that a good emergency plan must answer are:

1. **WHAT events would trigger the plan?** It is critically important that everyone involved understands that a certain event or combination of events will trigger your emergency plans without their asking anyone what to do. For "normal" home emergencies, things like a smoke detector alerting, the sound of an intruder, or the wail of a tornado siren would trigger planned actions for those events. Wartime

emergency plan triggers could be as obvious as FEMA radio alerts or air raid sirens or as subtle as rising tensions between hostile nations, the repositioning of emergency agencies, or changes in the economy.

2. **WHAT actions are required and in what order?** This is the most complicated part of the plan. You must cover all the critical actions but keep it simple and fast. The first element of the plan must be to stop or escape the immediate danger. For "normal" emergencies such as a home fire, this could involve using a fire extinguisher or just rapid evacuation. For a nuclear war, this would initiate evacuation or taking immediate shelter for urban inhabitants or sheltering in place for most living in rural locations. Except for impending and close nuclear detonations and immediate local combat shelter in place is usually preferable to evacuation through potentially hazardous environments.

3. **WHERE will you be and where will you go?** Obviously, the location you are in when disasters strikes will greatly affect your planning. A plan to react to a nuclear, biological, or chemical attack will be very different if you are at work or on the road than if you are at home. You also must consider your primary shelter or escape destination and your main rendezvous location where you will meet others and access your survival equipment. You may have selected several temporary storm or blast shelters (culverts, basements, etc.) along your daily route. You can hang on in these locations with your everyday carry survival items for a few days and then make your way to your home or other long-term shelter. Never assume that everyone will be at home and have access to all your supplies when disaster strikes.

4. **WHO is responsible for what actions?** In any emergency, it is critical that everyone does his or her job. Who grabs what packs and equipment? Who locks up the house? Who turns off the gas and electricity? Who gathers the children? Who brings the supplies? Who calls 911? Who provides first aid in the meantime? Who will stand watch? Make sure everyone is cross-trained to switch tasks or multitask as needed.

5. **WHEN to act and when to meet?** It could be hours or days before family or group members can move from shelter, evacuate the danger area, and get to a designated assembly point or rendezvous. You should have several alternative meetings places and a time each day that plan members would be there. Your plan might say that you would meet at the abandoned gas station on Highway 12 at noon, four days after the plan trigger event, and every day after that until all are assembled or after ten days have passed. If that location is unsafe (e.g. occupied, contaminated) the alternate location is the cluster of trees near the Wilson farm.

6. **HOW each action will be achieved?** While some actions may be self-evident (run, hide, carry) some actions may require more detail such as how to crawl out of a burning house or how to protect from radioactive fallout and need to be included in the plan. Lifesaving first aid actions, fire suppression, and armed and unarmed self-protection will require training for all plan participants. Good training requires less detail included in the plan. When fear and chaos reign, it is too late to read instructions.

7. **WHAT IF there are problems with the plan?** Plan on things going wrong and *try* to have a plan that can get you past these inevitable problems. What if your route is blocked? What if you must walk instead of drive? What if you can't get to your survival pack? What if you must evacuate instead of shelter in place? What if someone is injured? What if you or someone else cannot safely get home? You need alternate plans and backup equipment to deal with these inevitable challenges. Consider that one emergency may create several other disasters so that you may need to combine and alter plans.

EXAMPLE OF FAMILY WORLD WAR III SURVIVAL RESPONSE PLAN (SRP)

Trigger Events and Trends

American ground, air, or naval forces engaged in combat overseas. Any conventional missile attack on US territory anywhere. Any nuclear weapons use involving US or allied territory. Declaration of war between US or US allies and major foreign powers. Major movements of military and civilian emergency assets related to international tensions.

Any word could work so a code word such as *equinox* would be used in verbal, text or email messages to family and group members.

Preparatory Actions (move the disabled, pets, fuel, place supplies, prep shelters, 24/7 watch)

Elderly relatives and children would be relocated outside of major target areas. Equipment and supplies would be relocated to prepaid locations. Funds would be withdrawn from accounts. Vehicles would be fuel and packed. Radio communications with all family members would be established. Around-the-clock monitoring of local conditions, and emergency radio frequencies would be established.

Immediate Actions

Depending on the time available, evacuation by vehicle or on foot to pre-established locations would be initiated. If evacuation is impractical, taking shelter in the best location with survival gear and weapons. First aid, fire suppression, and rescue procedures initiated. Active self-defense as needed to protect life and property is justified.

Sustained Actions

Separated family members would rendezvous at preestablished location. Survivors would establish a base at home or at appropriate available shelter. Foraging for supplies, water gathering, and purification, nuclear fallout shelter, and decontamination procedures initiated. Ongoing war zone medical, combat and survival action sustained.

Responsibilities (Watch and Guard, Medical Care, Gather Gear, Defend)

Four-hour guard and monitoring shifts established and assigned to each adult family member. All adult family members are assigned duties for securing the property or bringing specific items during evacuation. All family members know where to take shelter, what routes to take in evacuation, basic first aid, and age-appropriate self-protection.

Essentially, emergency planning is the process of asking and answering these four questions:

1. What can happen? What if?
2. What can I do? Skills, knowledge, and training.
3. What do I have? Gear and supplies.
4. How will I do it? Execute the plan.

The Preparedness Triangle illustrates the three elements that must be applied to each anticipated threat.

TRAINING FOR WARTIME EMERGENCIES

During the Cold War, the old Civil Defense Department offered a variety of training programs for civilians, including radiological monitoring, shelter building, and first aid. FEMA is focused on training for professional responders. Even the Red Cross and the Boy Scouts have moved away from disaster response training. Public apathy and denial have eroded support and participation for disaster response and education. Although developed after 9/11 to train civilians for terrorist attacks, the Community Emergency Response Team (CERT) program provides excellent training for many war-related emergencies including light rescue, first aid, fire suppression, and safety. Unfortunately, it does not include security, defense, or radioactive fallout protection. Red Cross first aid courses, STOP THE BLEED, and CPR training are often offered by local police, fire, and medical agencies. NRA firearms skills and safety course are usually available through local shooting ranges. The Apprentice Doctor at www.theapprenticedoctor.com offers several self-teaching kits for advanced medical procedures. More and more preparedness advocacy organizations are offering in-person and online education programs. While outdoor and wilderness survival education can be helpful, most of it is not directly applicable to war related scenarios. Skill development and practice is a critical element in survival planning.

All emergency plans should be revised regularly to keep up with changing conditions. All family members should be thoroughly familiar with their duties as well as what others will be doing. It may be a good idea to assign each plan a code-name or an activation word that can be quickly communicated by voice, text, or phone. Code words will be covered in the communications chapter.

CHAPTER 15

NAVIGATION WITHOUT GPS

Within the past two decades, the civilian population has become dependent on GPS while basic navigation and map-reading skills have been relegated to novelties. Even the military have become GPS dependent. Cruise missiles, drones, combat aircraft and even ground forces and logistics systems all require GPS data from satellites to function. For this reason, the GPS satellites will be the first targets for electronic and kinetic assault in any kind of war. The United States, China, and Russia all have independent GPS systems and military backup GPS systems ready for activation when war in space becomes a reality. The survival of GPS navigation systems for civilians is highly questionable. This loss will significantly impact the supply chain and emergency services in all communities. Depending on GPS to get from point A to point B narrows the traveler's focus on just the immediate route rather than the surrounding terrain and alternative routes. Using GPS, we get there, but we lose awareness of where "there" is in relation to the surroundings. If we lose GPS, we are lost, but if we use a map with or without GPS we always know where we are and what alternatives we have. While wilderness campers, hunters, and backpackers may need detailed map and compass skills, the civilian needing to navigate roads, trails, and evacuation routes only needs to reestablish basic map reading knowledge and understanding to get around or get away under future wartime conditions.

MAP GATHERING AND USE

Not that long ago maps filled the glove compartments of most vehicles, and most folks owned a road atlas. Maps and road atlases are difficult to find today, although you can usually find free state road maps at highway rest stops. You can also pick up maps at tourist information stations. You certainly should have these basic maps in your vehicle. Unless you are not planning to leave your state, you should purchase a Rand McNally or National Geographic *Road Atlas* online or from a bookstore or truck stop. These cost about twenty-five dollars and provide detailed road maps of every state, along with street maps for larger urban areas. You should also have a DeLorme Atlas & Gazetteer™ for your state and any adjoining states you may travel through in an emergency. These are far more detailed maps showing elevations, buildings, roads, trails, backroads, waterways, and vegetation at a one-inch equals 2.4 miles scale. You can purchase them online or at most truck stops. While the internet is still functional, you should print out a collection of maps of local areas and potential evacuation destinations from Google Maps. Print out both map views and satellite views. Looking at or printing street views may be helpful in planning movement through unfamiliar areas. Always note the date on any printout. While Google's maps are usually more up to date than printed maps, they are refreshed less frequently in rural areas. Even as you still use GPS, get in the habit of using the maps to backup your planning. You may also find interesting alternative routes, shortcuts, or points of interest that GPS did not provide.

Road atlas, State Atlas Gazetteer, road map, Google Earth printouts and compass.

For the purposes of basic land navigation, the main function of the compass is to make sure that the map and you are always pointed in the right direction. You should acquire a rugged military-style lensatic liquid-filled compass. These are available at from fifteen to one hundred dollars at sporting goods stores.

Map Orientation

The top of the map is always north, making the bottom south, the right east and the left west. There is a difference between the north that the compass points to (compass north) and the actual geographic north (true north). This difference is known as declination. Declination is important for cross-country and long-distance travel, but less critical for using road maps or regional navigation. Compass magnetic north is usually indicated by an arrow pointing at an "N" and true north is indicated by an arrow pointing at a star. If you have a compass, you can align the top of the map with the magnetic north arrow. This will orient the map with true north. Practical map orientation involves matching the map in your hand with visible terrain features around you such as hills, buildings, and roads.

Matching a map with the terrain and structures.

Map Legends and Symbols

All maps will include a box showing the various symbols used to represent various roads and terrain features. Traditional road maps will show major and secondary highways and streets. Detailed topographical maps will show elevations, waterways, lakes, buildings, highways, trails, and other details.

TOPOGRAPHIC MAP SYMBOLS
VARIATIONS WILL BE FOUND ON OLDER MAPS

Primary highway, hard surface	Boundaries: National
Secondary highway, hard surface	State
Light-duty road, hard or improved surface	County, parish, municipio
Unimproved road	Civil township, precinct, town, barrio
Road under construction, alinement known	Incorporated city, village, town, hamlet
Proposed road	Reservation, National or State
Dual highway, dividing strip 25 feet or less	Small park, cemetery, airport, etc.
Dual highway, dividing strip exceeding 25 feet	Land grant
Trail	Township or range line, United States land survey
	Township or range line, approximate location
Railroad: single track and multiple track	Section line, United States land survey
Railroads in juxtaposition	Section line, approximate location
Narrow gage: single track and multiple track	Township line, not United States land survey
Railroad in street and carline	Section line, not United States land survey
Bridge: road and railroad	Found corner: section and closing
Drawbridge: road and railroad	Boundary monument: land grant and other
Footbridge	Fence or field line
Tunnel: road and railroad	
Overpass and underpass	Index contour Intermediate contour
Small masonry or concrete dam	Supplementary contour Depression contours
Dam with lock	Fill Cut
Dam with road	Levee Levee with road
Canal with lock	Mine dump Wash
	Tailings Tailings pond
Buildings (dwelling, place of employment, etc.)	Shifting sand or dunes Intricate surface
School, church, and cemetery Cem	Sand area Gravel beach
Buildings (barn, warehouse, etc.)	
Power transmission line with located metal tower	Perennial streams Intermittent streams
Telephone line, pipeline, etc. (labeled as to type)	Elevated aqueduct Aqueduct tunnel
Wells other than water (labeled as to type) Oil Gas	Water well and spring Glacier
Tanks: oil, water, etc. (labeled only if water) Water	Small rapids Small falls
Located or landmark object; windmill	Large rapids Large falls
Open pit, mine, or quarry; prospect x	Intermittent lake Dry lake bed
Shaft and tunnel entrance	Foreshore flat Rock or coral reef
	Sounding, depth curve Piling or dolphin
Horizontal and vertical control station:	Exposed wreck Sunken wreck
Tablet, spirit level elevation BM△5653	Rock, bare or awash; dangerous to navigation
Other recoverable mark, spirit level elevation △5455	
Horizontal control station: tablet, vertical angle elevation VABM△95⁄9	
Any recoverable mark, vertical angle or checked elevation △3775	Marsh (swamp) Submerged marsh
Vertical control station: tablet, spirit level elevation BM×957	Wooded marsh Mangrove
Other recoverable mark, spirit level elevation ×954	Woods or brushwood Orchard
Spot elevation ×7369 ×7369	Vineyard Scrub
Water elevation 670 670	Land subject to controlled inundation Urban area

Typical map symbols.

Map Scale

The term *scale* refers to how many inches on the paper map represent how many miles on the actual ground. This information is usually found in the lower part of the map indicated in both miles and kilometers. For example: a typical road map may be at two and one quarter inches per twenty miles, or two and one-eighth inch per kilometer. This is critical information in estimating time of travel and fuel consumption.

Map Elevation

Basic road maps do not show elevation so what appears to be one hundred miles in a straight line may be somewhat longer and more challenging going up and down hills or mountains. Topographical maps will include contour lines that show the elevation, steepness, and shape of the terrain. Depending on the scale of the map these lines will indicate so many feet of elevation between lines. The further apart these contour lines are the gentler the slop. Very close lines indicate a steep slope or a cliff-like drop-off. This information can be very helpful in establishing cross-country routes and possible locations for shelter or encampments.

The actual terrain on the left as indicated by the contour lines on the left make it obvious how important this information is.

SCOUTING THE TERRITORY

Modern transportation methods combined with GPS have tended to isolate citizens from their own communities and surroundings. There is an old military axiom that says that "the map is not the terrain." There is no substitute for having seen the actual roads, routes, and places. A map or GPS may get you there, but it also can take you through a very dangerous community, or near a site prone to looting, or into a location that could be a target for hostile nations or terrorists. If you have scouted your immediate community, you may find additional escape routes and shelter locations. Knowing the alleys, trails, underpasses, and abandoned buildings can be lifesaving. Scouting your immediate community and your potential evacuation routes by eye and with optics can greatly enhance your map knowledge.

To get more detailed map and compass skills, consider purchasing *US Army Field Manual FM 3–25-28 Map Reading and Land Navigation*.

CHAPTER 16

WARTIME COMMUNICATION METHODS

Once war develops or is declared, communication systems will be under constant assault. Radio and cellular communications will be subject to temporary or even permanent disablement, and all legal prohibitions on monitoring by domestic and foreign agencies will be removed. In a society where constant communications with anyone regardless of location has become the norm, the inability to communicate reliably and securely will have a major impact. Reestablishing reliable short-range communications and maintaining security under scrutiny will be critical as wartime challenges persist.

COMMUNICATIONS SECURITY

Code Words

Establishing code words to communicate emergency information quickly and clearly should be part of every family or group emergency plan. Code words or phrases should be easy to recognize by the intended recipient, but also easy to fit into an innocent sounding sentence if others are listening in. Below are examples of codewords for specific messages. I have used military radio lettering words, but any words or uncommon phrases will work.

Code Word	Meaning
Quebec	Help. I need help.
Yankee	I am captured, or under duress.
Papa	You are in immediate danger.
Uniform	Activate preestablished emergency plan.
Echo	Meet up at preestablished rendezvous point.
India	Evacuate immediately.
Sierra	Shelter in place.

Practical Codes for Civilians

Most of us can remember childhood simple transposition codes where "A" really meant "S," etc. Variations of these methods were incorporated into code machines such as the Enigma machine of World War II. Such methods were somewhat effective as long as the sending and receiving parties had the same machines or duplicate code books. Even cryptanalysis using primitive computers was able to break codes quickly. Today, supercomputers, quantum computers, and artificial intelligence systems make any form of transposition code useless.

Book Codes

Simple transposition codes can delay deciphering by untrained citizens but are no match for government computers. The unnecessary use of any kind of code may only attract attention and complicate communications. Book codes remain the most secure kind of code short of a supercomputer. Using a book code requires that (1) both sending and receiving parties have the same edition of the same book, and (2) no one else knows what book you are using. Since the number of book texts and editions is almost infinite, such codes are extremely difficult to break. The downside of this method is that the sender must find the desired word somewhere in the book and then write down the exact page number, paragraph number, line number, and word count from the left for each word in the message. This can be slow and tedious but very secure. So, if you find the word *emergency* on page 122, paragraph 2, line 7, and the fourth word from the left you write or send 122, 2, 7, 4. If you are really concerned about being monitored, don't buy the books to be used online or using a credit card, as that information might be used to "guess" what books you are using.

Tap Codes

Tap codes were developed and used in prisons and POW camps throughout the world. These codes (unlike Morse code) require only taps without dashes, so simply tapping on pipes or a tin cup against a wall can transmit the letters. For example: tap tap (pause) tap tap tap indicates row two, column three as "H," etc. A short pause indicates the break between the letter and a long pause indicates the end of the message. Rapid tapping is used to indicate that the word was not received or understood. The code can be tapped, blinked, winked, coughed, nudged, or communicated as finger movements. Of course, the letters can be moved around in the table to create more secure codes.

	1	2	3	4	5
1	A	B	C/ K	D	E
2	F	G	H	I	J
3	L	M	N	O	P
4	Q	R	S	T	U
5	V	W	X	Y	Z

Morse Code

The original telegraph code was named after Samuel Morse, the inventor of the telegraph. The code consists of a series of dots and dashes easily transmitted by taping or holding a telegraph key/switch. It is also readily transmitted via blinking lights are radio signals. Telegrams were a primary means of communication well into the twentieth century. Even after the ascendency of voice communications, being able to tap out Morse code was a requirement for radio licensure and a mainstay of Boy Scout training. If radio and cellular communications are interrupted or compromised, hard wire systems may survive and be more secure. Very few people today use or recognize Morse code so it may be relatively secure.

Basic Morse code dots and dashes, blinks and flashes can be used for emergency communications.

Hand Code

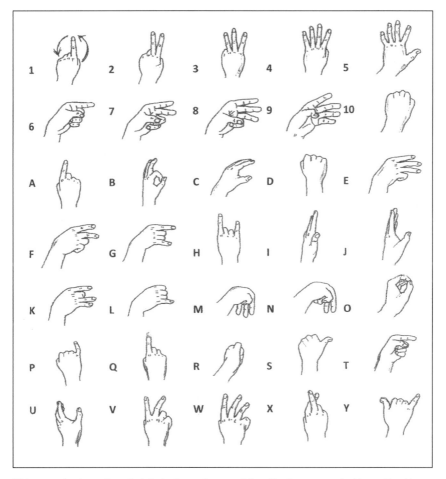

This easy-to-learn hand alphabet can be used for silent communications. For the letter Z, which is rarely used, make a Z-shaped movement with your index finger.

RADIO COMMUNICATIONS OPTIONS

Warfare of any severity will result in the interruption or complete breakdown of communication systems. Cell towers and satellites will be targets for kinetic and electronic attack in the early phases of combat. Various forms of radio communications may be the only means of monitoring events and communicating with family members and friends. Every family should own a radio capable of receiving AM, FM, and WX weather alert channels. A scanner that will monitor police, fire and other local emergency agencies would be a good investment. The FCC has set aside special frequencies for general citizen usage. These are the FRS (Family Radio Service), MURS (Multi-Use Radio

Service) and GMRS (General Mobile Radio Service) bands. Transmitting on the FRS and MURS band does not require a license. To legally transmit on any of the GMRS channels an FCC license is required but is easy and cheap to acquire online or by mail. You must be eighteen years old or older, an individual, not a business, and pay a small fee for a ten-year GMRS license. No test is required, but you must agree to follow all FCC regulations. These rules include:

- No hidden or coded messages, but the so-called 10 code as in 10–4 is permitted.
- No false or deceptive messages.
- No advertising or sale offers.
- No political campaign messages.
- No continuous uninterrupted messages (recording, music etc.).
- No international distress signals (mayday) unless in a vehicle in immediate danger.
- You must identify yourself using your assigned FCC call signal at the end and at periodic intervals throughout your transmission.

Most commercial walkie-talkies come with all twenty-two channels available and can be set for privacy codes between pre-programmed units using FRS or MURS channels. FRS Channels are 1 through 14, while MURS channels are 1 through 5. GMRS channels are 1 through 22. Acquiring a GMRS license and transmission capability would be highly beneficial under emergency conditions. Transmission on channels 1 through 7 is limited to five watts. Transmission on channels 8 through 14 is limited to one half watt. Transmission on channels 15 through 22 can be up to fifty watts. Range depends on the location of the transmitter and receiver and the number of obstructions between them. Obviously higher locations, higher transmission power and open terrain are best. These frequencies are not intended for long-range communications, but should be sufficient for family, neighborhood, and community communications. Sets of radios are available at sporting goods stores or online at reasonable prices and come with chargers. Extra batteries and a solar powered charger would be a good investment. The only way to determine range and reliability for your area is to test transmission reception at various locations further and further from your base.

Shortwave Ham Radio

Moving beyond local communications capabilities will involve a significant investment of time and funds. Even if you are not seeking to acquire transmission capability, having a good quality shortwave receiver will give you access to virtually all radio transmission locally, nationally, and internationally through a crisis. A good receiver should cover all AM, FM, VHF, SW, and SSB bands with over one thousand available channels. A high-quality set may run as much as five hundred dollars but will bring in weaker and more distant channels. Cheaper sets are available for as low as seventy-five dollars but with correspondingly lower performance and range. To obtain a general ham radio license you must provide a US mailing address and a social security number to the FCC. You can take an online or in-person class and take an online or in person examination. You must get at least twenty-six of thirty-five questions correctly to pass. Transmissions on these frequencies are subject to considerable national and international rules and protocols. Shortwave transceivers range in price from a few hundred dollars to over one thousand dollars, depending on desired range and options.

Baofeng Radios

One of the most versatile and popular radios among preparedness advocates is the Baofeng programmable, multi-channel transceiver. One of its major advantages is that it can operate in both licensed and unlicensed brands. The unit can be used as a basic walkie-talkie for short range communications and a wide range of ham radio frequencies including UHF and VHF for long distances. The unit can be used to monitor the weather band (WX), emergency channels, and local police bands as well. Multiple power settings aid in extending battery life. Optional extended antennas are available for greater range and larger batteries can be purchased. At only 4 × 2 × 1 inches in size, the Baofeng can be carried on a belt or in the survival pack. The basic units cost from fifty to sixty dollars and come with a charger, 110-volt adapter, and user manual.

Compact, programable, multichannel Boafeng transceiver.

Basic Radio Communication Protocols

- Identify with a call sign: If using a licensed frequency, give your FCC-assigned ID. Under other circumstances, use a preestablished call sign or "handle" to clearly identify yourself to the desired recipient while preserving anonymity.

- Pause a second after you press the talk button to avoid cutting off the first word of your message. Push first, then talk.
- Speak clearly, slowly, and concisely to ensure understanding.
- Avoid slang terms and lingo that may be misunderstood.
- When spelling out words, use the standard military alphabet.

A ALFA	B BRAVO	C CHARLIE	D DELTA
E ECHO	F FOX-TROT	G GOLF	H HOTEL
I INDIA	J JULIETT	K KILO	L LIMA
M MIKE	N NOVEMBER	O OSCAR	P PAPA
Q QUEBEC	R ROMEO	S SIERRA	T TANGO
U UNIFORM	V VICTOR	W WHISKEY	X X-RAY
Y YANKEE	Z ZULU	1 WUN	2 TOO
3 THUH-REE	4 FO-WER	5 FI-YIV	6 SIX
7 SEVEN	8 ATE	9 NINER	Ø ZERO

Using the pronunciations above provides clarity over often garbled radio transmissions.

Communication Preparedness

The subject of radio communications is far too complex to cover adequately in one chapter, but it is important to provide some basic information and starting points for establishing both communications security and alternative systems. Under gravest extreme conditions, FCC regulations are the least of your worries and having the capacity to communicate can be a lifesaving necessity. Developing networks, establishing repeater systems, and upgrading potential power and antenna capacities to be used only in emergencies would be prudent steps towards communication preparedness.

CHAPTER 17

WARTIME WATER STORAGE AND PURIFICATION

A ccess to clean, safe water is taken for granted, yet it is the most vulnerable and at-risk resource for urban and suburban populations. Pumping stations and filtration plants have minimal security, and the sources of water, lakes, rivers, and wells are virtually impossible to protect from deliberate damage or contamination. Drones and small missiles can bypass security to destroy pumping stations or deposit chemical or biological agents into the water supply. Hostile nations and terrorists can initiate a variety of cyberattacks that can interrupt water supplies or even damage equipment. Any kind of nuclear warfare will put radioactive fallout into lakes, rivers, and streams. Radioactive fallout will also leach into groundwater and wells. Damage to municipal water purification systems could initiate the spread of waterborne diseases including cholera, giardia, dysentery, salmonella, and hepatitis A. Safe water access is the Achilles' heel of any military, civil, or private survival plan. Any interruption of water supplies to highly populated areas would result in chaos, civil disorder, and massive fatalities within a week. In most cases the lack of running water would also result in the development spread of diseases, and uncontrolled fires. Every outdoor survival text devotes pages to finding and collecting water. Every disaster preparedness book focuses on storage and purification of water. Wartime water emergencies may range from periodic and temporary interruptions of supply to long-term loss of access to safe water. While the methodologies for water storage, filtration, and purification are the same, wartime conditions require greater storage and more sustainable purification methods.

WATER STORAGE

Depending on age, health, and level of activity and environment (e.g., temperature and humidity) the average person can only survive about three days without water. The average person under normal conditions requires at least one quart of drinking water per day. When reasonable sanitation and cooking needs are added, a minimum of one gallon per day is the absolute minimum. Under long-term wartime conditions, a two- or two-and-a-half-gallon per-day supply would be ideal. While in theory you can never store too much water, it is heavy and takes up a lot of room. If you anticipate that you will be staying at home and that your home will be safe from fire, floods, and other conditions, then you can store your water there. If, however, your home could be damaged or inaccessible you should consider storing water in a safer but reachable location. Consider whether you may need to carry your water. A fifty-five-gallon drum of water in your basement would be of no use if you have to evacuate. Plastic containers that were designed to hold water, juice, or soft drinks are good for storing water. Milk containers can be used but are flimsy and hard to clean. Never use containers that originally held soaps, solvents, or other chemicals. Containers should be rinsed thoroughly with clean water and then soaked in a mild (10 percent) bleach solution. As soon as you dump the solution out, fill the container with clean water and seal tightly. Most municipal waters can be stored without additional treatment. If you are storing well water or other water you are unsure about, add six to eight drops of household bleach to each gallon. Of course, you may simply want to buy bottled water at the store.

A two-gallon camping water carrier along with several repurposed plastic water containers and bleach for purification. While a drum of water and a hand pump is efficient for the home, multiple containers in multiple locations is also desirable.

CHEMICAL PURIFICATION

The two most common methods of water purification are chlorine bleach and iodine. Household bleach contains about 8 percent chlorine, so six to eight drops per gallon is recommended, but bleach loses strength over time, so ten drops per gallon, especially if the water is cloudy, may be a better choice. Tincture of iodine is another good method of purification and is recommended for use in southern and tropical environments. Add five drops of 2 percent USP (United States Pharmacopeia) tincture of iodine to a quart of clear water or ten drops to cloudy water. Mix in the bleach or iodine and let it stand for an hour before drinking. Chlorine and iodine water purification tablets are available from camping supply outlets. These are very small bottles that can be carried in pockets and survival kits and include instructions for use.

BOILING WATER TO PURIFY

Boil orders are common during disasters. While this method is effective for short-term purification, the need to use various fuels and the potential for fire make it impractical for meeting long-term, day-to-day needs. Bringing water to a vigorous boil for at least three full minutes will kill biological contaminants. You can add a pinch of salt or pour the water back and forth to aerate it to restore taste.

ULTRAVIOLET PURIFICATION

Ultraviolet light has been used for municipal water purification since the 1940s. UV light destroys microorganisms that cause diseases through the process of thymine dimerization. In recent years UV light water purification systems have become available to the public for home use and outdoors. UV devices use very little energy and do not involve adding chemicals to the water. UV light kills biological contamination but does not remove chemical and particulate contamination, so filtration is still necessary if these kinds of contaminates are present. Home systems can cost from a few hundred to a few thousand dollars. Portable pocket-sized UV water purifiers cost from fifty to a few hundred dollars and can be rechargeable.

Ultraviolet light from the sun can be used to purify water. You must know that the source water is not chemically contaminated, as UV will not remove them. Natural sunlight will kill microorganisms just as the UV light devices do. You need to start out with a clean, clear (no color) plastic bottle. Do not use glass, as it blocks UV penetration. Fill the bottle with water and place it in direct sunlight. Place the bottle on its side with the long side facing the sun to maximize exposure. For improved results place the bottle on a reflective surface such as whiteboards or aluminum foil. Leave the bottle exposed for at least six hours on a mostly sunny day, but if the days are partly cloudy you may need to leave the water exposed for up to two days to assure effective decontamination.

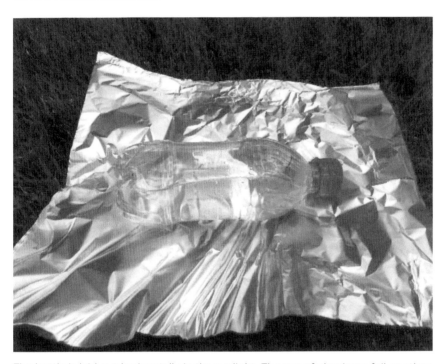

The bottle is laid out horizontally in the sunlight. The use of aluminum foil or other reflective backing is not necessary, but it will increase the effectiveness of the UV-A exposure.

PORTABLE WATER FILTRATION DEVICES

While clean water may be available from emergency agencies during peacetime disasters, a wartime scenario may overwhelm such agencies and the effects of warfare may necessitate mass evacuations while water sources are unavailable or unsafe. Every evacuation pack and vehicle should have at least one water purification device. There are too many commercial water purification systems to cover here. Pocket-sized LifeStraw® sell for about twenty dollars. Water purification tablets are easy to carry and sell for about fifteen dollars a bottle. Water filtering canteens and water bottles are available at sporting goods stores, and survival stores, for about thirty to forty dollars. The Katadyn® Vario system is designed for camping but can filter about two quarts per minute and up to five hundred gallons per filter, making it practical for home use as well at about one hundred dollars. Additional filters run from twenty to thirty dollars. These are a must-have item and are more practical for evacuation packs and short-term situations than long-term home shelter in place use.

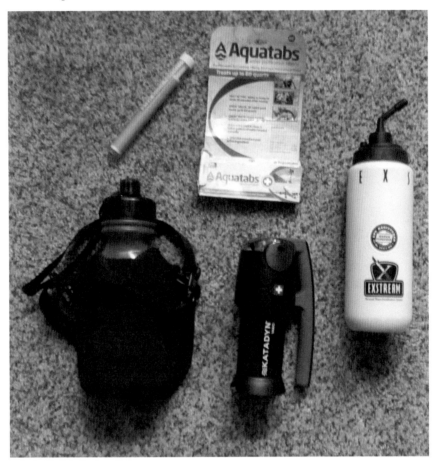

Top: Filter straw Anqatabs provide pocket sized but limited filtration capacity. Bottom left to right: Filtration canteen. Katadyn® large capacity filter pump device, and Exstream® radiological water filter bottle.

HOME WATER FILTRATION DEVICES

Under normal conditions municipal water is safe to drink, but as hostilities increase, the chances of system failure or deliberate contamination will increase. Home water filtration services are a good investment but are dependent on the service and a pressurized water supply. Without adequate filtration waterborne diseases including typhoid fever, cholera, giardia, dysentery,

e. coli, hepatitis A, and salmonella can spread rapidly. Large units for the home that can remove 99.999 percent of bacteria, viruses, and chemical contaminant at a rate of ten gallons or more per day can be found online or from survival supply outlets. Typical units range from $170 to $700. Stocking up on extra filters would be a good investment as well. One of the first steps in wartime emergency preparedness is to invest in a large capacity filtration system for the home and smaller ones for the evacuation pack.

Water filtration systems come in a variety of sizes and price ranges.

HOMEMADE WATER FILTERS

In addition to commercial water filtration devices, you may want to stock up on supplies to make your own filter systems. There are plenty of instructions on how to do this online and in self-reliance texts. Below are instructions for making a simple filtration device.

Homemade filters use alternating layers of sand and activated charcoal separated by coffee filters. After filtration, bleach is used for biological decontamination of rainwater in the rain barrel supplied from the roof gutter. Note that this filter is made from a solar tea bottle with a tap on the bottom.

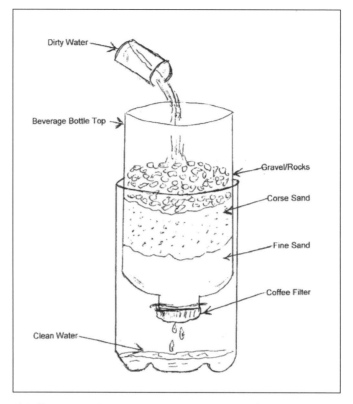

This filter uses a large plastic beverage bottle with the top cut and inverted. The top layer is clean gravel then coarse sand and then fine sand held in place by a coffee filter. The best source for clean gravel, clean sand, and activated charcoal is aquarium supply stores.

WATER COLLECTION

Once the water supply is interrupted you will have whatever water you were wise enough to store and the remaining water in your hot water heater and plumbing. Swimming pool and pond water can significantly increase your supply but will require treatment. Nearby ponds, lakes, and streams can be assumed to be biologically, chemically, and even radiologically polluted. The installation of rain barrels is highly recommended, but rainwater from any source must be filtered and treated to assure safety.

WATER CONSERVATION

Water that is not safe to drink may be okay for washing clothes or watering plants. Water that has been used for washing or is from an unsafe source can still be used to flush the toilet. Try not to use drinking water for anything but drinking, food washing, hand washing, and medical care. Reserve used water for non-contact applications and/or recycle it through filtration and purification if possible. Once the emergency starts you must gather every drop you can and make every drop count.

CHAPTER 18

HYGIENE AND SANITATION UNDER WARTIME CONDITIONS

I have spent some time talking with refugees from Russia, Britan, and Italy that endured bombings and urban war zone conditions during World War II. I even knew a Cossack who fought against the Bolsheviks during the Russian Civil War. I have also studied the experiences of civilians living in Berlin and other war-ravaged cities. The challenges of maintaining health and sanitation appeared frequently in our conversations. Hygiene and sanitation are often neglected survival priorities, but poor health and diseases can kill you just as dead as a blast or a bullet. The constant stress of wartime conditions combined with malnutrition increases susceptibility to illness. Municipal sewage systems are susceptible to cyberattacks, as well as sabotage, and direct bombings. Serious conventional bombings and nuclear detonations could open the sewers and even mix sewage with water sources. The recent pandemic caused labor shortages in trained people who knew how to run the sanitation systems. A true warfare scenario could leave critical water and sanitation systems understaffed or even abandoned.

PERSONAL HYGIENE

War is a dirty business. Photos of refugees from war-torn regions past and present show dirty, unkempt, unshaven, and exhausted civilians staggering through rubble-filed streets. If photos had a smell it would be that of human excrement, rotting garbage, and even decaying flesh. Maintaining basic hygiene under any kind of wartime, much less war zone, conditions is challenging but necessary. Dust, dirt, smoke, and pollutants are plentiful while clean water and cleaning supplies become scarce. Personal hygiene and cleaning supplies must be given a high priority to assure survival and as high-value trade and barter items in a wartime economy. I will not quantify the necessary items as you just cannot have too much. The pandemic shortages should have taught us not to overlook these items.

WARTIME SURVIVAL HYGIENE SUPPLIES

- Soap bars and liquid
- Toothpaste
- Toilet paper
- Lysol spray and liquid
- Laundry detergent
- Dishwashing liquid
- Shampoo
- Shaving cream
- Razors
- Isopropyl alcohol (70 percent)
- Listerine disinfectant
- Sanitary napkins
- Hand sanitizer
- Insect repellent
- N95 respirators

Tooth cavities and infections can become serious issues when a dentist isn't available. Left untreated, they can lead to serious and even deadly illness. Good dental maintenance before emergency disaster conditions prevail is an important survival preparedness step. Emergency toothache kits and temporary filling kits are available off the shelf at most pharmacies. If you have dentures, be sure to stock up on cleaning supplies and a repair kit. Keep old dentures as backup in case your primary set is damaged.

There are plenty of books on how to make soap, toothpaste, and other hygiene products. Having the necessary supplies and skills to do so can make you a valuable part of your community's survival and recovery structure. Below are just a few methods.

How to Make Toothpaste

Formula 1
- ⅔ cups baking soda
- 4tsp. sea salt
- 2 tsp. peppermint oil
- Mix to a paste and keep covered.

Formula 2
- 6 pts. baking soda
- 1 pt. vegetable-based glycerin

- 1 pt. hydrogen peroxide
- Mix to a paste and keep covered.

How to Make Soap

The most important element of keeping clean is soap. You should be able to make your own soap for family use and for trade once the commercial supply runs out. There are many kinds of soap-making kits and many ways to make soap, but I have chosen the original "pioneer" method because it uses lye that can be made from ashes and fat that can be rendered from cooking. These two materials would be available regardless of economic conditions. The addition of various herbs and scented oils such as from roses, lilacs, and mint can make the soaps more pleasant to use.

Ingredients
- Clean animal fat
- Lye
- Water

Equipment
- Clear 2-qt. plastic bottle (such as from juice)
- Rubber gloves, apron, and eye protection
- Wooden mixing spoon or stick
- Large 10–12 qt. pot (never use aluminum with lye)
- Candy or dairy thermometer
- Mold: heavy cardboard or wooden box lined with plastic or greased with petroleum jelly
- Insulation such as cardboard, foam, or blanket material
- Newspapers to protect working surfaces and floors

Instructions
1. Prepare the lye solution by slowly adding and mixing 13 oz. of lye into 2½ pts. of cold water. CAUTION! NEVER ADD WATER TO LYE. This solution will self-heat to about 200°F.
2. Let this solution cool to about 98°F.
3. Warm six pounds of fat to about 98°F. Do this in a tub of hot water, never over a flame.
4. Slowly pour the warm lye solution into the warm fat and stir until you have an opaque creamy solution.
5. Pour the solution into the mold about 1 to 1½ inch thick.
6. Cover with insulation to assure slow cooling.
7. When cooled and solidified, cut into bars.

Making Lye for Soap Production

Lye can be made by filling a barrel or other non-metallic container with wood ashes. You need to have a layer of straw at the bottom of the barrel to filter the liquid precipitate, and a hole at the bottom or low on the side to let the lye drip out. Then add boiling water slowly to the top and let it seep down through the ash until it starts to drip from the hole into a plastic or glass container.

Test the lye by cracking a raw egg into the lye. If it barely floats, the lye is usable to make soap.

CAUTION: Lye is a very corrosive material. It will damage your eyes and burn skin quickly. It is also particularly reactive with aluminum. Wear rubber gloves, rubber aprons, and goggles and have water to flush off splashes immediately and repeatedly. Use glass and plastic containers.

HUMAN WASTE DISPOSAL

Once humans began to inhabit permanent, large towns the accumulation and disposal of human waste became a problem. Open sewers, gutters, and "honey wagons" carried human waste to the nearest waterway and outhouses served the peripheral areas. Sewage limited the growth of cities to thousands or a few hundred thousand through the eighteenth century. In town, outhouses were common well into the early twentieth century. Early sanitation system systems depended on gravity to sustain a flow to the outlet, but as cities grew, it was necessary to pump sewerage and treat it before discharge. Most sewage systems today are dependent on constant maintenance and power.

Short-Term Waste Disposal

In short-term emergencies, the sewage system may still be functional for weeks, although the water to flush the existing toilets may be hard to spare. So-called "brown water" from bathing and cleaning can be used to flush the toilet. Dumping about one gallon of any kind of water will cause a toilet to flush. Rainwater, pond water, or any other water source can be used for this purpose. If the toilet is not available at all, you can improvise a toilet using a five-gallon pail lined with a heavy-duty plastic bag. As it fills, add some bleach and bury it in the backyard if possible. This is one of the reasons to have bleach, plastic bags, buckets, and shovels on hand. Waste can also be dumped into a pit with quick lime and covered. In Vietnam, the Army often burned human waste in oil drums using gasoline. While effective, it is unlikely you will have fuel to waste, and no one will appreciate the smell. Stock up on bleach and plastic bags while they are still available. Ten gallons of bleach should be maintained and rotated, as it deteriorates with age.

A basic "Port-A-Potty" kit consisting of a toilet seat mounted on a bag-lined five-gallon pail sells for about thirty dollars, or you can make your own for less.

Basic shallow pit toilets. Note the shovel to throw dirt in and handy toilet paper holder. Such facilities would be sufficient for short-term use or in temporary backyards and camps only and never near to or uphill from water sources and pumps.

Long-Term Sanitation Facilities

Small towns with gravity-operated systems and uphill well water supplies may do okay throughout a catastrophe. Most suburban areas and urban areas will experience traumatic population reductions through epidemics, famine, evacuation, and violence. The shortages of water, food, and other critical needs will probably reduce the population before the sanitation systems fail completely. Those having access to large lots can probably build outhouses. These "facilities" provide a reasonably safe and sanitary means of waste disposal. Screening and proper ventilation will keep flies out and prevent the accumulation of flammable gases. Yes, they can blow up! My grandfather had a permanent outhouse about two hundred feet from the house. He had a small toilet room inside for use at night and in cold weather. You had to haul the bucket out and dump it in the outhouse hole every morning. There was bucket of "quick lime" and a scoop in the outhouse. So, after you had dumped, you would throw in a scoop of lime to start breaking down the waste. If you don't have quick lime, you can use ashes from your fireplace instead.

GARBAGE DISPOSAL

The term *bonfire* was originally "bonefire" because garbage, bones, and waste was what was burned. Prior to the 1940s, the volume of trash and garbage generated by the average urban household was far less than it is today. Trash cans were usually small, galvanized containers. The contents were periodically emptied into dump trucks and hauled to the "city dump." Garbage consisted of mostly food waste and some empty cans and bottles. A wartime economy would drastically reduce the amount of packaging materials, and trash, but food waste and other perishable material would still accumulate. Manpower shortages, fuel shortages, and other disruptions could easily result in interruption or even cessation of garbage disposal. Garbage worker strikes in New York City and other locations provide a glimpse of what prolonged accumulation of trash could look like. During World War II, most homes had coal-burning furnaces that could burn up most of the paper, cardboard, and other combustible trash for heat. Open burning is still common in rural areas but prohibited in urban and most suburban locations. Such prohibitions would have to be ignored under wartime necessities. Garbage burning would generate significant smoke and pollution issues, but leaving raw garbage in the open would be even more unhealthy. Where large backyards are available, using steel oil drums or commercial firepits with spark screens well away from structure would be practical. In crowded urban environments, parks and open areas would need to be designated. The temptation to use barbecue pits or fireplaces to burn trash near to or inside of structures would lead to frequent fires when fire departments and water supplies might be unavailable. In all cases, burning locations should be free of brush, trees, debris, and other combustible materials, and water or fire extinguishers should be always on hand. Fires should never be left unattended.

INSECTS AND RATS

America's urban areas are already overrun with rats. Any kind of disruption in rat abatement, combined with failure of garbage collection and sewage treatment systems, would undoubtedly lead to full-scale rat infestation. Rat-borne diseases including plague, tularemia, rat bite fever, and even rabies could be a major source of fatalities. Rat and mouse feces can be the sources of some contact and airborne infection, so handling dead rats or materials that may be contaminated would require gloves and a dust/mist respirator. Of course, rats and mice will be hungry and could pose a significant threat to unprotected food stocks and crops. Kill traps and rat poison should be considered as part of preparedness for any long-term survival situation.

Mosquito-borne diseases including malaria, dengue, West Nile virus, yellow fever, tularemia, encephalitis, and dirofilariasis are common in third-world countries and disaster zones and only held at bay through good sanitation and insect abatement. Insecticides and insect repellents should be included in survival supplies. Mosquito netting is cheap and may be worth having to drape beds and camps during warm months.

LAUNDRY

Let's hope that your electricity stays on and the washer and dryer are working through wartime, but if things get rough, you may need to resort to hand laundering and air drying of your clothing. You can probably improvise washing equipment and methods, but here are some alternative lifestyle devices you may want to have on hand:

Washtubs: These are big, two-foot and larger diameter twelve-to-twenty-four-inch-deep galvanized steel tubs with handles. They come in many sizes from eight to thirty-five gallons. Granger, Harbor Freight, and many other suppliers still have these at about forty dollars each. You will need to have two or three of these, one for washing and one or two for rinsing. These are heavy when filled and will need to be pumped or bailed out, so put them on a strong stand or table so that the top of the tub is about waist high. Under survival conditions you may need to use these to gather rainwater when not in use. You may also need the used laundry and rinse water for other purposes.

Hand Washing Devices: These are replacements for the agitator, and they look like common plungers. In fact, you can use a plunger if nothing else is available. You just plunge the clothing in the soap water to force the dirt out. Not rocket science here. You will want to go easy on the soap because (1) it's valuable and (2) you need to rinse it out with the minimum of water. If you can hang it out on a rainy day, nature will rinse it for you, but you will have to wait for a sunny day to get it dry.

Scrubbing Boards: Washboards are made of corrugated tempered glass or galvanized metal. They provide a smooth, but wavy, surface against which to scrub tough dirt out of clothing. This is a must-have item but can still be rough on clothing and should be used sparingly. They cost about forty dollars today. A good soft bristled brush is handy for those dirty spots too.

Wringers: Hand wringing clothing is ineffective and tiring. Crank-powered wringers are much more effective and wrung out clothing will dry much faster indoors or out. Crank wringers are often sold by country stores and survival suppliers for from $80 to $150.

Drying Devices: Laundry poles were a common fixture of backyards well into the 1970s but are rare today. Clotheslines and clothes pins can still be found, as well as drying racks for indoor use. Even if you don't have all the other alternative washing equipment, you are going to find this item essential. Lines can be strung from trees, or structures, or in the basement. Lines should be strung tightly about seven feet high to compensate for the line sagging under the weight of heavy, wet clothing.

CHAPTER 19

WARTIME FOOD SOURCES AND STOCKING

A ccess to food under wartime or war zone conditions can be challenging. Even if the actual violent components of a war are limited to regions beyond our borders, serious shortages of food may develop. Cyberattacks can now cripple the food transportation systems, resulting in empty grocery store shelves and food rotting in trucks or in the fields. Certainly, the recent pandemic and supply chain issues demonstrated the fragility of the food supply system. Any level of warfare will result in shortages and probably rationing. Many urban areas already suffer from food insufficiency so that even a temporary interruption of the food supply would trigger civil unrest and looting that would spread into suburban and rural areas within a few days or weeks. While in theory a person can survive up to three weeks without food, food deprivation leads to increasing desperation and physical depletion within a week or less. The siege of Leningrad during World War II provides some idea of what food deprivation can do to normally civilized populations. There are photos of people looting a few turnips from a starved woman lying in the streets. People ate dried wallpaper paste from walls, and leather belts. Cats and dogs disappeared, along with rats and squirrels. Bodies were left in the street because there was no one strong enough to bury them. Anyone who had even a little food was hated even by relatives and former friends. Government-controlled food distribution inevitably leads to corruption and coercion by those in power. Criminal organizations will always take advantage of famine conditions by hijacking food trucks, intimidating farmers, and victimizing the public. Finally, any occupying force or foreign supported insurgent group might destroy crops and livestock as a tactic. Random poisoning of crops using drones could render all crops potentially unsafe to use. Ultimately, whoever controls access to food controls the population, and whoever can provide their own food retains freedom. Food is life and the procurement and protection of food is a life-and-death priority. Wartime rationing will come with significant regulations and requirements that may even mandate migration or travel limitation. Hoarding or home food production may bring confiscation. How much food you have stored and where it is kept should be extremely confidential information. Anyone with stored food would be well advised to have the means and the will to protect it against the malevolent and the desperate. Short-term survival packs and thirty-day food supplies are covered elsewhere in this book. Extended war conditions will require larger stocks of non-perishable food and the ability to produce and forge for sustenance beyond initial emergency supplies.

MALNUTRITION

While the recommended caloric intake ranges from sixteen hundred for inactive and up to three thousand for active adults, requirements depend on age, health, and body mass. Exposure to colder temperatures increases caloric needs as does high levels of stress. While the body can last only a few weeks without any food, it can survive for long periods of time on less than the ideal level of nutrition. However, prolonged lack of adequate food will inevitably result in malnutrition. When the body is deprived of nutrition to sustain energy and life, it compensates by breaking down its own tissues and shutting down functions. This begins with bodies fat stores and then moves on to the muscle, skin, and even the hair. The emaciated photos of World War II concentration camp inmates and starving children in Africa attests to this process. The immune system shuts down, making the victims prone to illness and wound infections. Heart rate, body temperature, and blood pressure drop, and the digestive system may atrophy, making it difficult for the victim to eat and digest what food they can get. Severe vitamin deficiencies can cause vision problems and softening of bones among other complications. For this reason, a year's supply of multiple vitamins should be a high priority in any wartime supply stocks.

FOOD STOCKING AND STORAGE

The most common method of assuring that you have food when you need it is stocking up and storing it. In the short term this is faster, cheaper, and takes less work than other methods. For home survival where weight and space are not a big issue, the best method is to simply stock up on various canned goods, and staples (e.g. sugar, honey, flower, rice, etc.) and rotate them into use. Most of these items last at least a few years, so you can have a year's supply of food without ever having any food in stock that is over a year old. Several preparedness supply companies provide prepackaged survival food and storage racks for such systems. Where space is limited or where weight is an issue, freeze-dried foods are more practical. These are more expensive but keep much longer and you can carry a lot more food if you need to evacuate. You do need to have a lot of safe water and fuel for heating and reconstituting these products.

Under emergency conditions, the ideal two thousand calories may have to be reduced and ideal requirements and limitations put aside temporarily but serious health issues will develop if less than two thousand calories is sustained for more than a few weeks. Fat, cholesterol, salt, and sugar limitations should not stop you from eating when you need calories, protein, minerals, and vitamins to stay alive and healthy. The list below is a good start on a home "survival pantry." These foods are economical, easy to store, and have a long shelf life. They are best kept vacuum packed and at moderate temperatures. To assure proper rotation, mark the storage date on each container. Since there really is no maximum amount of food to store, I have included a suggested minimum per person per year as a goal. I found wide differences in shelf-life estimates. The ones shown below are averages of several sources, but in all cases the use of vacuum packaging and cool dry storage will prolong shelf life.

- **Pasta:** Spaghetti, noodles, etc. are high in carbohydrates and easy to use in lots of dishes. Pasta has a shelf life of at least fifteen years. Minimum per person: twenty-five pounds.
- **Rice**: High in carbohydrates, rice is useful in many dishes. Store only whole grain rice as instant rice will not keep well. Minimum per person: twenty-five pounds.
- **Beans**: Pinto beans, black beans, garbanzo beans, red beans, lentils, and other types can be stored for twenty to thirty years, are easy to cook, and are a good source of protein. Minimum per person: thirty pounds.
- **Grits:** Grits are made from the cornmeal process and are a good source of nutrition. They can be used as cereal, fried, or in many recipes. You can use them to replace part or all of the recommended grain storage.
- **Nuts:** These are usually vacuum packed and can be stored for decades. They are a great source of protein and other nutrients. Minimum per person: about ten pounds.
- **Peanut butter**: A forty-ounce jar of peanut butter contains 6,650 calories. That's more than three days' food supply. It only has a shelf life of about three to four years, so you need to rotate it. Minimum per person: about four jars.
- **Whole grains:** Whole grains are often sold as survival foods. They do provide good nutrition, but to make baked good (e.g. bread, etc.) you need a grain mill to grind them into flour. Whole grains keep much longer than flour. Oats can simply be made into oatmeal or used in baking. Minimum per person: twenty-five pounds.

- **Dried fruits**: Dried fruits such as dates, raisins, apple slices, banana slices, figs, and apricots store for many years and provide important vitamins to the diet. Minimum per person: ten pounds.
- **Beef and turkey jerky**: Jerky or dehydrated meats are an important source of calories and protein to your diet. If you make jerky yourself, be sure to salt it and remove all the fat before drying. Vacuum-packed jerky should keep for at least two years and can be reconstituted in soups or stews or eaten as is. How many packages or pounds of jerky you need depends on your taste.
- **Powdered milk:** Powdered milk is a good source of vitamins and other nutrients. Store-bought products should be immediately vacuum packed for the best shelf life, but the vitamins degrade over time. Powdered milk specifically packaged in cans for storage will last up to fifteen years but should be repackaged in airtight containers once opened. Minimum per person: five pounds.
- **Powdered eggs** are nutritious have a shelf life of about ten years if kept in airtight or vacuum-packed containers. They can be used as scrambled eggs or in a variety of recipes. Minimum per person: five pounds.
- **Canned vegetables**: Canned vegetables such as spinach, corn, green beans, and carrots are essential to health and keep for four years or longer. Vegetables can be stored for many years, but canned fruits should be rotated every few years as the acid can eat through the cans over time. Minimum per person: fifteen to twenty cans.
- **Canned meats**: Canned meats such as Spam, corned beef, or Vienna sausage are very nutritious and store well. You can also stock up on canned tuna and chicken for variety. The recommended shelf life is two to four years, but I have used products that were as much as fifteen years old. Canned anchovies and sardines in oil keep indefinitely. Minimum per person: at least twenty cans.
- **Boullion and soup mixes**: Bouillon cubes and soup mix envelopes take up very little space and provide a way to create tasty soups from what you have stored and what you may be able to gather.
- **Honey**: Sometimes called the perfect food, honey really keeps indefinitely and can substitute for sugar in many uses. Minimum per person: two or three pounds.
- **Sugar:** Sugar is a nonperishable staple if kept in airtight and dry containers. It can be used in all kinds of recipes. I recommend keeping both white and brown sugar. Minimum per person: ten pounds.
- **Flour:** Useful in all kinds of cooking and baking, flour last up to ten years if sealed and dry. Minimum per person: fifty pounds.

- **Coffee and tea**: Depending on your tastes, these beverages offer comfort, warmth, and stimulation under any conditions. Great trade goods too. Minimum per person: twenty-four pounds of coffee or four hundred tea bags.
- **Vinegar**: Vinegar has many uses in cooking, food preservation, and even alternative medicine. You definitely want to have a few gallons.
- **Cooking oils and shortening**: A necessary ingredient in baking, frying. Minimum per person: two gallons.
- **Salt**: Used to enhance flavors and for a preservative. It will be in big demand during a prolonged emergency. Minimum per person: five pounds.
- **Spices**: A good selection of spices and sauce mixes can make otherwise bland "survival food" more enjoyable. The selection depends on your taste.
- **Other stuff**: There are lots of other options and additions. You can add freeze-dried meals to reduce storage space, spaghetti sauce to enhance the pastas, molasses in place of some honey, Bisquick™ (shelf life two to three years) or other baking mix in place of flour. You may want to add a few bags of hard candy for comfort and quick energy. Hard candy lasts a long time if kept dry and cool.

A number of options for food stocking. Left to right: (1) homemade food stock consisting of pasta, rice, beans, oatmeal, and other storable foods in vacuum packed bags, (2) stack of three ready-made, thirty-day containers of freeze-dried meals, (3) box of six #10 cans of survival foods from a preparedness supply outlet, (4) tote bins full of freeze-dried foods, MREs and canned goods.

FOOD STOCK PLANNING

One way to build up a food stock is to create a table like the one below and start building a month-by-month food stock up program. You can include canned goods, dehydrated foods, and nonperishable items. The sample table below is by no means complete. Try to stock up on foods you like to eat. Take advantage of sales and quantity discounts and buy store brands to save money.

	Jan	Feb	Mar	Apr	May	Jun	Jul	Aug	Sep	Oct	Nov	Dec
Canned Foods												
SPAM®	4	4	5	5	5	6	7	10	4			
Tuna fish	3	2	3	5	4							
Green beans	2	2	2	2	2	2	2					
Corn	1	1	1	2	2	2	2					
Soup	8	6	5	2	2	2	2					
Peanut butter	2	2	2	2	2	3						
Dehydrated Foods												
Potatoes, #10 can	2	2	1	1	1	2	3					
Carrots, gallon can	1	1	1	1	1	2						
Beef jerky Pkg.	4	4	5	5	7							
Nonperishables												
Pasta boxes 2 pounds	6	6	6	4	6							
Beans 2 pounds	4	3	2	4	5	6						
Peas 2 pounds	3	2	3	4	6	2						
Wheat 10 pounds	20	20	20	20	20	20						
Oats 5 pounds	20	20	20	20	20	20						
Staples												
Sugar 4 pounds	1	1	2	1	1	2						
Salt, 26 oz.	1			1				1		1		
Coffee, 26 oz.	1	2	1	2	1	2	1	2				
Cooking oil, 1 qt.	1		2		2			1				

You probably have five to ten days of canned and frozen food in the house normally before you need to start using your survival stocks. You can go with costly dehydrated foods if space is a problem, but otherwise stock up on dry and canned foods that you can rotate. Dried fruits, beans, lentils, rice, corn-meal, oatmeal, nuts, wheat, pasta, sugar, coffee, and other long-term storable foods can be further preserved by vacuum packaging. Vacuum packaging equipment and supplies can be purchased at survival supply and at hardware stores. Canned vegetables and meats (Spam® corned beef, beef stew, chicken and dumplings, pork and beans) usually have a two-year marked shelf life. They keep much longer, but rotation is recommended. Powdered milk can be kept for up to twenty-five years and condensed milk lasts well beyond its marked two-year limit. Things like honey, molasses, vinegar, and syrup, last indefinitely. See chapter 28 for a food supply list. In addition, I highly rec-ommend the chapter on food acquisition and preservation in my book *Total Survival.*

ALTERNATIVES AND LONG-TERM FOOD SOURCES

While stocking up on food for any emergency is the fastest and easiest way to assure adequate nutrition through an extended emergency, it is wise to have alternative methods of food acquisition and to be prepared to develop methods for food acquisition, production, and preservation. Consider the possibilities listed below.

- You may not have time or the funds to build up a full year's food sup-ply before economic and wartime conditions create food shortages.
- You may not have room at your residence to store the necessary quan-tity of food stuffs.
- You may be forced to abandon most of your stored food due to a fire, civil unrest, or necessary evacuation.
- Your food supply may be confiscated by government agencies or taken by criminals or looters.
- The war and associated economic disaster may last far longer than your one-year food supply.
- There is no room here to provide detailed instructions on the methods for gathering and preservation of foods, and the options available will depend on the reader's location, budget, and inclination, but develop-ing the potential for some of them would move from simple emer-gency survival to future self-reliance.

FOOD ACQUISITION AND PRESERVATION METHODS

- **Urban foraging:** While looting is a criminal act under normal conditions, gathering food that would otherwise go to waste from a bombed-out grocery store or restaurant is justified when starvation is the alternative. Abandoned homes and industrial facilities may have left food behind in haste. There may be opportunities for street trading for food with those who have sources. Various charities and agencies may also have food available. These sources can supplement your stored supplies, but don't put yourself at risk using them.

- **Natural foraging:** If you live in rural or semi-rural areas, there are many edible plants, nuts, berries, and roots available to those who can identify them. Buying a book and familiarizing yourself with the location of regional edible plants could be a good supplement to your food supply.

- **Gardening:** If you have a yard, establishing a vegetable garden is a healthy hobby and good source of long-term food supplies. Don't wait until the emergency arises to start gardening. Effective gardening is a skill that takes time. Build up supplies so you can expand your small garden to replace grass and flowers as necessary. Focus on easily preserved crops such as potatoes, carrots, beets, peas, and beans. Vacuum-packed seeds are available from survival supply stores.

- **Hunting:** Many hunters are overconfident in their ability to provide protein through an emergency. When a true food shortage develops, hunting season will be every day, everywhere, for everyone. Game will disappear within weeks and venturing into the woods where amateur hunters are shooting at everything that moves can be very dangerous. Responsible hunting can be a healthy hobby and a source for building food supplies prior to wartime conditions. Smoking, drying, and salting of game meat can build up your food larder and even provide trade goods.

- **Trapping:** Trapping is generally not legal but is justified under emergency conditions. Since traps don't discriminate between game and domestic animals and are usually painful to the animal, they should be considered a last resort in wilderness survival situations.

- **Fishing:** Food shortages will create thousands of first-time fishermen who will ruin fishing conditions. Wartime will probably suspend enforcement of regulations so that such techniques as netting, spearing, gigging, and even explosives may be used by desperate citizens. Fishing may be used early in an emergency to delay using up stored foods and for freezing or preserving catches for emergency stocks. Don't depend on it for a continuous supply once desperation sets in.

- **Canning:** Canning methods can be found in many "back to basics" and homesteading books, as well as the internet and community classes. Canning supplies are readily available at hardware stores and grocery stores. Canning is a great hobby, and you can use the technique to preserve produce from your garden or from quantity purchase at local farms. This is a great way to build up your emergency supplies, save money, and establish a sustainable food supply. Canning requires boiling a lot of water, so a sustainable source of fuel is a prerequisite.
- **Smoking:** Smoking is an excellent method for preserving meat and fish. Smokers can be purchased at most outdoor and sporting goods stores. A variety of woods and seasonings are also available. You can smoke game and fish that you have gathered or purchased. This process facilitates the preservation of meat when freezing is no longer available.
- **Drying:** Drying is probably the oldest method of food preservation and requires the least amount of skill. You can dry meat, fish, fruits, and some vegetables. Some things can even be sun-dried if kept from insects. For instance, green beans can be threaded like popcorn and hung in a warm dry place to dry. Home food driers can be purchased from survival supply outlets or you can build an outdoor dryer that uses a wood fire. Food that can be dried include beef (jerky), sliced carrots, sliced bananas, beans, and apples.
- **Salting:** Salting is an effective method of preserving meat and fish. This method is more complicated than just dumping salt on foods. Salt draws the moisture out of meat and fish, thereby making them more resistant to fungus and bacteria. The two methods of using salt are "dry salting" and "brining." Basic instruction can be found in most self-reliance books and the internet. Salt should be stored in quantity to provide this reliable method of non-refrigerated food preservation. Be sure to seal stored salt in moisture proof containers.
- **Pickling:** Pickling, like salting, can be used to preserve a variety of meats and vegetables. The process basically involves submerging the item to be preserved in vinegar. Pickled cucumbers, pickled beets, and pickled herring are common off-the-shelf items. If you plan on utilizing this method, stocking up on vinegar by the gallon would be advisable.

SUPPLY CHAIN INDEPENDENCE

The importance of access to food cannot be overstated. War has always brought famine or at least some form of food shortages. Hunger has always bred desperation and violence. Access to food can be used to coerce and control the population and limit freedom. Empty stomachs have no conscience. Being able to feed yourself and your family throughout a short-term or long-term emergency without dependence on the supply chain or emergency response agencies not only secures your life and freedom, but also leaves more food for others and provides a safer and faster recovery from any war-related deprivations.

CHAPTER 20

ALTERNATIVE POWER UNDER WARTIME CONDITIONS

At the very beginning of World War II, German bombers targeted the natural gas storage tanks of Warsaw, Poland. Russia has consistently targeted Ukrainian generating stations with missiles and drones in an attempt to leave civilians in the cold and dark. Even the US targeted Bagdad's generator stations in the first minutes of the "Shock and Awe" campaign. It is virtually certain that any type of military conflict will involve both physical and cyberattacks on the electrical generation and distribution systems in America. While most local emergencies and regional disasters can result in localized and short-term power interruptions, warfare may result in frequent and extended outages. A nuclear war or the use of so-called electromagnetic pulse (EMP) weapons could disable the grid for months or longer. Most emergency preparedness plans include the use of battery and liquid propane (LP) gas powered lights and small appliances, but extended wartime deficiencies will call for more robust and sustainable sources of electricity.

ALTERNATIVES AND RECHARGEABLES

The first level of energy interruption preparedness is to have adequate short-term lighting, cooking, and heat sources. There are plenty of tactical flashlights, battery-powered lanterns, and emergency radios available. Gas camping stoves and camp heaters can get you through a few days or a week without electricity. Rechargeable flashlights and crank, solar, or battery radios will give you more sustained, but limited power. Investing in a solar battery charger and extra batteries can keep your lights and radio going for prolonged periods. It is always best to avoid dependency on one source of anything. Gas, oil, and kerosene lanterns, and plenty of candles can supplement your electric lighting system.

The next level of alternative power is to be able to provide electricity to run essential appliances such as sump pumps, water pumps, furnace fans, refrigerators, and freezers. Large natural-gas powered generators are efficient and popular. They offer seamless switching to alternative power and enough power to run all appliances and lights, but these may be too expensive or impractical for many. The next alternative is smaller gasoline and multi-fuel (gasoline, LP, natural gas) generators. These come in a variety of sizes priced from a few hundred dollars to $3,000 or more, depending on wattage output. They need to be run periodically and the gasoline should be changed at least annually to assure that they will run when you need them. In most towns there are limits on how much fuel you can store, and fuel may be rationed or unavailable under wartime conditions, so don't be dependent on this source of power beyond a few weeks or beyond your fuel storage capacity. Always store flammables away from the house in safety cans and in steel cabinets. Carbon monoxide is a significant hazard from running a generator, so plan on having it running well outside of the house and away from intake vents. In many cases the natural gas supply will continue even when the electricity is off but modern furnaces will not run unless they have adequate electrical power. If you have a large gasoline or multi-fuel generator, consider having an electrician install a transfer switch so that your furnace, hot water heater, and other appliances can run off of your generator.

The 100-watt generator on the right is easy to move and uses only a little fuel. I ran a sump pump and a small freezer alternately for several days on just a few gallons of gas, but of course I had to rely on solar lamps and candles for lights. The larger 3,500-watt generator can power most of the home appliances but burns a lot of fuel in the process. More modern multi-fuel generators can reduce dependency on just one fuel source.

Portable "power stations" and backup power systems are essentially batteries with voltage regulating systems. The older systems were small automotive batteries that could jump-start a vehicle and included 12-volt and USB outlets. Modern systems use advanced power storage technology and are available with a wide range of capabilities. While basic units are designed to keep computers and other low-voltage appliances running for a few days, advanced systems can keep a refrigerator running for fifteen to twenty-seven hours. These are smart batteries that need to be recharged every few days, so they are only useful if the power outages are temporary or intermittent.

SOLAR POWER STORAGE AND RECHARGING SYSTEMS

While battery-powered lighting and radios supplemented by a multi-fuel generator may be adequate to get through most disaster-related power interruptions, more sustainable power sources will be necessary for the potential long-term effects of assaults on the power grid. A strategy of reducing dependency on electrical appliances while increasing access to solar power generation is the only practical and sustainable course of action. Portable systems including foldout solar panels, storage batteries, and control systems are available through camping supply and survival supply outlets. While gasoline generators are noisy, cannot be used indoors, and are dependent on fuel supply, solar power systems are safe and can even be used from apartments or in camps. These units can be part of your home preparedness system but can also be placed in your evacuation vehicle or kept at your retreat location.

The Grid Doctor™ solar generator system shown above sells for less than $500 including the one-hundred-watt solar panel and power storage unit. This one can be charged from the solar panel, a wall outlet, a USB cord, or an automobile lighter adapter. It can run lights, laptops, TVs, a fan, and even a mini fridge for various lengths of time. A second solar panel can be added to shorten charging time. Larger but less mobile systems costing just under $3,000 can run larger appliances such as refrigerators, microwaves, and washing machines.

STAYING WARM WHEN THE POWER GOES OUT

Coal and charcoal (used for heating) theft was a major activity throughout Europe during World War II. In the first winter of the Russian-Ukrainian war, Russia used missiles and drones against the Ukrainian electrical, gas, and fuel grid to try to freeze the civilian population into submission. Two-thirds of America is subject to prolonged periods of cold and subfreezing temperatures. Electric, natural gas, and even propane delivery systems are vulnerable to direct attack, sabotage, and cyberattack. Prolonged cold exposure can lead to hypothermia even at temperatures well above freezing. Cold conditions combined with inadequate nutrition can wear down the immune system and have severe physical and psychological consequences. In Russia, they depend on "general winter" to defeat invaders when bombs and bullets fail. If you are a winter camper you may have what you need, but if not, you must prepare for prolonged periods of reduced heat or no heat. Well-heated homes tend to discourage having heavy blankets. Preparedness must include having both wool blankets and cold weather–rated sleeping bags for the whole family. One of the best approaches to winter survival at home under grid failure conditions is to erect a tent in your living room or basement and use camp heaters. If you have a stove or fireplace, seal off the room that it is in with plastic sheeting to conserve the limited heat. In all cases, have a working carbon monoxide detector nearby. Even if you have a wood stove, or camp heater, long-lasting war-related grid failure will exhaust your fuel supply. A tent and sleeping bags will help conserve body heat, and hot food and drinks will help to prevent hypothermia. Homeless people survive this way through the worst winters. You can too.

SUN OVENS AND SOLAR COOKERS

Your gas stove may or may not be working during a crisis and you will eventually run out of fuel for your camp stoves. Cooking over a campfire may or may not be practical in your location, but hot food and beverages are essential to survival in cold weather when heating resources are limited. Solar cookers and sun ovens cook food by concentrating the heat of the sun onto the food or a cooking utensil. The larger the reflective surface the more heat is concentrated. Solar ovens or sun ovens can provide limitless cooking capacity without fire hazards, smoke, or the use of limited fuel resources. Larger ovens can even bake pizzas and bread. Solar ovens come in a variety of designs priced from $50 to $400. Some are rather bulky, while others are foldable or compact. Instructions for making your own solar cooker are available online and involve using aluminum foil, cardboard, plastic wrap, black paper, and other easy-to-find materials. Larger ovens will cook faster and be more effective in winter conditions.

ACCESS TO POWER

Wartime preparedness must include alternatives for everything that the peacetime grid provides. While normal disaster preparedness anticipates temporary and regional disruptions, war-related grid failure may be widespread and long-term. Immediate access to battery and fuel powered lighting, heat, and electricity is essential but must be enhanced by more sustainable methods for generating and storing electricity and for cooking and heating. While stocking up on short-term power, cooking, and lighting sources remains an important survival priority, solar power systems and solar ovens can provide long-lasting access to power generation and cooking capacity.

CHAPTER 21

SURVIVING IN A WARTIME ECONOMY

I have addressed various aspects of wartime economics in other chapters, but economic warfare and economic survival issues are a critical element of the developing war. During World War II, the American economy was virtually immune to attack. Everything we needed we made in the USA and almost every critical natural resource was directly accessible here. Countries like England and Japan were dependent on imported goods and material. England came close to surrender due to a handful of German submarines decimating their shipping. Japan was virtually starving as American submarines sank most of their cargo ships. Today the United States is dependent on imports for virtual every commodity and product and our potential enemies already own the manufacturing facilities and the ships. We experience just a glimpse of our vulnerability when the supply chain malfunctioned during the COVID pandemic. In any declared or undeclared war, the supply chain would virtually cease to exist. On day one of any war, everything you own and possess would multiply in value exponentially, while the cost of everything you need would also multiply exponentially.

I knew several people who lived in the USSR through the Cold War. The USSR and their vassal states operated as a war economy. Throughout that period the black market became the primary economy. The so-called oligarchs that rule Russia today rose from the black-market cartels of the Cold War period. The Mafia in Sicily arose from similar roots. Even in today's failing US and world economy, criminal cartels are taking root in most major urban areas. The recent emergence of well-organized theft rings is no accident. These operations "liberate" goods from trucks, shipping containers, warehouses, and stores and market them through their own outlets to the public. As they drive prices up and legitimate retailers go out of business, they drive citizens to buy from them. This is a foretaste of what a wartime economy may bring even to secure communities.

Once the government initiates a controlled economy and the black market expands, it will be challenging for the individual citizen to maintain a self-reliant lifestyle or safe economic activities. In addition to price controls, massive inflation, and rationing, the government may outlaw hoarding of critical supplies and label prepared citizens as unpatriotic. Jealous neighbors may even be tempted to turn in those who have too much food or other supplies. Black marketers will not appreciate competition from those engaged in honest trade and barter or alternative economy activities. Violent theft, vandalism, and protection rackets always flourish in a wartime economy, and the government seldom acts to protect the private citizen. These are the realities based on wartime economics in Europe, Asia, and South America. Once introduced into a region or nation, the level of corruption control is difficult to extinguish. Well-organized communities and trade and barter networks backed up by responsible, law-abiding security associations may be necessary to preserve the integrity and safety of the economy.

One thing about our long relationship with the global economy is that everyone has too much of everything. Before the end of World War II, almost everything was repairable and durable. There were no mountainous waste dumps. While we may not encourage hoarders who hang on to useless junk, the wise economist should stop wasting and start selective retention of salvageable goods. Things that can be repaired, lubricated, painted, repurposed, or recycled can be used directly or as trade items. Citizens that have the skill and the tools to repair damaged or worn items will be in great demand. We get almost all our clothing from foreign sources so "out of style" clothing will be "in style" when nothing else is available. Socks can be mended. Tears can be patched. Knives can be sharpened. Motors can be fixed. Stocking up on spare parts, lubricants, cloth, thread, and other repair supplies is highly advisable. Being able to maintain what we have and do without new items for a while may be necessary to get through the early stages of economic warfare.

Like survival knowledge, practical skills weigh nothing, take up no space, and can be carried anywhere you go. In his book *Defiance*, Nechama Tec describes how the Jews who had escaped the Nazis and set up a whole economy in the Naliboki Forest in Eastern Poland welcomed mechanics, seamstresses, doctors, and carpenters, but rejected lawyers and bankers. They also welcomed those with military experience, especially if they brought their own weapons. Unfortunately, our throwaway society and loss of manufacturing jobs has created a deficit in practical skills that will handicap survival and recovery. The old adage "make yourself useful" will go double in a wartime economy.

TRADE AND BARTER SUPPLIES

In addition to home survival supplies, and evacuation packs, wartime preparedness should include the accumulation and storage of equipment and supplies that will have high trade value during wartime. Some potential trade and barter supplies are listed below in no particular order.

- Over-the-counter painkillers and other medications
- Prescription medications
- Antibiotics
- Disinfectants
- Toilet paper
- Diapers
- Sanitary napkins
- Medical alcohol
- Repair items: duct tape, glue, wire, rope, etc.
- Automotive supplies: tire patch, oil, coolant, filters, etc.
- Bleach
- Water purification filters, tablets, etc.
- Batteries (all sizes)
- Flashlights and lanterns
- Plastic sheeting and tarps
- Sugar
- Coffee
- Flour
- Salt
- Vinegar
- Cooking oil
- Matches and lighters
- Oil lamps and lamp oil
- Candles
- Battery-powered radios
- Sewing supplies
- Vegetable seeds
- Fuel that can be safely stored, including LP gas, kerosene, and gasoline.
- Any kind of firearms
- Ammunition: particularly 9mm, .38, .45, .40, .22 calibers, and .308, 5.56 NATO and 7.62 Russian rifle ammunition. Twelve-gauge shotgun shells will also be in demand.
- While not true necessities, alcoholic beverages and cigarettes will be in huge demand by dependent individuals and therefore will be high-value barter items.

While survival items for personal use can be kept surreptitious, trading will disclose that you have high-value items and inevitably attract the attention of black marketeers, looters, and even government regulators. Trade networking and security associations will be necessary to avoid being pillaged and intimidated. The Chinese symbol for disaster and opportunity is the same. Many a shrewd entrepreneur have risen from poverty to wealth using survival skills in wartime.

LIVESTOCK

During World War II it was common for people to raise chickens and ducks in small coops in urban backyards. In fact, between the "victory gardens" and chicken coops, many homes resembled small farms. Vegetables and eggs were a common neighborhood trade item back then. The country was just recovering from the Great Depression and a lot of folks that lived in the cities had been raised on farms or their parents had. Most urban and suburban areas have regulations that prohibit such practices today, but these prohibitions are under review in many regions, and would be rescinded or unenforceable in wartime. Today, urban and suburban citizens are far removed from the sources of food and the skills of farming, but "back to basics" and "alternative lifestyle" movements have preserved the fundamental information and sources for establishing mini-farms. Chickens, geese, rabbits, and even goats can supply food for home and trade again during wartime, but the modern citizen will need to establish these small livestock facilities before full-scale hostilities create shortages of stock and feed. As with other survival and self-reliance supplies, livestock would need to be protected against human and animal predators.

CHAPTER 22

WARTIME SHELTERS AND RETREATS

Nuclear fallout shelters have been addressed elsewhere in this book (see chapter 9). Here we will focus on the various shelter options available under desperate circumstances other than nuclear. Along with air, food, and water, shelter is a prime survival priority. Under war conditions it will often be the immediate priority as protection from projectiles, blasts, heat, and other war effects. Exposure to excessive cold, heat, and moisture can lead to death within hours or a few days. The efficacy of modern homes depends on heating, air conditioning, and structural integrity to protect occupants, but worst-case scenarios may compromise these protections. In the gravest extreme, the survivor may be forced to abandon their primary home and seek alternative shelter.

HOME FORTIFICATION

Modern homes are neither designed nor intended to function as combat for-tifications. Ideally, a real masonry construction home with minimal windows and a basement can offer some defensive potential. Frame buildings with-out basements are virtually impossible to defend against bullets, blasts, and incendiary devices. Individual homes that are well spaced may be defendable against unorganized assaults, but closely spaced buildings and apartments are virtually indefensible to an individual or family facing any kind of organized attack. If actual military operations are anticipated in your community, evac-uation to more defensible locations is the only safe option. The actions below can prepare for home fortification if that is your best option.

- Secure military-style long guns and plenty of ammunition, along with ballistic vests and helmets, for all family members.
- Identify potential locations where hostile shooters might take up sniper positions or assailants might hide and launch an assault from. Think of ways to make these locations undesirable or unusable.

- Identify blind spots and covered approaches to your home Think of ways to make these locations undesirable or unusable.
- Make up chicken wire screens that can be placed over windows to repel rocks, Molotov cocktails, and grenades.
- Clear away shrubbery and other obstructions that could provide cover and concealment for criminals or combatants approaching your home.
- Consider the installation of fencing that will inhibit access but permit you to observe and engage potential threats.
- Stock up on smoke grenades to facilitate your movements or escape.
- Stock up on barbed wire, tools, sandbags, and other supplies needed to fortify your home. If you are going to use barbed wire, be sure to purchase special gloves and barbed wire tools.
- Make a home defense plan and an escape plan that includes all family members.

When and if your community cycles from wartime to war zone conditions that justify significant and immediate fortification efforts, here are a few suggested actions:

- Position weapons and ammunition for quick access at all firing positions.
- Position heavy furniture and appliances to protect firing positions.
- Barricade doors and position obstacles on exterior stairs and approaches.
- Install premade wire screens over window to repel rocks, Molotov cocktails, and grenades.
- If available, use barbed wire or other items to create obstacles and tripping hazards on approaches to your home.
- Knock loopholes in walls below exterior eye level or just above basement ground level to provide firing positions.
- Have fire extinguishers, water, and first aid kits ready.
- If sandbags are available, position them near your firing positions.
- It may be tactically necessary and justifiable to occupy adjoining homes or dig foxholes in yards to effectively repel an assault.
- Move vehicles into garages or away from the homes as they will provide cover and concealment for assailants and a serious fire hazard.

Home fortification may be able to deter criminals and encourage bypassing of some paramilitary units, but making your home the site of a battle with well-armed and trained soldiers will result in the destruction of your home and probably the annihilation of you and your family. One grenade, artillery shell, rocket, drone, or heavy machine gun burst will overwhelm most small-arms defenses. Being part of a community defense program or retreating to a more defensible location may be the wise choice. In you are forced into house-to-house defense, the following illustration from *FM 90–10 Military Operations in Urbanized Terrain* may be of value:

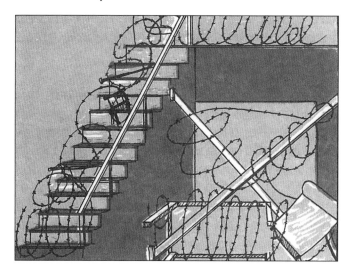

This illustration shows how barbed wire might be used to deny access to doorways and upper floors.

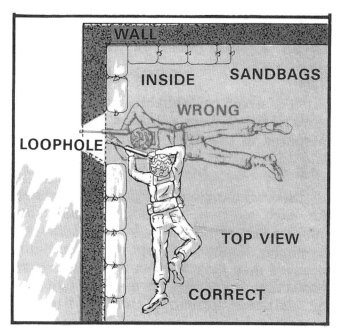

This illustration shows how to and how not to shoot from a fortified loophole or window.

This illustration shows how a basement can be fortified.

APPROPRIATED SHELTER

Desperate times justify desperate measures. If your home or your community are overrun or untenable, it may be necessary to occupy more secure and remote dwellings or commercial structures. Adequate shelter is a critical need. Under wartime conditions there should be plenty of abandoned homes and buildings available. While breaking and entering and damaging property is illegal and wrong under normal circumstances, protection from attack, cold, wet conditions, or radioactive fallout trumps any moral or legal concerns. However, attempting to forcefully occupy an inhabited home is not justifiable and should be avoided. Carrying bolt cutters, hacksaws, crowbars and an axe in your vehicle can facilitate access to locked gates and doors. Mastering the skills of lockpicking can be useful as well. A broken-down door lets others know that you are in there whereas picking the lock leaves no evidence of your occupancy. Under such conditions, the appropriation of essential food and medical supplies may also be justified. Taking items beyond survival necessities is looting and places you with the reprehensible criminal element. Where practical, leave cash or an IOW in your wake.

PREESTABLISHED RETREATS

While the heroes of popular survival fiction always seem to have a fully stocked retreat in the mountains, most of us cannot afford the luxury of such a facility. Unoccupied cabins in remote areas tend to attract looters and vandals even during normal times and may be ravaged by desperate refugees before you get there. Extremely remote and well-hidden shelters may be too

far away or too difficult to access. The hazards of exposure to weather, dangerous people, and even radioactive fallout may prohibit extended travel. If you
have relatives in an accessible location outside of the immediate danger zones,
consider making arrangements with them and storing essential supplies at
their location. They may welcome the extra help and security you can provide, but you must be able to provide enough supplies and skills to earn your
keep. So-called "self-storage" facilities are common. These are often located
in semi-rural areas and accessible from major evacuation routes. These units
come in a variety of sizes and are reasonable secure. Survival supplies, food,
fuel, tentage, tools, and even an alternative vehicle can be kept in such a cache
at a reasonable cost.

IMPROVISED SHELTER

The subject of improvised sheltering is more applicable to wilderness survival than it is to wartime survival where occupiable structures are usually
available. Basic evacuation packs will include some form of tentage or tarps
to provide temporary shelter. Military survival texts and wilderness survival
books devote some detail to the construction of shelters using natural materials. Such shelters are intended for use by downed pilots, or lost hikers awaiting rescue. Civilian refugees might find it necessary to retreat into the forests
with limited supplies and need to construct temporary shelter as protection
from the elements. These designs can be enhanced by the use of tarps, or plastic materials, but should be considered last-resort and temporary habitation
until more substantial shelter is constructed or located.

This commonly used shelter design is constructed from available branches and
thatched with pine boughs, grass, or other material. The main cross-support is
run between two standing trees. It should be three to four feet high, six to seven
feet wide, and about four feet deep. It can be floored with available leaves, grass,
or pine boughs for comfort and insulation. Be sure that the open end faces away
from the prevailing wind. A small fire and reflector placed about three feet from
the opening can provide warmth, but be cautious not to set the shelter on fire.

Whenever possible, use natural conditions to provide shelter. Here, a fallen tree provides the primary support and pine boughs and branches are used to create the shelter sides.

This three-point design is strong and fast to erect. The open end should be about three feet high by three feet wide. The depth needs to be about seven feet to accommodate the occupant far enough into shelter to cover the head and shoulders.

SURVIVAL CAMPS

The book *Defiance* by Nechama Tec describes how Polish Jews escaped and defied the Nazis during World War II by establishing an elaborate self-sufficient and defended survival camp in the Naliboki Forest. In the movie *Red Dawn*, resistance fighters called the Wolverines operate from a survival camp. If habitable communities and structures become dangerous, then long-term survival camping in remote areas may be the only option. If you are a camper and have already acquired tents, stoves, packs, sleeping bags, and other camping gear, you have an advantage at home and an option for sustainable shelter in extreme emergencies. Beyond backpacking gear, camping gear for long-term habitable camping is usually too heavy to carry very far. You will want durable, large tents, sleeping pads or bunks, sleeping bags and blankets, camouflage nets, stoves, weapons, cooking gear, and other bulky items in addition to food and supplies. If you have a vehicle capable of off-road travel and it is able to get to your selected site, you are lucky. Carts or bicycles with trailers are other options. Preselecting one or more potential camp locations and prepositioning the heavier items near there may be the best idea if you can do it. You may be able to plan and prearrange with a private campground owner for an emergency site and store some items there, but remember that known campgrounds and state parks may be swamped with desperate families and would-be looters. A secluded location well away from the main roads, but with access to water, would be ideal. Establishing a survival camp may be practical for groups or multiple families to divide the workload and security duties.

This hasty abatis made up from deadfall trees and branches can slow down or prevent unwanted intruders approaching your camp. Trenches, sharpened stakes, and tripping hazards can also be created. Of course, camp occupants must know the exit routes and the routes should zigzag to not be obvious from the outside.

You may also need to forage in nearby towns and abandoned buildings, etc. for materials such as wire, plastic, cloth, rope, containers, metal, and other materials. Depending on the situation, you may or may not want to interact with other survivors or occupants in the area. Remember that these folks may be in desperate situations and may not welcome your foraging and hunting in the same area. Of course, there may also be openly hostile and criminal groups roaming about that you want to avoid. You probably will need to set fires, and some noise and odors will be unavoidable. But keep fires and smoke to a minimum and do not wear trails to and from your camp. Worn trails, trash, and signs of foraging will all attract attention. These are particularly troublesome in fall and winter when there is less foliage and tracks in the snow are very hard to conceal. The gathering of firewood and building materials will soon clear the area of deadwood and branches, giving more evidence of your camp. After a few weeks your impact on the area will be hard to conceal. Here are two solutions to these hazards:

- Move your camp every few weeks. Doing this gives you fresh foraging and hunting territory while reducing your risk of being raided by hostile groups. You should search out and designate your next campsite as soon as you settle in the current one. You may even want to cache some supplies there and make it your emergency evacuation assembly point.
- If constant moving of the camp is impractical, you can minimize your foraging, hunting, and other activities within a few miles of the camp and go out on foraging and hunting expeditions to remote areas well away from your camp.

Another feature of the survival camp is that it justifies the time and effort to establish basic fortification. You should be able to set up and man a lookout post that will spot intruders well before they can detect the camp. You can use deadwood, branches, ditches, and other material to slow down any form of intrusion long enough to be identified, resisted, or for you to evacuate. You should consider having trenches or other bullet-resistant "cover" available for all camp members. Finally, you must have a plan for evacuation and a plan for camp defense established and practiced.

Sanitation is another issue that becomes critical in a long-term camp. Human waste, cooking waste, and the offal from cleaning fish and game will attract unwanted insects, animals, and disease that will soon render the camp untenable. These wastes must be buried well away from the occupied camp and water supplies. Clear procedures must be in place as soon as the camp is established. Since waste disposal and personal hygiene issues will probably be addressed outside of the camp's main defensive perimeter, it will be necessary to have an armed guard accompany anyone visiting these facilities. It is standard procedure for a hostile intruder to take down a person who is outside the camp and then infiltrate wearing their clothing as if returning.

CHAPTER 23

WARTIME ETHICS

What a cruel thing war is . . . to fill our hearts with hatred instead of love for our neighbors.
—General Robert E. Lee (1807–70)

The concept of ethics is distinguishable from morals in that ethics are much more practical.

Morals are ideas or opinions that are driven by a desire to do good. Ethics are rules that establish allowable actions and correct behavior. An ethical code may or may not be definably moral as it is just an established set of rules. Under normal circumstances a citizen has preestablished moral principles and ethical standards provided by society and laws. Under wartime chaos and war zone violence, citizens will be faced with moral dilemmas and ethical conundrums without guidance. While the trained soldier has orders to follow and a chain of command to sort out moral and ethical conflicts, the civilian caught in a life-and-death combat situation must make decisions and cope with conflicting emotional consequences alone. Survival ethics is guided by the basic survival imperative, but the ethics of survival in wartime and in a war zone is more complicated. The difference between right and wrong can be clouded by ideological, ethnic, racial, religious, and national affiliations. One's location, social, or family relationship render philosophical neutrality unfeasible. While natural disasters or a singular foreign enemy may unite a population, more complex modern conflicts can create all manner of division, paranoia, and distrust.

Under wartime deprivations, normally honest and law-abiding citizens may resort to theft, or black-market dealings. Citizens with weak moral codes and selfish tendencies are inclined to commit a full range of criminal acts once the prohibitions of effective law enforcement are removed. Soldiers and citizens exposed to the violence and trauma of actual warfare often become desensitized or even malevolent and violent as a result. It is no accident that gangs of the Wild West, and the gangsters of the Roaring Twenties followed the Civil War and World War I. War releases the most terrible inclinations of humanity. Be aware that there are "nice people" but there are also people who are just being nice. Ultimately the citizen must establish his or her own code of ethics. A few examples of ethical and moral challenges follow:

- **Use of force:** Police are often caught in a lose-lose scenario where using force can be seen as brutality, and failure to use force can result in failure in their duty to the law and the community. For the citizen the question is, "Is the use of force or threat of force" justifiable and reasonable under the circumstances? You may need to use force against family members or neighbors to get them out of harm's way or to prevent them from endangering yourself and others because they are obstinate or unaware of danger. You are doing the seemingly wrong thing but for a good reason.

- **Use of deadly force:** Using any kind of deadly or potential deadly force is an extremely drastic action. Unfortunately, modern media and video games have trivialized killing and desensitized the public. No responsible citizen should look forward to taking a human life, but during the gravest extreme of wartime, such an act may be inescapable. Terrorists imbued with hatred and extreme views will kill innocent civilian men, women, and children without the slightest hesitation. Criminals simply have no moral code or empathy for victims. Finally, previously peaceful citizens enraged, shocked, or misled by wartime and war zone conditions may become predators. If using deadly force is the only way to save yourself and others, be mentally prepared to do it. Failure to act may result in your death and the death of those you care about. Regardless of the justification, using deadly force will probably result in your having regrets and guilt for life.

- **Looting and foraging:** During periods of civil unrest, looters are simply opportunistic criminals using excuses to justify theft and destruction, but in some cases such illegal and immoral behavior may be fully justified. Should cold and homeless refugees from a bombed city pass by an intact home along the road? Should groceries be left on the shelves of an abandoned store while children are hungry? One example of laws vs ethics is a case where elderly were being evacuated from a flood. The local fire department was prohibited from "opening" the convenience store across the street to access supplies for the patients even though the flood waters would soon destroy the supplies. If it makes you feel better, leave an IOU.

- **Taking sides:** During World War II it was simple, as it was the allies versus the Nazis and Japan. Your side was determined by your location. In today's fractured, globalized, and multiethnic society, factions, regionalism, and media generated divisions can cause hostile and potentially violent conflict between friends, neighbors and even family members. At one time Jews and Arabs lived peacefully in Palestine. South Koreans have family in North Korea. Russia and the Ukraine have much in common. Once violence has been initiated by one side and responded to by the other, they become implacable enemies. This is a horrible situation. If you don't pick a side everyone will regard you as an enemy and your situation will be untenable. Of course, acts of hate, brutality, violence, and oppression by one side may help make your choices.

- **To help or not to help**: Should you share your food, water, and medical supplies with friends, neighbors, or strangers who have not prepared themselves? Should you render aid to the injured if it puts you or your family at risk? These are two classic survival ethics questions. There is no absolute right or wrong answer, but the "do what you can, if you can, when you can" ethical principle applies. Note that that police are trained to bypass injured civilians and move on to neutralize the threat. You cannot be your brother's keeper unless you are able to be your own keeper.

ESTABLISHING YOUR CODE OF ETHICS

Survival ethics come down to life and death. Your life and death and that of others you encounter. Do you save life, risk life, or take life? A primary question that everyone must answer is how do you define your life? Are you *what* you are physically or *who* you are morally and spiritually? Are you about how you look and what you have or are you about what you believe in and stand for? While your body is mortal, your values and ideas are immortal. So, does your survival action justify your continued physical survival or does your survival alone justify your action? Is what's best and safest for you also best and safest for what you stand for?

In survival, laws are not an issue. You are left with your own moral code and ethical concepts to make life and death decisions. You must ask yourself:

- What is the right thing to do based on my values?
- What is the best thing to do for me?
- What is the best thing to do for others?
- What represents my values and ideas?
- What is my duty?
- Would I want others to do this to me or *for* me?
- How will others that I care about judge my actions?

Yes, the answers to each question may be conflicting. What *can* you do? What *should* you do? What do you *want* to do? In the heat of a survival situation, there will be no time to engage in a philosophical discussion. Most true survival situations are about risking your life or risking or taking the life of others. You must have an idea of where you draw the lines. In a situation where you may need to choose to risk or even sacrifice your own life, when would you do it?

- Never. Even if it would protect those I care for or values I stand for.
- Only if absolutely necessary to protect the lives of others that I care about.
- To defend the life of others being attacked or abused.
- Only if necessary to defend my values and ideas.
- Only if necessary to remain free.
- To defend my property.
- To maintain my pride and honor.
- Rather than live an unpleasant life.

If you know when you would be willing to put your own life on the line, have you established when you would take a life or put the life of others at risk?

- Never. Not even to defend my life and that of those I care for.
- Only in the immediate defense of my life and those I care for.
- To defend the life of others being attacked or abused.
- To defend my personal freedoms and rights.
- To defend my values and ideas.
- In order to remove potential threats to my life and freedom.
- To defend my property and lifestyle.

For the purposes of the above questions and answers, taking or risking life is not just about shooting or being shot at. Risking your life could be the act of sharing your food, entering a danger zone to rescue someone, or stopping to help instead of keeping moving. Taking life could be just failing to aid others who are in need of food or water they need to survive.

We may look at our moral code as a compass that directs us towards the right action, but ethics is the map that guides our route. Ethical choices must be free of fear, anger, hate, pride, and other negative emotions. Flexibility and adaptability are key concepts in survival psychology. Rigid moral codes that are valuable assets during "normal" times may conflict with survival imperatives under emergency conditions. The lines between right and wrong can become blurry in the heat of survival and conflict. What can you live with and what would you die for? The true survivor must know themselves and have a firm ethical foundation upon which to base life and death decisions. How and why, we survive is as important as *that* we survive. These kinds of situations have only lose-lose solutions, but they are easier for those who have considered them in advance and balanced the risks and values. Many such decisions will be difficult to live with regardless of the outcomes.

CHAPTER 24

RESISTANCE IN AN OCCUPIED AMERICA

The flies have captured the flypaper.
—A term used in John Steinbeck's book *The Moon is Down* about
the Nazi occupation of a Norwegian town during World II and the
resistance movement it engendered.

The first sentence of the 1965 book *Total Resistance* by Swiss Army Major H. von Dach Bern reads, "The author is fully aware of the fact that he has touched upon a difficult and unpleasant subject." While his book was intended for citizens resisting a Soviet occupation, the subject of resistance is always fraught with controversy and misinterpretation. While most of the chapters in this book include detailed instruction on how to perform various survival techniques, I will not risk enabling potential terrorists or extremists with information about how to improvise explosives, derail trains, or disable the power grid. There is plenty of information available on the internet and easily available military manuals, and I have no interest in contributing to indiscriminate violence and destruction in our communities. Resistance is justified and motivated when a population is oppressed and abused by an occupying force. American citizens can anticipate three forms of hostile occupation:

- **Military occupation** has been the consequence of lost wars for centuries. A foreign army will physically place troops in the cities and towns of the defeated nation and take control of all government and private institutions. All travel, communications, and commerce would be strictly managed. This form of occupation is expensive for the occupier, and usually is accompanied by using collaborators and surrogate forces to maintain control. The Soviet Union occupied East Germany, Czechoslovakia, Hungary, Poland, and other countries for decades, but was eventually defeated by constant resistance the cost of maintaining control.

- **Domestic occupation** is accomplished when a foreign power manages to impose its authority and ideology onto the population of a previously free and democratic state. Basic Communist strategy favors this kind of occupation. The preconditions for such occupation include the creation of internal division and chaos within the potential victim state. As Abraham Lincoln famously stated, "A house divided cannot stand." Lincoln also said that if America were to fall, it would be from within. Such an occupation might occur surreptitiously or through a revolutionary act. Even a revolution "for freedom" might well have the opposite effect. Historically, domestic occupations are more oppressive and violent than those imposed by victorious foreign armies.
- **Technological occupation** is a new and more insidious possibility. The terms of a surrender might include access to all internet systems, surveillance systems, and economic records. Everything a citizen does, everywhere a citizen goes, and everything a citizen buys could be controlled remotely. Acts of noncompliance might result in loss of employment, loss of housing, and loss of the ability to purchase goods just by the action of a foreign power's AI system. Technological occupation would certainly be an integral part of military occupation or a domestic occupation.

There are two levels of resistance that need to be considered. Passive resistance is noncooperation, noncompliance, avoidance, strikes, slowdowns, and other methods of resistance that do not involve any level of damage or violence. Active resistance includes underground publication, poster, slogan painting, and some levels of sabotage, intimidation, and armed resistance to oppression.

Passive resistance would be justified by:

- Forced gun registration.
- Restriction of the types of guns, ammunition, and magazine capacities.
- Special taxation of guns, publications, organizations.
- Confiscatory taxation.
- Regulation of the press, radio, TV, or internet content.
- Restriction or harassment of non-government organizations.
- Prohibition of self-reliance and preparedness supplies and training.
- Invasion of privacy through facial recognition, tracking, artificial intelligence, and other methods.
- Repressive medical system control and manipulation.
- Rigged or manipulated election processes.

Justifiable methods of passive resistance would include.

- Strikes, work stoppages, and slowdowns.
- Boycotts.
- Demonstrations and marches.
- Noncooperation and noncompliance with regulations.
- Black-market and underground sales of survival items.
- Underground press, radio, and internet programs.
- Placement of resistance posters and flyers.
- Support for those persecuted or prosecuted and their families.
- Funding of resistance candidates.
- Building up for potential active resistance as a deterrent to further oppression.
- Active support for town, county, and state governments that resist and refuse to implement unconstitutional laws and regulations.
- Labeling those who actively support oppression as "collaborators" as was done in occupied countries in the past. Collaborators can be identified by listing in underground publications and by various means of marking.

Active resistance would be justified if these levels of oppression are initiated:

- Occupation by foreign military forces.
- Foreign control of American economic and surveillance systems.
- Mass arrests and relocation of political dissenters.
- Disbandment of nongovernment organization.
- Suspension of the constitution.
- Gun confiscation of any kind.
- Subjugation of the state and county governments in order to implement unconstitutional laws. This would include armed occupation of states, counties, or towns in order to force compliance with regulations that those entities refuse to implement. Any action to replace the Electoral College that would effectively render the states subunits of the federal government and major population centers.
- Mandated carrying of government-monitored cell phones as in China.
- Foreign intervention in any aspect of American political or economic procedure with or without the consent of the American people.
- Active suppression of publications, broadcasts, or internet communications by resistance-oriented groups.
- Alteration of the election process or the Electoral College system.
- Confiscation of books and publications that pose a danger to the control of the population.

- Confiscation of survival and emergency preparedness supplies.
- Imposition of martial law.
- Open borders that effectively negate the rights, safety, and privileges of American citizenship.
- Uncontrolled lawlessness, crime, and destruction of private property when the state and federal government cannot or will not restore safety and order. Defunding the police and failure to protect the lives and property of law-abiding citizens negates the legality of the government.

Methods of active resistance include:

- Sabotage of government and private vehicles and equipment.
- Blockading access to government facilities and opposition events.
- Support for state and multi-state secession movements.
- Confrontation with those attempting to implement oppressive programs arrest resistance personnel or confiscate personal property.
- Active intimidation of "collaborators" and cooperating officials.
- Actively aiding people and families that are victims of unjustified prosecution or hardship caused by noncooperation.
- Tagging (painting) with slogans and resistance symbols in public areas to demoralize collaborators and encourage other would-be resistors. Such tags tell others that they are not alone, and this is not over. Seeing tags and posters can encourage more resistance and demoralize collaborators.
- Armed preparedness and resistance may be necessary.

It is important that any resistance movement avoid actions that will harm the public or endanger good citizens. Collateral damage should be avoided at all costs. Be the solution, not the problem. Certainly, there will be efforts to discredit any resistance movement as criminals and rabble. An oppressive state will initiate reprisals against entire groups or geographic regions. Reprisals may include denial of medical care, confiscation of property, or even interruption of power, water, or food supplies to noncompliant regions. Such actions will only serve to justify and increase resistance. Passive and active resistance should always be justified and in balanced response to oppressive and violent actions taken by an occupation agency. Any programs that can be initiated to provide food, medical help, or other forms of aid to the public will be more effective than paramilitary actions.

Past resistance movements involved structured organizations and chains of command. The introduction of drones, tracking devices, cameras, and other technology make many of these tactics obsolete. Less centralized and nonhierarchical organization (or non-organization) practicing multiple and independent actions by individuals and small groups has proven to be the most effective method for modern resistance operations. One idea, one goal, many methods, many agents.

Let me be clear: I am not advocating any form of violent or illegal resistance activities at this time, but the potential for events that might justify such actions in the future can no longer be discounted. Life and liberty are in more danger now than they were in the late Cold War era and almost any scenario for social and political disaster must be considered as a possibility. It can be hoped that the *potential* for resistance will be a deterrent to oppressors foreign and domestic.

CHAPTER 25

WARTIME UNARMED COMBAT

The average citizen is not a trained combatant. Even those who may have had limited unarmed combat training while serving in the military may no longer have those skills. Hand-to-hand combat skills require regular training. Most citizens are not trained in military combat and will simply flail and fail under combat assault situations. Even if hostile military forces are not on American soil, surrogate paramilitary groups, criminal gangs, and even desperate citizens may create hazards to innocent citizens. War at home or abroad may dramatically increase the chances of being assaulted by individuals and groups. Obviously, being armed at all times can greatly reduce the need for hand-to-hand combat, but unarmed combat may be unavoidable in some situations. Physical combat skills cannot be learned from a book, but this chapter will attempt to provide some basic tactics, principles, and techniques that can aid the citizen in surviving, escaping, or minimizing injury. It is highly recommended that citizens acquire basic self-defense training wherever available. It may also be important to keep in mind that wartime self-defense combat is usually "mortal" combat where the assailants intends to kill you if you fail to kill or disable them. There are no rules, and no place for subtility. Certainly, such desperate situations are best avoided, but once initiated you must have the will to endure injury, inflict trauma and survive. Military hand-to-hand combat training involves complex movements, grapples, and throws that require physical conditioning and repetition. The civilian combatant should focus on mastering the delivery of disabling blows against vulnerable targets using all parts of the body.

IMPROVISED WEAPONS

While one must be prepared for "unarmed" combat, any kind of weapon is preferable to using parts of your body to strike parts of your opponent's body. Obviously, a knife or a gun trumps a fist or a foot in most combat situations. If you are not armed, it does not mean you do not have access to weapons. Anything hard or sharp can be used to improve your chances of survival. Your keys, a tightly rolled magazine, or a pen can be used to jab at the eyes. A coat can be used to blind or distract. Soil or liquids can be thrown into the assailant's eyes. Pipes, boards, or other items can be used to jab or strike. Sharp metal or glass can be employed as cutting weapons. Bricks or rocks can be used as striking objects or thrown. If you are caught in a high-risk situation without access to a formal weapon, improvisation could be your only advantage.

YOUR BODY AS A WEAPON

The average citizen tends to think of the fist or the hand as the primary striking weapon in a fight. While the fist may be effective in some situations it is limited in range and effectiveness in many combat applications. In reality, there are many parts of the body that can be used as effective weapons. In a real fight, being able to strike at multiple targets with multiple weapons is the key to survival.

- **Fist:** It is important to make a proper fist. Do not curl the finger over the thumb or let a finger protrude. An improper fist will result in injury to your hand and fingers. Lock your wrist straight with the forearm and top knuckles in line. Punch with your whole body. The power should come from your legs, then through your hips, and finally from your shoulder, all going straight into your fist. In some cases, the fist can be used as a hammer striking downward with the outer edge of the fist.
- **Palm:** By curling the fingers tightly back and up, and the thumb to the side you can use the palm wrist as an effective striking instrument. This weapon can be used to strike upward at the chin or other vulnerable targets.
- **Palm edge:** The edge of the hand can be used against the throat or back of the neck but is not as effective as seen in karate films. The so-called spear hand with fingers locked together and the thumb tucked under the palm can be used against the throat, below the nose, and at the eyes.
- **Fingers:** Fingers can be used to claw at eyes, pull clothing, or grasp the groin. Fingers are delicate and should not be exposed to force. Fingers moving towards the eyes will cause the opponent to instinctively bend backwards, exposing the groin to a knee kick. Getting hold of the opponents' fingers and bending them backward can give you control of the fight.
- **Forearm:** One of the most overlooked body weapons is the forearm. It can be used against threats from the front and rear. You can use your

arm as you turn your body to get a backswing towards the opponent's face and neck. The forearm can be used as an effective block to be followed with an elbow or hand strike to the face.

- **Elbow:** In close quarters the elbow can be used against the assailant's abdomen, groin, and face. You can lock your hands together to use both arms to add force to an elbow strike.
- **Knee:** A knee to the groin can be very effective. If the opponent instinctively bends forward to avoid the knee, they will present the face, head, and neck for various hand strikes. If you can force the opponent's head downward, then an upward knee to the face can be very effective.
- **Foot:** Kicking by an untrained person can be awkward and leave you off balance. A slow, poorly delivered kick can wind up with your assailant holding your foot. Strong back kicks to the rear can be effective against a rear holding attack. A forceful sideways thrust kick to the front of the kneecap can disable a threat. Kicking the back of the knee can take an opponent down but must be followed by stomps to the abdomen or throat.
- **Head**: In close quarters, a strong headbutt to the face, particularly the nose or jaw, will force the opponent to disengage. A backward headbutt will have the same effect.
- **Teeth:** Survival is the only rule. Biting a nose, ear, finger, or arm will usually at least get the opponent to disengage long enough to give you another chance to win. Don't bite to hurt, bite to bite it off.

Impact Weapons of the Body

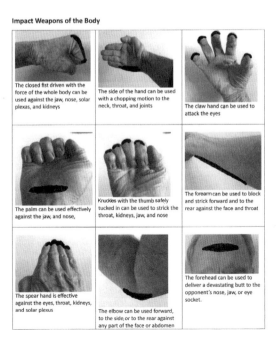

The closed fist driven with the force of the whole body can be used against the jaw, nose, solar plexas, and kidneys

The side of the hand can be used with a chopping motion to the neck, throat, and joints

The claw hand can be used to attack the eyes

The palm can be used effectively against the jaw, and nose,

Knuckles with the thumb safely tucked in can be used to strick the throat, kidneys, jaw, and nose

The forearm can be used to block and strick forward and to the rear against the face and throat

The spear hand is effective against the eyes, throat, kidneys, and solar plexus

The elbow can be used forward, to the side, or to the rear against any part of the face or abdomen

The forehead can be used to deliver a devastating butt to the opponent's nose, jaw, or eye socket.

TARGET FOR ATTACK

There are many parts of the body that can be struck with little immediate effect. It is important to use your available weapons against the most vulnerable parts of your opponent's body with the most force possible. Regardless of what you hit with, you must aim to go through the target and finish the fight as soon as possible. The longer the fight goes on, the more likely you will be disabled or exhausted. Time is not on your side in any fight. Immediate unlimited application of violent force is the only viable response to a deadly and imminent threat. The most well-defined targets for any kind of punch, strike, or kick are described below.

- **Eyes:** Any scratch or poke to the eyes will at least temporarily blind the opponent. This potential for blindness initiates an instinctive defensive reaction that leaves other targets vulnerable.
- **Nose:** A hard strike to the nose is very painful and can temporarily blind and disorient. A powerful upward strike can disable or kill.
- **Jaw:** Any powerful strike to the jaw line can break the jaw, dislodge teeth, or render the opponent unconscious.
- **Throat:** A spear hand thrust, side hand chop, forearm, or elbow to the throat can crush the windpipe and disable or kill the opponent.
- **Neck:** In addition to the trachea (windpipe), the major blood supply arteries and veins pass through the neck. A stranglehold of the neck will render the opponent unconscious in about thirty seconds.
- **Solar Plexus:** This area lies just below the ribcage and contains the floating rib and the xyphoid that are easily broken.
- **Elbow, knee and finger joints**: Grasping arms and forcing the elbow backward can dislocate the joint. Strong sideway kicks to the front of the knee can dislocate that joint. Bending a twisting finger and thumb joints can force the opponent to release you and disable the hand.
- **Abdomen:** Elbow strikes, kicks, and punches to the abdomen can inflict pain, but are generally not disabling.
- **Kidneys:** Hard multiple hook punches or kicks to the kidneys will produce chronic and disabling pain.
- **Groin:** Any kind of force applied to the testicles will result in distracting or disabling injury. Kicks delivered upwards are more effective than from the front.
- **Shins:** A hard kick or stomp and drag down the shins can be extremely painful. This is particularly effective if in close quarters or being grabbed from the rear.

- **Feet:** Stomping on the foot and toes can temporally cripple the opponent but must be followed with more disabling kicks and sticks.

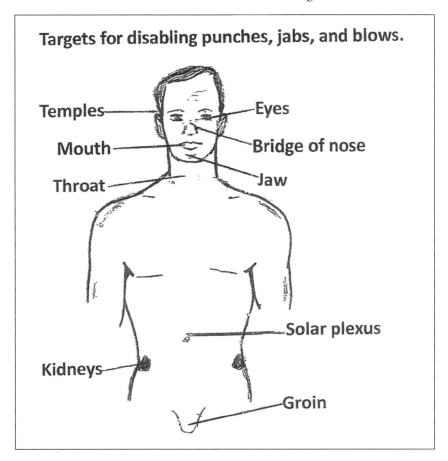

Targets for disabling punches, jabs, and blows.

Temples

Mouth

Throat

Eyes

Bridge of nose

Jaw

Solar plexus

Kidneys

Groin

HAND-TO-HAND COMBAT TACTICS

Unlike street crime and civilian assault situations, where breaking away or temporarily disabling an assailant is the goal, wartime combat must assume that every assailant has lethal intentions and that there are no moral or legal restraints related to use of force or methods of combat. When the streets become combat zones, the citizen must think and act like a combatant. Awareness and good tactics can nullify some of your opponent's physical advantages. Hesitancy and civility have no place in life-or-death combat.

- Be hyperaware of sounds, shadows, silhouettes, and anything out of place that may indicate lurking assailants. Think "what if?"

- Do not get ambushed or caught by surprise. Anticipate where, when, and how you are most likely to be attacked. Have a plan and be ready to use any weapons you have, along with movement to respond and overcome.
- Be aware of the actual or potential direction of an assault and the terrain, buildings, trees, and other obstacles to avoid being cornered and maintain escape routes.
- Don't get caught in a defensive, reactive mode. When the first moves towards assault are detected, instantly respond with maximum force and violence. Take the initiative and take control of the fight. This is the only way to survive military-like combat.
- If justified, initiate a preemptive assault. While starting a fight or assaulting first is illegal under "normal" conditions, and initiating combat when it can be avoided is a bad tactic in most situations, war zone priorities may justify and even require initiating a surprise attack on an individual or individuals that clearly represent an unavoidable threat to you or your family. A surprise assault, ambush, or trap may be the only chance you have against a superior and malevolent threat.
- Never leave an armed or capable enemy behind you. Every opponent must be totally incapacitated, immobilized, and disarmed before you move on.
- Never get distracted or tunnel visioned by one threat or even one wounded friend. Be sure that all threats have been identified and dealt with before rendering aid. This is basic scene safety.
- Never leave a room, door, or window unsecure in your rear. Consider any unchecked room, door, or building as a possible source of danger. Cover your six.
- Whenever possible, avoid close contact and hand-to-hand combat. Regardless of your physical skills, hand-to-hand combat can always lead to serious injury or death.
- If the opponent has a pole or club or a longer reach than you do, get inside their swing radius and deliver blows to the face, throat, and kidneys.
- Avoid tripping or being knocked down. Keep your balance. This is why boxers focus on footwork. Stay on your feet, but if you go down, kick, roll, and get up fast.
- Avoid knife fighting. Even if you win you will almost certainly sustain one or more cuts. Don't fight a knife-wielding opponent fairly. Use a gun, club, spear, or anything else to get an advantage. Use a chair or other item as a shield. Do whatever it takes and do it fast.

- If you encounter more than one assailant, maneuver and keep moving so that they cannot close in or get behind you. Use available obstacles to your advantage. Keep them off balance. If possible, use doorways, stairways, and other chokepoints to force them to come to you one at a time and inhibit their movements.
- It is always preferable to be in a group and move in a formation that is mutually protective. There is no "fair play" in this kind of combat. If you have a numerical advantage over the enemy us, it. Fight as a team, all together, not one at a time.

MENTAL AND PHYSICAL CONDITIONING

Obviously, reading this chapter will not prepare you for serious unarmed combat, but rereading these recommendations frequently and thinking through how you would use them in various situations can provide mental conditioning for combat. Physically practicing these techniques can instill muscle memory that will initiate under combat scenarios.

Recommended reading: *U.S. Army Combatives Hand-to-Hand Manual FM 3–25 or 21–50*, and *U.S. Marine Close Combat Fighting Handbook*.

CHAPTER 26

ARMED COMBAT IN A WAR ZONE

Japanese Admiral Isoroku Yamamoto is alleged to have said, "Never invade America. There will be a rifle behind every blade of grass." Whether he said that or not, the fact is that America is the only nation where private ownership and control of firearms is legal. In most countries, the state has exclusive control of most or all firearms. Ukrainian citizens did not have access to firearms until they were issued by the state. It is doubtful whether Russia could have occupied the Crimea and eastern territories if the citizens had been armed at the beginning. Although Israeli citizens are all trained, members of the military reserves' private ownership of firearms is strictly regulated and getting a permit is very difficult. This is why Hamas was so successful at overrunning civilian settlements and taking hostages. Even a former Israeli general had only a handgun and a few rounds of ammunition to rescue his family. The flood of refugees from South America is driven by corrupt governments and allied gangs and cartels that have access to deadly weapons while the law-abiding civilian populations remain unarmed. America's founders were aware of the importance of an armed civilian population. The much misrepresented Second Amendment says nothing about the right to go hunting, or the right to self-defense. It specifically refers to "a well-regulated militia" so it is specifically intended to protect ownership of military type weapons. It is important to note that the term *regulated* as used in the eighteenth century meant trained or organized rather than controlled by laws. The generic term *arms* is used rather than more specific terms for muskets, or flintlocks, because it was assumed that weapons technology would evolve, so that what was then a musket in 1776 is now an AR-15. The civilian must have no doubts regarding his or her moral and legal right to possess these weapons.

Although Founding Father George Mason stated that "the militia is the whole of the people," that does not make every citizen a soldier, but any citizen may be thrust into a military combat situation and may need basic armed combat skills. Responsible and law-abiding citizens may be forced to confront organized criminal gangs, paramilitary extremists, or even foreign infiltrators or invaders. The rules and exigencies of war zone versus domestic self-defense combat are quite different. Under worst-case war combat situations, legality and safety must often be balanced against the sheer necessity of staying alive. The material presented in this chapter is limited to basic armed combat techniques and principles that will be helpful to the untrained citizen preparing to survive in a war zone.

PREPARING TO FIGHT AND SURVIVE

There are five essential steps to improving survivability in a potential combat zone. Even if you are already armed in some ways or have had some training with handguns or long guns, these steps can help reevaluate and upgrade your preparedness level.

1. Acquire the best weapons for your personal situation and potential combat scenarios.
Your survival weapons battery will depend on the kind of combat you anticipate, your physical capabilities, and your budget. Of course, any discussion of weapon types and calibers engenders controversy, and there are countless combinations, but the four alternatives below represent practical choice for the non-shooter citizen, preparing for an armed combat scenario.

Just One Gun
Because the citizen's combat applications will be primarily defensive and evasive, a large capacity handgun must be the first "go-to" weapon. Revolvers are reliable for self-defense, but their limited capacity makes them impractical for serious combat use. While .22 caliber rimfire weapons are useful for survival hunting, they lack the power to penetrate obstacles and disable adversaries quickly and effectively. If you are an experienced shooter, a .45 ACP or .40 Smith &Wesson may be good choices, but a 9mm Luger is recommended for

The two handguns pictured here are just examples of the many high-capacity handguns on the market. While well-aimed shots are preferable, being able to fire multiple rounds rapidly is often necessary under combat conditions. Sometime quantity has a quality all its own. Two or three shot "bursts" have a much higher probability of disabling an adversary than one shot.

its availability and reliability. Semi-automatic handguns should have a minimum ten-round magazine capacity and preferably up to sixteen rounds per magazine. Under potential combat scenarios, at least four magazines should be purchased and carried full in pockets or magazine pouches.

Shotgun and Handgun

In most civilian survival combat situations, the combination of a large-capacity handgun and shotgun will be most effective for urban and home defense situations. Shotguns have amazing versatility. You can perforate a vehicle with buckshot or stop it with a slug or armor-piercing round. You can use breaching rounds to open doors or use exploding or incendiary rounds to discourage attackers or clear your escape route. Compared to good handguns and combat rifles, shotguns are relatively cheap. You can get a good new combat-style pump shotgun for around $400 or $500. Shotguns are often less regulated than handguns and rifles and attract less attention. Accessories are available for most Mossberg, Winchester, and Remington shotguns at most sporting

Top: KEL-TEC KSG, 12-gauge tactical shotgun that has two six-round fixed magazines allowing the user to switch ammunition types without reloading is a good choice. Note the attached flashlight. Lower: Mossberg Camper 12-gauge with added folding stock and shell holder. Specialized rounds include law enforcement rounds (short), double-ought buckshot, slugs, armor -piercing, flamethrower, fireball, breaching, and non-lethal rubber rounds.

goods stores. More recently, specialized combat shotguns have begun to appear on the markets. Short pump shotguns such as the Mossberg 500 JIC Flex or the Kel-Tech KSG can be had for from $500 to $900. More exotic, magazine fed pump and semi-auto shotguns provide more rapid fire and the opportunity to switch ammunition in combat. Regardless of your budget or choice, a shotgun remains the most versatile, fearsome, and effective home defense weapon. A wide variety of ammunition is available for all occasions.

Sub rifles and Handguns

Sub rifles are short rifles that fire a handgun round such as 9mm or .40 S&W. The longer rifle barrel provides greater velocity and range from the small round, and greater accuracy. Having just one type of ammunition is less complicated, and some rifle/handgun combinations even have interchangeable magazines. Sub rifles are compact and some even break down or fold up.

The Kel-Tec SUB-2000 in 9mm folds down to just 16 × 7 inches and fits in a backpack. Note the variety of magazine sizes. It can be paired with any good 9mm large-capacity handgun to give the civilian combatant survival firepower.

Combat Rifle and Handgun

While military and paramilitary combatants may be focused on taking objectives and combating enemy forces, the civilian combatant will more often be caught in a war zone and need to counteract or defeat a threat to life and property generated by any combination of criminals, or rough military groups. In these worst-case combat situations only a true "battle rifle" combined with a reliable handgun and plenty of magazines and ammunition will suffice.

The AR-15 style rifle above is just one of dozens of variations of the design. Prices range from less than $1,000 to several thousand dollars. Plenty of parts are available but restrictions may be anticipated, and draconian war-justified restrictions can be anticipated.

2. Stock up on ammunition and parts for your weapons

Most self-defense scenarios involve the expenditure of less than fifty rounds, but in a war zone or extended period of combat it is easy to go through a thousand rounds or more. Civilians may face multiple armed assailants blasting away from multiple directions. Shots may come from windows, doorways, vehicles, or trees. Specific targets may be elusive but return fire may discourage the attackers or force them to take cover long enough for you to move or escape. My recommendations are a minimum of five thousand rounds for each handgun, ten thousand rounds for each rifle, and five hundred rounds of various types of shotgun ammunition. This primary stock should be high quality, name brand, high velocity ammunition. Off-brand and reloads can be used for backup stocks, trade and barter, and training. Be sure to have a cleaning kit, bore cleaning solution, and lubricant for each firearm. Follow the instructions for disassembly and cleaning that come with a new weapon, buy a manual, or download one from the internet. Store weapons and ammunition in a dry, safe location. It may be advisable to store extra ammunition in separate locations or cached along potential escape routes. Unlike military personnel, you will not have trucks to bring your ammunition, food, and supplies if you are engaged or on the move. Ammunition is heavy and every pound takes away your food, shelter, water, and medical supplies. While ammunition stocks at home can be almost unlimited, evacuation under fire can severely limit how long you can sustain combat before you run out of ammunition. Consider this reality in your planning. Always store ammunition in watertight military surplus or commercially made ammunition cans.

3. Practice safety and security procedures for firearms of all kinds

Possession of a deadly weapon is a human right, and necessity for the protection of life and freedom, but it is also a major responsibility that should not be taken lightly. Every gun owner should take basic firearms safety training. Weapons should be secured and locked when not in use. Every precaution must be taken to assure that a firearm does not fall into the hands of untrained persons, children, or criminals. What a misplaced, or stolen firearm does is still your responsibility. Here are a few basic firearms safety rules;

- Always treat every firearm if it is loaded regardless of how sure you are that it isn't.
- Never point a firearm at anyone unless you intend to shoot.
- Always know who or what your target is before you shoot.
- Be aware of your backstop. Before you shoot, know who or what lies behind that may be struck by bullets you fire. Will your bullets be stopped or go through the wall to strike others?
- Store weapons and ammunition separately when not needed.
- Use extra care for safety and where the firearm is pointed when climbing or negotiating obstacles.
- Be sure you are using the proper ammunition for the weapon you have.
- Keep the muzzle free of dirt and obstructions.

4. Get training and practice marksmanship however and whenever possible. Spending a week at one of the many combat weapons schools is certainly the best way to prepare for war zone combat, but this may be beyond the budget and time limits of most civilians. The next best option is to join a local gun club or spend time at a local firing range with a qualified instructor. Some gun clubs and gun stores may have available combat simulators. These devices place the student in a space with multiple onscreen simulated combat "shoot or don't shoot" scenarios. The student then can engage the targets with a variety of simulated laser weapons. If that is not practical, Airsoft guns can provide a training aid that can be used in a basement or outdoor

range. High quality Airsoft guns firing 6mm plastic pellets come in scores of realistic simulations that mimic the size, weight, and feel of almost every popular handgun, rifle, and shotgun. Prices range from less than fifty dollars for spring operated guns to a few hundred dollars for electric, full auto, or up to $700 for Co2 guns with high velocity and simulated blowback operation. The major advantage is that you can train at home or outdoors without the noise or danger. You can even set up combat courses. The major drawback is that the lack of noise and the recoil is not realistic, and the fact that they are relatively safe can instill bad safety habits. The last resort is to practice dryfiring your actual weapon at home targets or in simulated combat scenarios, being very certain it is unloaded. Below are a few basic concepts that apply to accurate shooting.

BRASS stands for Breath, Relax, Aim, Slack, Squeeze and is the mantra of target shooting. If you practice a lot, it will be a natural part of your combat shooting habits, but you will not have time to remember it or go through it when someone is shooting back. Practice bringing your weapon (handgun or long gun) to position, and smoothly aiming and firing.

1. **Breathe:** Take in a normal breath and let it out normally. Then stop breathing while you take all of the next steps.
2. **Relax:** Let your body muscles relax, avoid tensing up.
3. **Aim:** Line up your sight, focusing on the top of the front sight as below.

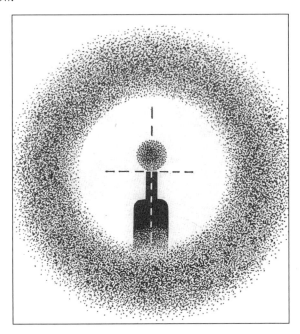

4. **Slack:** Take up the slack on the trigger until you feel a bit of resistance.
5. **Squeeze:** Add steady pressure to the trigger (don't pull or jerk) until the weapon fires.
6. Exhale and follow through by holding the weapon on target for the next shot as needed. Relaxing too soon after a shot can result in dropping the shot.

These are target shooting techniques that may not apply under combat conditions, but will build good habits, confidence, and muscle memory that will aid in effective shooting under any conditions.

Stance and Grip

There are several popular stances for combat shooting. The most popular is the Weaver stance developed by Los Angeles County Deputy Sheriff Jack Weaver. This is an aggressive forward-facing stance with the non-shooting foot about ten inches forward of the foot on the shooting side. Both feet are facing at about a 45-degree angle, the elbows are bent and slightly outward. The supporting hand is bent downward at the elbow at a 45-degree angle and pulls in towards the shooter while the shooting (trigger) hand pushes outward from the shoulder, creating a solid stable grip. The weapon is raised, and the sight picture is acquired just before firing.

Weaver stance grip with left hand supporting and pulling against the right hand and the right hand pushing outward from the shoulder.

Regular practice will improve your speed and accuracy. Your targets can tell you a lot about how to adjust your sight picture, grip, and stance.

Read Your Target

When shooting handgun or long gun your shot pattern and groups can tell you a lot about what you are doing wrong and how to improve your accuracy. You may think you are doing everything right, but unless you consistently get tight groups on the rang you will be shooting wild under combat pressures and when someone is shooting at you.

A split group like this indicates that you may have changed your stance or position a bit. Be sure to hold your hand, arm, elbow, and body steady through multiple shots.

A verticle group may indicate an inconsistancy in your eye placment. Keep your head still and your sight picture correct

Any kind of diagonal grouping usually means that your trigger hand is not tight on the weapon and/or the butt of the rifle is not firm against your shoulder

One shot out of the group can indicate can be caused by your sight picture or body position shifting. Failure to follow through and hold through past the last shot can cause this issue.

A scattered group like this one is caused by not following the same procedure for each shot. Focus on each step each time. Practice and consistancy will get you there.

A tight group like this one is what you are aiming for. If you shoot like this on the range, you will shoot well under combat conditions.

5. **Plan and practice for combat scenarios:**
   - Anticipate various combat scenarios in your home, and community. Consider how you would move, take cover, and if necessary, fight in these places.
   - Learn some basic formations, ambush reaction tactics, and fire and movement techniques in case you are caught in a war zone–like situation.

- Get in the habit of holding on target after shooting to be sure it is neutralized.
- Avoid tunnel vision under combat stress. There may be multiple threats and hazards. Sweep the area and stay alert and in cover if possible.
- While single shots are good for target practice, the so-called double tap to the center mass of the opponent's body is far more likely to hit and disable effectively. Practice two-shot groups and multiple two-shot groups.
- Check and clear each room and space before moving past it.
- Under war zone rules, assume everyone is hostile until proven otherwise and disarmed.
- Never leave an unsecured, wounded hostile behind you. Be sure they are bound or disabled.
- If possible, avoid running a magazine dry or having a partially loaded magazine in the weapon when further combat is likely. If there is a break in combat, exchange the partially used magazine for a full one so you don't go empty in the middle of combat. Keep the partially filled magazines handy if you need them and refill them as soon as conditions permit. Practice combat reload techniques for handguns and long-guns.

Tactical Reloading

While normal self-defense combat usually involves a limited number of shots fired, combat zone situations usually involve the expenditure of dozens or even hundreds of rounds. The necessity of matching the opponent's volume of fire to discourage assault or facilitate movement to cover will often require changing empty or partially empty magazines with full ones while under fire. The two most common methods of doing this are the tactical reload (TAC) and the reload with retention (RWR). TAC takes a bit more practice and involves holding the full magazine in the hand while dropping the empty or partially empty magazine to the same hand as you insert the full one. This can be a tricky maneuver with shaking, sweaty hands and can result in dropping both magazines. RWR is simpler and easier to master. In RWR the shooter removes the used magazine, stows it in the available pocket or pouch, and grabs a full magazine and inserts it.

CHAPTER 27

MILITARY SKILLS FOR CIVILIANS

T hroughout this book I have included various military skills as they apply to civilians coping with war zone survival scenarios. At the beginning of World War II, Great Britain was faced with the possibility of an invasion and responded with the creation of the Home Guard and the publication of *Home Guard Fieldcraft Manual* by Capt. John Langdon-Davis. Directly after the Pearl Harbor attack, American citizens formed informal military organizations to oppose anticipated Japanese raids and invasions along the West Coast. Magazines of the time even featured some military tactics and techniques. In past decades, populations faced with the potential of combat on their home soil have had an existing reserve of combat trained former soldiers from previous wars. After many decades of limited military recruitment and reliance on small units and technology to fight remote wars, very few civilians have any level of combat skill or experience. George Mason, author of the document that inspired the Bill of Rights, defined the militia as consisting of "the whole of the people except for a few public officers." While the term *militia* has been much misapplied and maligned, Mason's definition and principle still apply. The whole of the people have the right and the duty to defend their homes and homeland in time of war. Having covered home defense, weapons, camouflage, and armed and unarmed combat in other chapters, we will focus on safe movement, ambush reaction, and basic combat tactics that can be used for advancing or retreating under fire.

MOVEMENT IN A COMBAT ZONE

Movement under combat conditions is always risky. The advantage always lies with the potential ambusher or sniper. If possible, avoid moving through any potentially hostile area. Stay put or take a longer and safer route if possible. If you must move about do so in a combat-ready condition. Whether you are moving in daylight or at night, strict noise discipline is essential. Talking in normal tones is prohibited and whispering is only used for essential communications. Everyone's gear must be secured so it does not squeak, rattle, or clang. Have everyone jump up and down before starting out to detect and secure any noise sources. Any shiny or glowing objects should also be covered. If extreme stealth is needed, rags or old heavy socks can be placed over shoes. Of course, only muted or camouflage colors should be worn. This includes shoes and socks. White flashlights are never to be used at night. Red-lensed flashlights, preferably covered under ponchos or coats, can be used to consult maps if necessary. Cell phones are strictly prohibited. Bunching

up or lack of attention is an invitation to assault. Even if there are just two or three people in the group, they must maintain a distance from each other and a staggered formation so that they cannot be taken or shot all together. The distance depends on the terrain and the visibility. Each member should maintain a distance of at least four to six feet from others in all directions. This distance can be a bit further in open terrain but may need to be closer on dark nights. Members should always be in a position to support and protect each other in a

Mixed family group lines up in double column preparatory to moving down a road. Such formations support alertness and facilitate response to emergencies.

staged formation that permits firing in multiple directions without endangering fellow members.

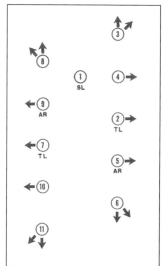

Basic double column formation with leader in the center. Arrows denote the direction of responsibility.

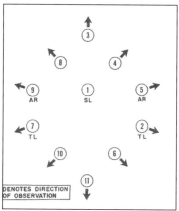

Basic diamond formation provides for 360-degree defense and can change direction of movement without changing formation.

A skirmish line prepares to enter wooded area. Each
person needs to maintain contact with those on each side.
This is also good formation for search and rescue.

One person on the move must stop, squat, and slowly turn around and
listen every few minutes. A group must have clearly assigned directions of
responsibility such as front and right flank, left flank and rear, etc., to ensure
360-degree coverage. Larger groups will send out a point man and have a
designated rear guard. A flank security person or team may be needed in some
kinds of terrain. The point man's task is extremely fatiguing, as it requires
constant vigilance in all directions and even for trip wires. This task should be
rotated frequently. Normally the point man should be just in view of the lead
person in the group. The rearguard usually is closer to the group but must
stop periodically and turn around to watch for adversaries. The people at the
rear of the group should always be checking to be sure that those behind are
still there and safe. In a single file column, every other person keeps guard on
the opposite side with the front person watching ahead and the rear person
regularly checking behind. In a double column the right row covers the right,
and the left row covers the left side. Frequent rest stops are necessary but are
not a time for conversation or bunching up. Select a well-concealed spot off
the roads and paths. Put out 360-degree security. If a small group stops, they
should all face outward not inward while resting.

CROSSING LANES

Crossing roads, railroad tracks, and other open lanes is particularly hazardous under hostile conditions. Anyone looking down that lane has a clear field of vision and fire. Cross at a narrow point or a sharp bend where your action is least visible. There are two schools of thought about crossing. You can send one scout across to secure the opposite side and see if they are shot at. This may only alert the enemy that more are coming. The other tactic is to all rush across at once before an enemy can react. Both methods have advantages and risks. You do not want to wander across or loiter. If you know the crossing will be opposed and cannot find another route, you can fire your weapons and maneuver by having half the group fire to pin down the enemy while the other crosses and then fires to cover the second group's crossing; this is something a survival group should practice. If you have smoke bombs, these can be of great help in such crossings.

DIVERSION AND MISDIRECTION

Diversion and misdirection are key military skills. Smoke or fireworks can be used to draw attention away from you while you escape or maneuver. A false campsite can attract looters and raiders while your real site remains hidden. Dummy defenses and bunkers can draw fire away from your true location. False trails can be laid away from your true route.

POINT PERSON AND SCOUTS

If a group is moving down a road or trail it is important to have someone move in advance of the group to spot potentially hostile people, or hazardous conditions. This point person will usually be far enough ahead of the group to spot danger before the whole group walks into an ambush. Usually, the point person stays visible to the leader of the group and can stop and signal or move back to warn the group. If the point person is out of visual contact with the group, radio communications should be established. The point person is always at high risk needing to look in all directions for dangers, maybe even needing to look up for snipers and down for tripwires. This can be exhausting work. The task of point person should be rotated frequently. A scout or scouting group can be used to reconnoiter a route or location in advance of the group. Scouts may be sent out just ahead of the group or well in advance of the group's movement. Scouts or scouting parties should have good maps and good optics to facilitate detection and location of threats, obstacles, and routes as well as sources of water, food, and shelter. Scouting reports should be specific and detailed. A report of "some guys down by the bridge" is unacceptable. The report should be more like "there are three men on the south end of the bridge with a truck, and they all have long guns." In this case the scouts should also be able to offer suggestions on how to approach the bridge or get past the hazard without being engaged.

COUNTER AMBUSH TECHNIQUES

The ambush is the deadliest situation a group can find itself in. The best way to avoid being a victim is to avoid movement, especially at night. The advantage always lies with the ambusher who chooses the place and time and remains hidden.

Since it is most likely that the citizen will not be encountering well-trained and heavily equipped ambushers that would be using automatic weapons and mines, basic ambush avoidance and counter ambush methods should be effective.

An ambush may simply be a group of shooters hiding along the side of the road or in buildings where they have good concealment. A more sophisticated ambush would involve a roadblock or debris to stop the group in the kill zone. Sharp turns in a road or path can permit ambushers to fire down the length of the road or trail as well as from a flank. These are the locations that a group on the move must be especially aware of. The point man should be constantly alert for signs of activity, noises, shadows, etc. and signal the group to halt if anything looks or feels suspicious. Since the group may already be in or near a kill zone it may need to back out and consider ways to avoid or eliminate the threat. There are several counter-ambush tactics that are effective depending on the situation. The survival group should be well trained in each counter ambush drill. Basic counter-ambush techniques include the following:

- If the group has not entered the kill zone, the best action is to back out while maintaining good order and fire if necessary. You can then opt to go around the ambush or flank them and flush them out of the position.
- If the group is well into a kill zone and under fire, you may be able to fire on the ambushing location while quickly running out of the danger zone or crawling to safety. The use of smoke bombs may be very helpful.
- If quick escape is not an option, then your only other choice is to charge the ambush site with all the firepower you can bring to bear in hope of overrunning or dispersing the ambushers.

- The one thing you do not want to do is remain in the kill zone and engage in a fire fight. The leader must call the counter ambush and the team must execute it immediately. Regardless of training, being caught in an ambush almost always results in casualties. If the ambushers turn out to be well trained and/or numerically superior, you may expect very serious losses.

- When any kind of counter-ambush drill is executed, your group is going to get dispersed. This is particularly true in heavy forests and/or at night. Always establish a rally point and passwords while on the move. All participants must know where to regroup if lost or dispersed and have an established password and countersign to prevent accidents.

BASIC MILITARY MANEUVERS

Fire and maneuver is the most basic military drill and should be understood by any group that anticipates a combat situation. The British call this tactic "bounding over watch." Simply put, one person or team shoots at the enemy while the other moves to a better position. In an offensive situation, the fire team pins the enemy with fire while the maneuver team moves closer. Then, they change tasks so that the maneuver team becomes the fire team while the fires team maneuvers even closer until the objective is taken or flanked. In withdrawal, the same alternating persons or teams execute the maneuver until they are out of range or into a safe position. While fire and maneuver can be used to facilitate a straight-in assault or straight-out withdrawal, flanking to the right or left should always be preferred if possible. Frontal assault or a running retreat is generally costly and often disastrous. Civilians that truly anticipate combat situations should be trained in execution of fire and maneuver.

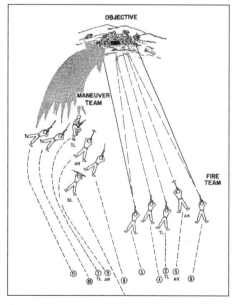

Once a group (even just two people) comes under fire, they must be ready to implement a fire and maneuver engagement either moving forward or to extricate themselves.

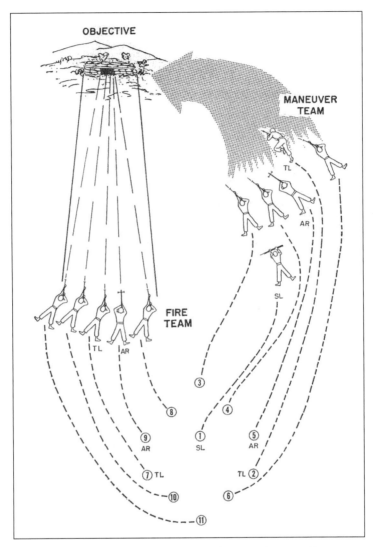

The original maneuver team (or person) has now become the fire team as the other team closes in on the objective here. If the objective is not critical or the defending force is strong, the fire and maneuver should be rearward.

FIELD FORTIFICATIONS

Field fortifications are a necessary skill for survival. Failure to dig in has doomed many complacent military units in the past. Trenches, foxholes, and improvised bunkers provide the defender with a great advantage against even a superior force. When time is short or the ground is hard (rocky or frozen), scraping even a shallow, low spot with some dirt, rocks, and debris in front is far better than lying in the open. A pile of dirt in front of a trench or foxhole may give away your location, so try to camouflage them with leaves and debris. In general, foxholes should hold no more than two people but be close enough to each other for mutual support. Trenches should zigzag or curve. While barbed wire may not be available, interlaced tree limbs and sharpened stakes can be used to slow down assaulters. Fortifications of any kind should be located so there is a clear field of view and fire in front of them. Rocks, low ground, or close trees and brush would permit an enemy to get close without risk. Clear tall grass shrubs and other obstruction out to at least fifty yards. Even plain wire can be strung at ankle height to trip and slow approach. Empty cans with stones inside can be attached to these obstacles to make noise at night. Below are a few simple types of field fortifications that could be used to protect a survival camp or other position. A day practicing digging and using these kinds of fortifications would be time well spent.

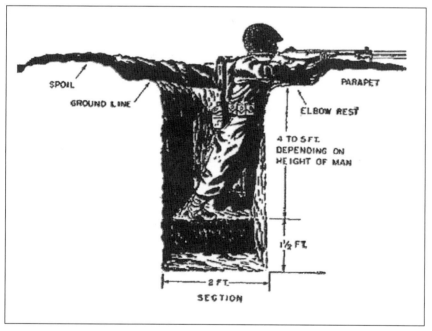

A simple foxhole. This can be enlarged to hold several defenders. Note that it is designed for 360 degrees, all-around defense.

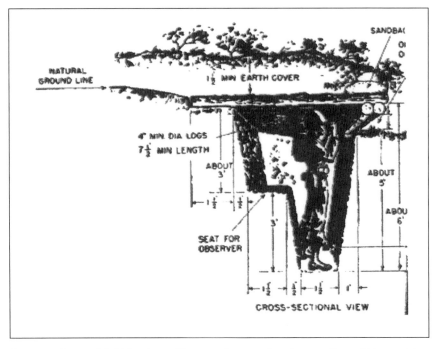

A more advanced field bunker with an earthen roof and camouflage. This would be practical for an observation post or camp defensive position if the location is to be held for an extended period.

Urban combat is to be avoided whenever possible. The cost and risk of this kind of combat far exceeds the value. Extensive training is necessary to have any level of proficiency and even the best military units take heavy losses in urban environments. For a citizen, home defense and/or a fighting escape are the only urban combat necessities. The same principles of stealth, camouflage, diversion, fire and maneuver and counter-ambush apply, but are all more complicated. Multistory buildings add a third dimension to threats. Hiding places are everywhere for you and for the potential enemy. Route selection must take into account how you are exposed, where you can use concealment, where you can find cover, and where threats may lurk. Open streets are almost always the worst route. Moving house to house, yard to yard, or alley to alley is much slower but often much safer.

Defending your home against a few unorganized criminals is achievable with good weapons skills and constant vigilance, but defense against organized assault will be extremely difficult. The military would simply flatten the adjoining houses and cut down the trees to clear fields of fire for automatic weapons. You do not have these options. Adjoining houses may be occupied by shooters or set on fire to drive you out. Walls and fences will provide cover and concealment for shooters to get closer. While older brick homes are basically bulletproof, frame houses and brick veneer homes can be riddled by rifle fire. Once a group of more than two or three attackers has decided to besiege your home, you are in serious trouble unless you have organized a block or community defense team. You should have evacuated already or have an escape plan to execute before you are trapped. There is one other option. Instead of waiting for the miscreants to get to your home, you can go out and help your neighbors by engaging oncoming marauders and assailants before they can launch an organized assault on your home. Obviously, such a tactic would have to be justified by a clear and present danger demonstrated by such forces.

PHYSICAL SECURITY

A single citizen cannot remain at full alertness for twenty-four hours a day. The entire family or group must be capable of sentry duty at home or in a camp. Ideally, sentries should be on duty just one or two hours, but no more than four hours per shift and in twos if possible. They may be assigned to just look out from fixed positions or walk a perimeter or both. If a perimeter patrol is established, it should be done at irregular intervals and routes. A clearly understood procedure for challenging intruders must be established and include a consistent challenge phrase and password. These should be changed daily. Sentries are never, ever stationed or permitted to sit around campfires or in lighted areas and they should avoid using flashlights as this will give away their location while ruining their night vision. The sentries must be armed and have a method of alerting the other members if a threat is imminent, night or day. The family or group should be ready and have an assault response plan in place. If personnel are available, patrols can be sent out to detect signs of activity in adjoining areas. Obstacles, barricades, and warning devices can be used to inhibit surprise entry into a building or camp. Since firebombs are often used by looters and criminals, all combustibles should be moved away from windows and wire screening can be nailed over windows to deflect such devices. Most important, multiple large fire extinguishers should be available.

THE CIVILIAN MISSION

While most armies' missions involve taking and holding ground and the elimination of enemy forces, the mission of any civilian military activity is the safety and survival of civilians. Taking a hill or holding a building may be a valid military objective but is of little value if it is at the cost of friends, family members or neighbors' lives. How the war will develop and whether it will involve combat on American soil is yet to be determined, but history tells us that civilians are often forced or motivated to engage in military activities once hostilities come to their towns. Throughout history, civilians have chosen to risk life in defense of home and freedom.

Note: It must be kept in mind that in an age of infrared and night vision equipment and drones, well-equipped and authorized military and police forces have much greater advantages than any unofficial force in the field and under extreme circumstance they could consider any noncompliant group (no matter how peaceful) as hostile.

CHAPTER 28

WARTIME SURVIVAL GEAR AND SUPPLIES

Specific supplies for specific situations are covered elsewhere in this book, but some redundance of recommendations is unavoidable. Most survival texts include lists of home preparedness supplies and various evacuation packs and kits. These recommendations are intended to meet the immediate needs of citizens coping with natural disasters. Even FEMA lists assume that the survivor will be rescued or will reach government provided shelter and aid within a few days or a week. Under modern wartime conditions, emergency services may be delayed, deficient, or completely dysfunctional. In addition to damage and violence created by hostile activities, civil disorder, looting, disease, and grid failure may add levels of misery to the citizen trying to survive and protect loved ones. While the lists to follow are based on the basic needs associated with regional natural disasters, they have been modified and enhanced where needed to deal with the challenges of a potential long-term national and international conflict.

EVERYDAY CARRY

As wartime and civil disorder increases, the prepared citizen will need to go about his or her everyday tasks but be prepared to cope with a variety of emergency situations. While basic everyday carry has been an established survival practice for decades, wartime developments may require modification and upgrading. The survival principle of "It's not what you have, but what you have with you that counts" applies here. Because of the added complexity of today's survival threats and impending war, the development of multilevel lists to respond to multiple threat levels becomes necessary. While one should carry increasingly tactical-like gear, it is important to blend in. Fortunately backpacks and camouflage are not unusual in some settings. The survivor should endeavor to be tactical without looking tactical.

Everyday Carry Level One

This level is adequate for what we now call "normal" times. The items included are intended to cope with a variety of natural emergencies such as storms, earthquakes, fires, accidents, and assaults. These items can generally be kept in pockets or a purse without attracting attention or being uncomfortably bulky.

- **Pocketknife:** Depending on the clothing you wear, this can be a small two-inch blade or a larger three-inch blade. Good "survival folders" come with a seatbelt cutter and a glass breaker for escape and rescue work. Some even include a flashlight and magnesium fire starter. A knife imparts a major survival advantage in many situations.
- **Cell phone:** These still have utility if the services are functional. If you live in an urban area, you may want to carry a second, fully charged "throw away phone." Most carjackers and robbers will want your phone so you can give them the throw away and use the other to call 911 after they depart. Even if they get the good, connected phone, you can still call 911 on any charged cell phone.
- **Mini flashlight:** Don't depend on the cell phone. These miniature flashlights could be critical in a blackout or smoke-filled building. They can even be attached to your key ring.
- **Whistle:** A loud whistle can attract the attention of rescuers far better than your voice.
- **N95 folding respirator:** Safe air is the first need of survival. When buildings are falling, things are burning, biohazards are in the air, or radioactive fallout begins, these basic respirators will offer some protection. While they do not protect against poison gases or chemicals, they are better than nothing and immediately at hand. Charcoal-impregnated N95 respirators can be had that provide limited protection against chemical contaminants.
- **Fire starter:** While small magnesium fire starter sticks can be used to get a spark that can start a fire with dry tinder, a flame beats a spark in most cases. A simple butane lighter can get a fire started or provide a bit of light as needed. The torch-like lighters sold at convenience stores are very effective and safe.
- **Bandana:** Cloth bandanas can be used as a bandage, tourniquet, improvised respirators, and other survival devices.
- **Defense device:** Your choice here depends on your environment and lifestyle. Any kind of loaded firearm around children is an invitation to disaster. Safety first, but if this is not an issue, a subcompact firearm is certainly an everyday carry need in many locations. Taser

and pepper spray devices are better than nothing but seldom effective when surprised by one or more assailants.

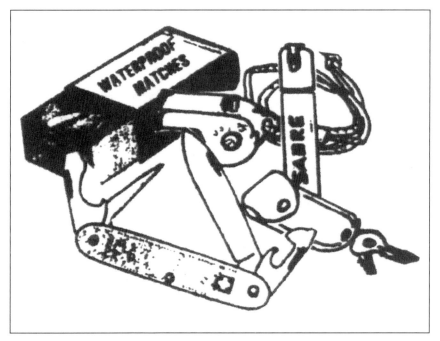

Basic level one everyday carry items, assuming that carrying a firearm is legal in your region.

Everyday Carry Level Two

This level brings a significantly higher level of daily preparedness for response to more violent and prolonged threats that might develop during wartime. These items can help cope with civil disorder, organized assaults, chemical, biological, and nuclear hazards, and the necessity to flee through high threat environments. Items can be distributed in pockets, pouches, or a vest without attracting much attention or being too bulky for everyday activities. In addition to the N95 respirator, whistle, cell phone and bandana, the following items should be added:

- **Multi-tool.** You can replace the knife or have this in addition to your knife. These tools enable the owner to improvise, repair, and escape. They come in a wide variety of sizes and tool combinations. The bigger the better.
- **Rain poncho:** A small plastic rain poncho can provide protection against wind, rain, and airborne contaminants. Just staying dry can prevent hypothermia. Keeping chemicals and fallout off the skin can

be critical. Not as good as a full body covering, but a big advantage over nothing.

- **Tourniquet device:** At this level of hazard there is a serious chance of major injury. All police and military personnel now carry tourniquets. These come with a handy belt or ankle pouch.
- **Hand sanitizer:** A small bottle of alcohol-based hand sanitizer can be used to help start a fire, clean off contaminants, and sanitize wounds.
- **Water purifier:** Hydration is critical, but you may need to use questionable sources. Having a few water purification tablets can provide some protection. They can also be used to make up safe wound flushing and cleaning water.
- **Larger flashlight:** A larger five- to ten- LED flashlight is advisable. Some come with adjustable beams and colors.
- **Firearm:** At this level, always carrying a firearm is just common sense. There are plenty of compact handguns with from six- to ten-round magazine capacities. Carrying at least one extra magazine is advisable.

Level two everyday carry items include a torniquet, water purification, multi-tool, and a larger pistol with extra magazines. In addition to pockets, this would probably require a belt pouch or two (center) or fanny pack.

Everyday Carry Level Three

At this level the items are intended to help survive when actual war zone conditions develop. Such conditions could include shooting, explosions, fires, interruption of water, food, and medical services, rampant civil disorder, and even radioactive fallout. These items are intended to provide immediate and basic needs to facilitate survival, escape, or evacuation in a worst-case scenario. Short of carrying a full survival pack and dressing like a combatant, a butt pack or a shoulder pack will probably not attract undue attention under these conditions. In addition to the aforementioned level one and two items, the following adds and upgrades create the level three everyday carry list:

- **Heavy-duty poncho:** A larger vinyl poncho that is more durable and effective will be necessary if you need prolonged protection from the elements and contaminants.
- **Rescue blanket:** These aluminized blankets will provide additional protection for you or another person and can provide shelter and warmth for cold weather. They are a must have for shock or hypothermia victims.
- **Eye protection:** Flying debris, dust, and contaminants can endanger your eyesight and introduce infections. Normal glasses are insufficient protection. A pair of folding googles will be helpful.
- **Energy bars**: Under high stress and prolonged survival exertions exhaustion can render you vulnerable. A few energy bars can provide nourishment and comfort.
- **Water bottle:** The bulk of carrying at least a pint or two of water is fully justified under these conditions. There are bottles that include a filtration system, or you can carry purification tablets to refill your bottle as needed.
- **Multi-band radio:** Small multi-band radios are available that can be tuned to emergency channels, citizens band, and even preestablished family or group communications networks. This may be your primary information and communication source as the cellular systems and commercial radio and TV networks go down (see chapter 16).
- **Monocular or binocular:** A small monocular will give you a chance to see trouble before you encounter it. Are those friends or potential assailants? Is that a safe route? What's leaking from that rail car? Is he carrying a gun?
- **Tactical flashlight:** You will want a heavy-duty, military-grade flashlight with at least 2000 lumens of brightness and an adjustable beam. There are plenty of options available.

- **Mini first aid kit:** In addition to the torniquet, you can add a variety of hemostatic blood stopper dressings, self-adhesive bandages, antibiotic ointments, and pain relivers.
- **Firearm(s):** At this point the sight of an armed civilian should not be unusual. A full-sized handgun with at least four extra magazines may be necessary to get you through a serious situation. Learn how to change magazines under fire. If things get that bad, carrying a pistol in a holster and/or carrying a rifle or sub rifle may be considered normal and justified for everyday use.

At level three a large fanny pack (bottom) or small backpack is necessary. A full-sized pistol with extra magazines, more first aid items, a monocular, and a two-way radio are added. This is still everyday carry, but just short of going full battle rattle.

You can add or combine items as needed to create an everyday carry system that meets your needs and environment. The key to survival is having what you need, where you need it, when you need it. Everyday carry means every day and all the time, starting now. If you only carry some items some time, Murphy's law will get you.

WARTIME EMERGENCY FUNDS

A wartime economy may evolve over several years with galloping inflation, rationing, and even a totally controlled economy. The welfare system may be expanded to control all income and expenses through a federal debit card system. War could also break out suddenly, accompanied by a stock market crash, bank accounts evaporating, and a collapsed supply chain. Any kind of war and cyberattack can render online banking, and credit cards useless. Most experts recommend that citizens have at least a $2,000 cash emergency fund on hand in addition to any emergency funds in banks or safety deposit boxes. Some experts advocate having some or all of this in gold, but this may be difficult to use under disaster conditions. Cash may not be king, but it may be more useful than credit or shiny metal in purchasing food, and other critical necessities. Cash should be kept in small bills for easy negotiations and stored in separate locations throughout your home and property. Keep in mind that your home may be set on fire, looted, or inaccessible. Keep no more than 20 percent of your emergency cash in any one location. Place cash in waterproof containers, in well-camouflaged and unlikely locations. Check on your cash caches regularly so you don't forget where they are. You may need to gather them up quickly in an emergency. Obviously, more emergency cash is better, but any emergency cash is better than nothing. A thousand in the hand will be more important than a million in the bank when adversity strikes. If you can't pull the funds from existing accounts, establish a budget to build up your on-hand emergency fund and stick to it.

EVACUATION SURVIVAL PACKS

The concept of "survival packs" predates the preparedness movement and the FEMA "evacuation pack" lists. Every survival book includes some kind of pack list ranging from outdoor "survival kits" through large, long-term "survival packs" intended to facilitate basic self-reliance when the citizen is never going to go back home. Survival supply vendors offer complete packs, that are sufficient for short term (three-to-five- day) emergencies. FEMA recommendations are intended to support evacuation to government-provided shelters during regional disasters. All these lists provide for the basics of water, food, shelter, and other necessities, but do not cover the potential needs for self-defense or extended survival under national emergency and wartime conditions. The following list is based on existing recommendations but modified to cover these additional needs. Your pack will be of little value if you can't carry it far enough to be safe. Basic *need* must trump emotional *want* in item selection. The pack itself matters, so buy a good quality pack with multiple pockets, and well-padded back shoulder and waist straps. Take the pack out for a bit of a hike. You should be able to carry it without resting for at least one hour.

The Get Home Pack

The get home pack is intended to get you home within one or two days through dangerous and possibly hostile conditions so it is necessarily heavy on first aid, respiratory protection, and self-defense and lighter on food, water, and other long-term needs. This pack can be kept in your vehicle but must be a backpack in case you have to walk home. You may want to keep a change of clothes and hiking boots with your pack. If the potential for movement through high-threat regions exists, you may also need to have a long gun, or sub rifle and extra full magazines stored with your pack. Of course, if you use public transportation the contents of your home pack will be much more limited.

- **Two or more N95 respirators:** Terrorist attacks, chemical incidents, fires, and many other situations will result in an unsafe atmosphere. If the potential for serious chemical exposure along your escape route exists you may want to include a full or half-face chemical respirator, but it will be a bulky addition.
- **A heavy-duty plastic rain poncho:** This item will protect you from airborne contaminants, rain, and wind.
- **A first aid kit:** Many types of emergencies will result in injuries. Basic bandages, a tourniquet, pain relievers, antiseptic ointment, and hemostatic gauze pads should be included.
- **Self-defense weapons:** Disaster situations can result in civil disorder and looting. If possible, include a small handgun and extra magazines of ammunition in your kit. If this is not an option include a large can of pepper spray and possibly a taser. Better to have it and not need it than need it and not have it.
- **A good pocketknife and/or multi-tool:** These have many critical applications during a survival situation.
- **A small AM/FM/WX band radio:** Knowledge of developing situations will be critical to your reaching home safely.

- **A small monocular or binocular**: Seeing hazards and checking rout safety in advance will be an important advantage.
- **A hand-held GMRS walkie-talkie:** If you have established a plan with your family this could be used to communicate with them as you get close to home.
- **A tactical flashlight:** Disasters frequently result in power outages. You may need to move through darkened areas at night or signal for help.
- **A loud whistle:** Always handy for signaling for help.
- **Several days' worth of your prescription medications:** You can never be sure how long it will take before you can get more.
- **One or two pints of water:** Water may not be critical during short-term escapes, but some should be carried. Adding a few water purifica-tion tablets or a Survival Straw may be a good idea, just in case.
- **A lighter, matches, or magnesium stick:** Starting a fire may not be a priority, but it's better to have the ability, just in case you need to camp in cold weather.
- **Short-term energy food:** While you don't need to have cooking gear and meals, you do need fast energy and nourishment. So-called energy bars, protein bars, and trail snacks for two to three days along with caffeine—5-hour energy drinks are a must.
- **Navigation aids:** Maps, compasses, and GPS devices are only neces-sary if you are unfamiliar with the routes to your home.

Survival Evacuation Packs

This pack starts with the basic evacuation pack but is modified for wartime situations and the possibility of evolution to long-term survival. It can be kept in the home or vehicle. Each family member should have a pack suitable for their ability to carry it. Children can have smaller bags as well. In most cases evacuation is a last resort, but the items in the pack can be used for home emergencies as well. If multiple packs are carried, redundant items like stoves, first aid kits, shelters, and water purifiers can be distributed so there is more capacity for food, water, and other consumable supplies.

- **(4) 16 oz. water bottles:** this can be replaced by one or two canteens and should be supplemented with a package of water purification tablets.
- **(1) Collapsible stove with heat tablets:** The folding Esbit® stove is ideal for this application.
- **(1) Metal canteen cup or Sierra cup:** Being able to prepare hot drinks is important for maintaining energy and morale.

- **(1) Fifty-hour candle:** This can be substituted with a solar rechargeable mini-lantern.
- **(1) Tactical flashlight:** Consider one that has multiple power levels and/or is solar rechargeable.
- **(1) Multi-band radio:** This should be AM/FM/WX weather band, preferably crank and solar powered.
- **(1–4) Food bars**: High-calorie, high-protein food bars and trail foods that have long storage life. Consider lifeboat rations that provide 2,500 calories.
- **(1) Large rain poncho**
- **(2) N95 dust/mist respirators:** these provide protection from airborne contaminants, but also help retain respirator warmth.
- **(1) Space blanket:** While cheap rescue blankets are lighter, the much more durable space blankets provide better shelter.
- **(1) Multifunction knife:** A Swiss Army–type knife or a multi-tool will come-in-handy for many purposes.
- **(1) Box waterproof matches:** You may want to add a lighter or a magnesium spark striker to be sure you start a fire.
- **(1) Bottle hand sanitizer:** The type that is alcohol based can serve as an aid to fire starting.
- **(1) First aid kit:** Include bandages, hemostatic gauze pads, antiseptic and pain relievers.
- **(1) Pair extra glasses:** If you normally need glasses this is a must.
- **(1) Spare pair of heavy socks:** If you will be walking a long distance this is important. Sore, wet feet can stop you in your tracks. Socks can also serve as mittens in cold weather.
- **Extra prescription medications:** Take as much as you can since you cannot depend on resupply in an evacuation.
- **(6) Light sticks:** FEMA recommends these, and they could be useful.
- **Copies of:** Birth certificates, deeds, mortgages, titles, insurance papers, medical, and contact information.
- **Self-protection device** (optional but recommended): Under some conditions, the evacuee may be subject to criminal assault and looting. Options range from a pepper spray to a handgun. Be aware that government shelters probably will prohibit and confiscate weapons.
- **Optional food:** Your stove can be used to heat up coffee, tea, instant soups, and other beverages, so consider adding instant coffee, tea bags, sugar packets, and bouillon cubes to your pack. If you include oatmeal or thick soups, don't forget a spoon.

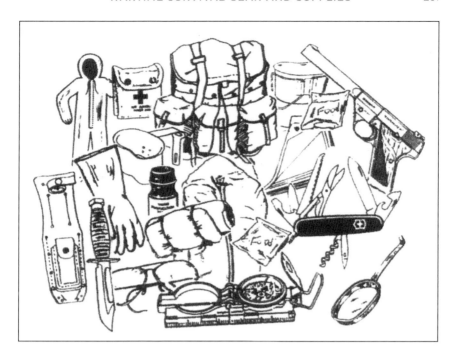

Long-Term Survival (Bugout) Packs

Survival packs, often referred to as "bugout bags" are generally considered the ultimate expression of self-reliance. Unlike survival kits and evacuation packs, the survival pack assumes that (1) no help will be forthcoming and (2) the disaster situation may be of extended or indefinite duration. The major weight and space increases result from the requirements below.

- The survival pack should have sufficient food and water purification capacity to last at least six to ten days. Add dehydrated meals sold for backpackers to the above supplies of energy bars, jerky, and nuts.
- The survival pack should have adequate sheltering and warmth items for extended outdoor survival in cold and wet conditions. This may include a bivouac tent and a compact sleeping bag, space blankets, or tarps.
- The survival pack should have tools necessary for self-reliance and survival beyond ten days, such as shovels, axes, fishing gear, game traps, firearms, ammunition, etc.
- The survival pack should have enough medications and first aid items to maintain health without outside help for extended periods.
- If you're not an experienced and trained "survivalist," consider adding one or two comprehensive survival books as you're not likely to have access to online information sources.

- If you're evacuating under war conditions, you are going to need to add and carry some serious weaponry. Your sidearm will be a large-capacity semi-automatic, and you will need to carry a military-style long gun. Shorter rifles or combat shotguns may be ideal for urban areas, while full-length, large-caliber AR-15 variant rifles are more suited for open-field combat situations. Unfortunately, ammunition for these is heavy and potential defensive combat may require the expenditure of one hundred or more rounds. Unlike military personnel you will not have sources to resupply. How "paramilitary" you are willing to go is a personal choice. Military load-bearing vests, plate-carrier, bullet-resistant vests and even Kevlar® helmets could be worth considering in some scenarios, but the more military you look, the more hostile attention you are likely to attracts. As in all things survival related, risk-vs.-benefit analysis should be applied here.

WHAT TO HAVE AT HOME

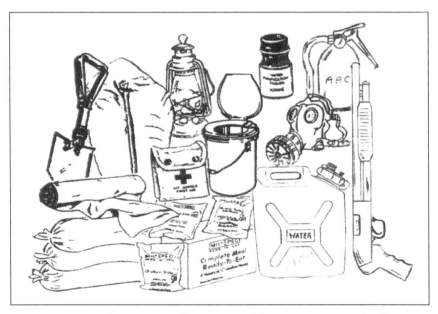

In most cases it will be safer and more desirable to stay home and ride out an emergency. If things get really bad you have your packs, but here are some of the items you will want to have at home. The goal is to be able to hold out for at least thirty days without outside sources of food, water, fuel, defense, medical aid, heat, or power. A specific list of items would depend on the number of people in the home, the climate, the available family budget, and the location. So, the following guide is provided.

Stored Water: While thirty gallons of water per person is recommended, it may not be practical. Five gallons for each person stored in one or more plastic containers with four to eight drops of bleach added to each gallon is recommended. Keeping water in anything over five-gallon containers is not recommended. What if that one big barrel leaks? What if you need to move the water supply? You also have drinkable water in your hot water heater. You just cannot have too much water purification and storage capacity. This should include:

- At least ten two-gallon full water jugs and five five-gallon water jugs at all times. Fifty-five-gallon water barrels with hand pumps are available from survival supply outlets but may be difficult to store or move.
- Ten gallons of household bleach
- 50 iodine water purification tablets
- One large capacity water filtration system with extra filters

Water purification: There are all kinds of water purification systems available. Tap water may be contaminated and you do not have fuel to boil it. You may have to use rainwater, pond water, river water, or sump water. A good water filtration and purification system will be critical for emergencies lasting longer than four to five days. If you do not have a filter system, you can use coffee filters and eight drops of bleach per gallon, but a good high-capacity water purifier is essential for long-term home survival (see chapter 17).

Food: Normally, you probably have five to eight days of canned and frozen food in the house. You can go with costly dehydrated foods if space is a problem, but otherwise go with dry and canned foods you can rotate. Dried fruits, beans, lentils, rice, corn meal, oatmeal, nuts, wheat, pasta, sugar, coffee, and other long-term storables can be further preserved by vacuum packaging*. Canned vegetables and meats (SPAM®, corned beef, beef stew, chicken and dumplings, pork and beans) usually have a two-year marked shelf life. They keep longer, but rotation is recommended. Powdered milk or condensed milk. Things like honey, molasses, vinegar, and syrup last indefinitely. A thirty-day supply of meals of approximately 2,000 calories per day is recommended. Below is just a sample list of items to consider (see chapter 19).

- 10 cans of SPAM® or other canned meats
- 10 cans of sardines and tuna
- 10 pounds of powdered eggs
- 20 pounds of rice
- 20 pounds of potato flakes
- 50 pounds of red beans

- 50 pounds of lima beans
- 50 pounds of wheat
- 50 pounds of oatmeal
- 50 pounds of dry milk powder
- 50 pounds of white beans
- 50 pounds of rye flour
- 50 pounds of corn meal
- 20 pounds of raisins
- 20 pounds of figs
- 10 pounds of prunes
- 10 pounds of mixed nuts
- 20 pounds of coffee or tea
- 20 pounds of sugar or honey

* Vacuum packing devices and reusable bags are available at most hunting supply stores and kitchen supply stores ranging in price from $50 to $500.

Sanitation Supplies: You are going to need bleach for water purification, sanitizing body waste, and possibly decontaminating equipment. Have always at least three to four gallons on hand. Rotate to keep a full-strength supply. Hand soap, toilet paper, dishwashing and clothes washing soaps, clothesline, clothes pins, toothpaste, and mouthwash are other things you should always be overstocked on. Have a package of heavy-duty plastic bags and a shovel. Remember the toilet may not work and the garbage will not be picked up.

Cleaning: Four gallons of bleach, ten rolls of toilet paper, ten bars of soap, two gallons of laundry detergent, fifty feet of cloths line, fifty clothes pins, six boxes of large trash bags, four bottles of dishwashing liquid.

Heat: Most furnaces will not run if the power is off and generators big enough to power the furnace fan will eat a lot of gasoline. You can light your oven (if you have gas) manually to heat the kitchen. Buy two or three good camp heaters and lots of fuel cylinders. Have a good two-burner camp stove.

Light, etc.: Several good LED flashlights are a must. Crank-powered flashlights, lanterns, and emergency (AM/FM/weather) radios provide long term light and information without needing extra batteries. Stock up on good long-burning candles and matches. Good glass-enclosed candle lanterns are recommended for safety.

Electricity: Electricity is a luxury but not a necessity. You need enough power to run your refrigerator and/or freezer until you use up the contents or the power comes on. You may need power for a sump pump or water pump. Stay small and stretch your fuel supply. A 2,000–3,000-watt generator should be plenty. Even a 1,000-watt generator will run a sump pump and alternately run a small deep freeze. Don't get dependent on a generator for long term situations as fuel may not be available or may be too costly (see chapter 20).

Shelter: Have lots of plastic sheeting and duct tape to cover damaged roofs and windows. Pick one room in which you will live, cook, eat, and sleep. Seal this room off to maintain heat from your heaters. You cannot heat your entire house with your limited heaters. Use them to heat one room and keep pipes from freezing if you can. Have good sleeping bags for every family member capable of keeping everyone warm down to the lowest temperatures in your area. Consider having a dome tent that can be put up inside your house. It will be much easier to keep warm, light, and safe than the entire house.

Fire Protection: You cannot afford a fire. Using candles, camp stoves, and heaters greatly increases the risk of fire and of carbon monoxide. Be sure your smoke and carbon monoxide detectors are working in the living area. Have several ABC fire extinguishers on hand. A garden pump sprayer filled with water is good for putting out wood, paper, and brush fires.

Defense: Choice of home defense weapons depends on where you live. While you may need to consider the weight of the weapon and ammunition for the pack, this is not a problem for home defense. If you live in the city or semi-urban areas where crime and looting are the main concern, a combination of a large caliber handgun such as a Glock, Sig Sauer or Smith & Wesson in 40 or 45 caliber or 9 mm and a reliable (e.g. Mossberg, Ithaca, Browning) pump, 12-gauge shotgun are recommended. For home defense, select shotguns with 24-inch barrels. You will want at least two extra magazines for the handgun and lots of extra ammunition for both weapons. If you live out in the country, you probably already have some firearms. If you have just one weapon, make it a 12-gauge shotgun. Any length is okay since you will probably use it for hunting also. A reliable handgun to carry is still recommended, but a good rifle is more practical in the countryside. This is way too broad a subject to cover here but select a reliable rifle for which parts and ammunition will be most available. This means 5.56, 223 Remington, 308 Winchester, and 30–30 for rifles like the AR-15 Mini-14, and M&P 15.

First Aid:

First and foremost, stock up on your prescription medications. Hoard any antibiotics and painkillers while you can. Although most medications expire in two years, they are often effective for much longer, especially when vacuum packed and kept cool. You must have a basic first aid book to ensure proper procedures. The following is a partial list that could be expanded depending on your needs and skills.

- 1 pkg. of blood stoppers (Celox™, QuikClot®, and HemCon®) powder or dressing
- 1 (8-oz.) tube of antibiotic ointment (e.g. Neosporin 9tm)
- 1 (8-oz.) tube of hydrocortisone cream
- 1 (8-oz.) tube of burn ointment
- 1 bar antibacterial soap
- 12 alcohol swabs
- 1 bottle of nonprescription pain medication (e.g. Tylenol™)
- 1 bottle of nonprescription antacid
- 1 bottle of nonprescription antidiuretic
- 1 bottle of nonprescription laxative
- 1 bottle of nonprescription cold and allergy medication
- 1 (3-oz.) bottle of eye drops
- 1 (2-inch) elastic bandage
- 1 (3-inch) elastic bandage
- 2 triangle (cravat) bandages/slings
- 24 assorted small bandages (Band-Aids®)
- 12 (2 × 2-inch) gauze pads
- 12 (3× 3-inch) gauze pads
- 12 (4× 4-inch) gauze pads
- 12 safety pins (large)
- 1 pair of EMT shears
- 1 pair of splinter forceps and/or tweezers
- 4 single-edge razor blades or scalpel blades with blade holder
- 1 toothache kit (available at drug stores)
- 6 pairs of latex gloves your size.
- 1 roll of 1-inch self-adhering tape
- 1 roll of 2-inch self-adhering tape
- 1 roll of ½-inch medical tape

Miscellaneous: Hopefully you have a stock of tools at home, but you may need big crowbars, good shovels, hand saws, heavy hammers, axes, and tools that do not require electricity. Be sure you have the right wrenches to turn off gas and water valves in a hurry. A chainsaw may come in handy (while you have fuel) to clear fallen trees and cut firewood. Have an old-fashioned coffee pot to replace that useless coffee maker. If your basement floods or you get your water from a well, you need to consider hand-operated or solar-powered pumps for long-term use.

CHAPTER 29

TEN PRINCIPLES OF WARTIME SURVIVAL

Si vis pacem para bellum. (If you would have peace, prepare for war.)
—attributed to Publius Vegetius Renatus

Reviewing the ten principles of survival as they apply to wartime and war zone scenarios is a good way to wrap up this book and provide a focused review of the essential concepts that apply to all categories of emergency preparedness and disaster survival. These principles apply to everyday life as well. While it is impossible to predict how a war will develop, what kinds of challenges it will present to the individual citizen, or how severe the effects will be on the civilian population, the application of these principles throughout preparedness, planning for, and responding to the exigencies of war and wartimes will be valuable. The ten principles are:

1. Anticipate
2. Be aware
3. Be here now
4. Stay calm
5. Evaluate
6. Do the next right thing
7. Take control
8. Have what you need
9. Use what you have
10. Do what is necessary

1. Anticipate the development of warfare. The very idea of a Third World War is repulsive to the human psyche. Natural denial and the "normalcy bias" resist even the contemplation of such a horrendous event. Even as we observe other civilian populations experiencing the spreading war, and growing tensions and threats developing between nuclear powers, the predominant reaction is avoidance and complacency. Unfortunately, World War III is not only "thinkable" it is already developing. Cyberattacks, economic warfare, psychological warfare, weapons development, and deployments are all under way. The same pattern of military, economic, and diplomatic events that presaged the beginning of World War II are once again obvious to anyone who knows where to look. You cannot hope to survive a threat until you accept that it is real and imminent. World War II was fought in other lands and did not directly reach America civilians, but none of the factors that kept war away from American streets in 1941 apply today. The immigration of rogue and conflicting ideologies, global economics, intelligent weapons, and a technologically dependent population guarantee that any kind of war will bring some degree of violence, destruction, and deprivation affecting every civilian. Anticipation of war's effects is critical, and time is short.

2. Be aware of wartime threats and hazards. War may develop through a series of events or a singular violent attack. Conventional nuclear bombings are obvious and immediate hazards, but civilians will be victims of more indirect and subtle effects of any type of war. Truth is the first casualty of war. Russia, China, Iran, and homegrown agents of chaos will sow division and confusion among the population, causing us to defeat ourselves. Dependency on Chinese goods will result in economic collapse and a "peace at any price" mentality. War in space and cyber warfare will result in the loss of GPS systems, and grid failure. Shortages, rationing, and a black-market economy may develop. Various factions may resort to street violence, sabotage, and even revolution. Fire, EMS, and police services may be delayed or even totally unavailable while crime and looting goes unabated. Even limited or unlimited nuclear war is no longer unthinkable. Civilians must face and prepare for these possibilities. Gather information about international events, national events, and local events that may affect your survival. Be your own intelligence service.

3. Be here now, focused on the immediate war zone here and now. As new threats develop, and wartime conditions prevail, situational awareness becomes critical. Your senses need to be tuned into your surroundings at all times. The military mnemonic "OODA" meaning observe, orient, decide, and act, must apply to wartime and war zone survival. On a deeper level, listen to your instincts and trust your gut. Your deep mind instincts are there to protect you. If it doesn't feel right or the hairs on your neck are standing up, pay attention.

4. Stay calm as you prepare for and face the challenges of wartime survival. Staying calm when the air raid sirens are going off, or you hear blasts or shooting down the street may seem impossible. An untrained civilian with no combat or disaster response experience will get a massive spike in adrenalin, accompanied by a fight or flight impulse and the development of tunnel vision. All of this can lead to impulsive behavior and poor decisions. The military and police conduct intense and realistic training and drills to partially immunize combatants against panic. Anticipating the dreadful possibility of war, being aware of how it may affect and endanger civilians, and focusing on preparedness and planning for worst-case scenarios can help the civilian avoid panic and get from denial to effective lifesaving action under pressure.

5. Evaluate the threats, needs, and challenges you will face as war develops. Everyone's situation is different. Consider the dangers and consequences of developing situations. Compare what you need or will need with the skills, equipment, and capabilities you have. Consider your income, family obligations, location, and environment. Do a "what if" analysis on each potential situation. Always assume that Murphy's law will apply and have alternative plans and backup gear. Be realistic about your capabilities. You're not Rambo, and neither was he.

6. Do the next right thing to survive in a war zone. Overreacting or doing the wrong thing at the wrong time can be disastrous under survival conditions. Knowledge, training, and planning can help to avoid these errors. Freeze, run, or take cover are all actions that can save your life or get you killed. In a combat zone, one must be constantly planning on action based on available cover and concealment. You may need to decide to shoot or not to shoot within nanoseconds. Based on your first aid training, you may have to triage multiple injuries and decide which ones must be treated immediately and which ones can be delayed. Indecision and procrastination kill.

7. Take control and manage your situation under chaos and combat scenarios. Anticipation and preparation enable you to own a situation instead of just reacting to it. Opportunities lie within the chaos of a war zone. You can minimize the injuries and damage. You can organize and lead through hard times. By planning a preparing, you are happening to future hazards before they happen to you. If you are trapped or under assault, you may be able to turn the tables. Think about what you need to do to improve your situation and win. Passivity and reaction must be replaced by intelligent initiative and constructive action.

8. Have what you need to survive, fight, and recover during developing wartime challenges. Basic safety and disaster preparedness gear is not enough to meet the needs of long-term wartime or war zone challenges. Under worst-case scenarios, the civilian may have to cope with violence, grid failure, and deprivation without hope of support from normal disaster relief, police, fire, and EMS agencies. While military organizations will have logistical support and organized defenses, the civilian may be isolated and become collateral damage. Every basic survival need for food, water, shelter, and first aid must be expanded to cover an indefinite period. Supplies need to be protected and dispersed to survive various levels of destruction and the possible need to abandon the primary shelter, or camp. While normal disaster-related weaponry is limited to self-defense and hunting, a war zone or wartime situation dictates a higher level of armament and a much larger ammunition supply. Good basic survival skills must be supplemented with more advanced armed and unarmed combat skills, and trauma-related medical skills.

9. Use what you have and improvise as needed to get through hard times and hazards. Unless you have an unlimited budget, you are going to need to create, repair, and invent tools and methods to meet survival and defense needs. Nature provides materials for shelter building, camouflage, and fuel. Junk such as wire, rope, tarps, bottles, cans, and plastic bags are examples of things that can be repurposed for survival needs. Bombing, looting, and general chaos can leave behind all sorts of useful items. Always carry a knife and/or a good multi-tool that can be used to fix what's broken and improvise what you need.

10. Do what is necessary to survive regardless of pain, discomfort, or reluctance. In the gravest extreme, the survivor may be forced to choose between two or more extremely undesirable courses of action. While some people are able to avoid or delegate such decisions, they will be inescapable for survivors in a true war-like disaster. You may have to abandon your home. You may have to use deadly force against looters and even desperate and hostile neighbors. You may have to sell or trade valued items for essential needs. You may be forced to do things that are illegal and against your normal moral code to save yourself or others. You may need to kill another human being who possess a threat to you and those you care about. Doing these things takes bravery and fortitude. If you are normal, you will suffer regrets and second thoughts for the rest of your life but do what must be done.

In addition, the most important principle of survival is never give up. It is easy to be overwhelmed by an emergency, or a disaster, and the stress generated by wartime conditions and war zone violence can generate confusion, depression, and hopelessness. History is filled with examples of "hopeless" situations being survived by sheer determination. Being able to take losses, suffer pain, and keep going is the essence of heroism. Just doing the next right thing, taking one more step, holding on just one more hour has saved many individuals and groups. If the unexpected can doom you, the unexpected can save you. History is filled with tales of people who have suffered gunshots to the head, abdomen, and chest and have survived without surgery or antibiotics. People have fallen from aircraft thousands of feet in the air and survived. Hopelessly surrounded and outgunned military units have held out and been rescued or had the enemy just withdraw for no reason. Groups have been stranded in Antarctica without hope of rescue long before radios, or rescue aircraft were invented, and yet they survived. Doomsday is the day that you give up. Hang on and do your best. Believe in yourself and care about what you believe.

CHAPTER 30

POST-WORLD WAR III ADAPTATION AND RECOVERY

As soon as the fighting stopped, people crept out of their holes and started life all over again.

—Soviet war correspondent in Berlin, 1945

No one could have guessed what the world would be like at the end of World War I, but in retrospect it is difficult to say that anyone won, and the seeds of another war were already planted. Certainly Germany and Japan did not foresee the outcome of World War II as they planned their aggression. A detailed study of that war shows that dozens of small incidents and accidents determined the outcome more than all the grand plans of politicians and generals. As the saying goes, "Man plans, and God laughs." World War III would be even less subject to planning and predictions. There are so many moving parts, political and religious dogmas, special interests, and technological developments involved that how World War Three will develop and be fought is impossible to predict. Anything can happen except world peace and civilian safety. The argument can be made that wars never end; they just change in intensity and location. While wars are waged for various "causes," victory for the civilian is just staying alive, saving his or her family and remaining free. World War III has the potential for the annihilation of civilization and sufficient devastation to the environment that only the most primitive life would remain. Short of that doomsday scenario, there are numerous ways in which the war will be fought and how it will end. There are three certainties: (1) no one will really win (2) it will be the end of the world as we know it (3) civilians will suffer and die in great numbers. Through this book we have explored the effects of war on various aspects of human survival. Here we will attempt to look at the effects of victory, defeat, or stalemate on coming generations. Win, lose, or draw, your children and grandchildren will live in that postwar world order.

A LOST WORLD

World War II had a clear ending and defined winners and losers. The end of World War III may not be so well defined. If the war escalates into massive and prolonged physical combat with conventional weapons and military forces, it may only end when one side is exhausted or destroyed. The losing side might or might not be physically occupied, but its economy would be unable to continue the struggle and its population would no longer have the will to resist. If the conflict goes nuclear, the war could end simply because there is nothing left to fight for, and everyone is left just fighting for survival. The low-intensity war that is already underway could expand to include more remote, surrogate wars and cyberwars. At some point, one side would gain the upper hand and force concession and submissions on the other. If America is economically and militarily defeated, the victor would demand access and control of all government and corporate data, surveillance systems, and financial institutions. Public disarmament and total control of all communications and news media would be required. Any involvement in unions, clubs, religions, or private enterprises would put you in a reeducation camp. Ideas like self-reliance, alternative lifestyles, and survivalism in general would meet with immediate and violent repression. In China, all citizens are required to carry a cell phone so they can be tracked, 50 percent of all the cameras in the world are in use in China watching its citizens, and a DNA database for the entire population is being developed. Is this the world of the future? Individualism is the opposite of collectivism. A true Orwellian dystopia would engulf the late great free world. During World War II, the oppressed in Europe and Asia looked to the United States for hope and many escaped the Nazis, and the Communists for a freer, better life, but if America is defeated where will we go? Who will save our future? During World War II, underground movements flourished in occupied nations, but in today's wired and watched society, such activities would be much more difficult to sustain. Certainly, the enemies of freedom are working to achieve a cultural and moral victory in advance of a military and economic conflict. It is possible that the free world as we know it will be defeated without even recognizing that fact until control, oppression, and economic domination is well established. Citizens have lost some liberties and suffered economically even when the Free World was victorious, but at least they retained hope and most liberties. A loss at this point in history could change the future in permanent and disastrous ways.

PERPETUAL WAR

In George Orwell's book *1984,* there was a perpetual state of war between three world powers. Occasional battles and incoming missiles kept the population fearful and obedient. It could be argued that such a state already exists. Considering the complexity of the world economy and modern military technology, a stalemate is the most likely outcome of World War III. The war may never be officially declared, and it may never officially end. Any form of victory or defeat may be difficult to define or recognize. Ongoing battles may decimate the world economy. The world population may be significantly reduced by combat and civilian casualties. Freedom and security could be surrendered to a foreign power or to domestic agencies in the name of national security. The third-world population would be starved and decimated, initiating mass migrations. The progress in human health and living standards could be reversed for decades. Such a conflict could involve shifting alliances, and cycles of violent combat interspersed with periods of economic, technological, and ideological struggle. Short of nuclear annihilation, a prolonged and indecisive World War III could be the most destructive and civilization altering development of the current developing conflict.

A NEW BEGINNING

Technology is the sharp sword of the modern state.
                                    —Chinese President Xi Jinping

It is far easier to win a war than to win a peace. France technically *won* World War I but was economically and morally exhausted. The nation never recovered and was easily defeated a few decades later. England *won* World War II but emerged with a ruined economy and a lost empire in a world dominated by superpowers. A militarily victorious United States would still be in a recovery mode for decades. Each past war has resulted in expanded government power and reduced individual liberties. Losing nations might still recover better and rise again as Germany did after the First World War. Anything short of total victory and the establishment of freedom and democracy throughout the major world economies would guarantee a future war in which a weakened United State might be decisively defeated. With these history lessons in mind, this generation must be dedicated to being even greater than the "greatest generation" to secure the future of life and freedom on this planet. While this war is already ending the world as we know it, a true victory by the Free World could offer the possibility of making the beginning of a world as we want it to be. While oppressive regimes are using technology as a "sharp sword of the modern state" technology can be used as tool to bring about a renaissance of individual liberty and self-reliance. The human spirit and the will to survive physically, psychologically, and spiritually will determine whether victory is meaningful or Pyrrhic. Ultimately it is up to you and your generation.

SPACE WAR

World War III will be the last *world* war. It may even begin in near space as satellites kill other satellites, and space-based weapons rain down on cities. Unless mankind is thrown back into a true Dark Ages, conflict will continue in near and distant space. Whoever dominates space will be the true victor in World War III and the arbiter of the future of mankind. Such are the stakes of today's conflict.

ABOUT THE AUTHOR

James C. Jones was born on the South Side of Chicago at the beginning of World War II. An impoverished and chaotic childhood made him a natural survivalist from an early age. He put together his own survival pack at age twelve and often spent time in the woodlands and swamps that adjoined the city at that time. Working two jobs while living in one-room and attending high school in the tough South Side added more real-world survival experiences. Starting as a technician at a large chemical manufacturing complex, his passion for safety led him to become an award-winning safety manager. While acquiring certifications in emergency medicine, hazardous chemical handling, radiological monitoring, safety management and training management related to his job, he energetically pursued survival related activities including rock climbing, caving, rafting, horseback riding, and survival camping. In the late 1960s he founded Live Free USA and helped it evolve from an outdoor survival club into a broad-based, national preparedness and self-reliance education organization. During the 1970s and 1980s he was a leading voice in defending and defining responsible survivalism on national television and radio and even the BBC.

Jones is the author of *Advanced Survival, Total Survival, 150 Survival Secrets,* and *The Prepper's Medical Manual* and has developed and conducted hundreds of survival training events and seminars over the past forty years. He has written hundreds of articles for Live Free's *American Survivor* newsletter as well as national several national magazines. He is now retired and living in Indiana but continues to author articles for the AmericanSurvivor.org website and newsletter, while continuing to teach a variety of survival courses and make presentations at major preparedness expositions. He can be contacted at survivorjj@aol.com.

INDEX

protective suits and masks, 52–54
treatment, 54–55
use of chemical agents, 49
chemical weapons, 49, 50
chest, flail, 117
chest wounds, sucking, 115–116
Chicago, fire in 1871, 90
children
in emergency planning, 122
keeping firearms away from, 206, 222
pre-evacuation planning and, 26, 29
protection from radiation exposure, 66
relocation outside target areas, 123
survival evacuation packs, 229
during WWII Britain, 25
China
cell phones and DNA database, 244
chemical and biological warfare, 3
crime syndicates, 10
crippling of banking accounts and finances, 21
deployment of false social media, 7
drones, 38
economic warfare, 2
hackers against USA, 6
nuclear warheads, 56
purchase of America's economic institutions, 9–10
social media and press in, 16
social media as weapon to wage war on America, 22

tactical nuclear weapons and, 39
testing anti-satellite weapons, 23
in twenty-first century, 2
use of "agents," 19
use of non-symmetrical methods against USA, 20
use of psychological warfare, 3
Chinese military mask MF-11, 53
chlorine bleach and iodine, for water purification, 142
chocking agents, 50
Churchill, Winston, 24
civil defense and survival. *see* drones
Civil defense Cold War training materials, 71
Civil Defense Department. *see* FEMA
civil defense drills, during World War II, 17
Civil defense fallout shelters and system, 56
civil defense instruction material, 71
civil disorder or insurrection planning, 121
Civilian Emergency Response Teams (CERTs), 17
civilian life
impact of war on USA, 11
WWII challenges for, 12–18
civilian mission, 219–220
Civilian Survival Conditions (SURCON), 29
Civil War of 1861-1865, 1
cleaning supplies, 234
close contact, avoiding, 197
closed and oppressive societies. *see* China; Iran; Russia

shotguns, 202–203

shovels, 74

sides taking, 184–185

Sierra cup, 229

sight level, importance in escape and evasion, 86

silhouette, as element of camouflage, 83

"Simulating Nuclear War," Science & Global Security (Princeton University), 57

skeletal injuries, in war zone, 110–114
   principles of splinting, 111
   splinting methods for hand, arm, and leg, 111–114

sledgehammers, small and large, 74

slow movement, in escape and evasion, 85

smoking, for preserving meat and fish, 164

soap, making, 150–151

"social activists," 8

"social influencers," 9

social media
   as China's weapon to wage war on America, 22
   disinformation, 7
   false deployment, China and, 7
   Russia, China, Iran, and, 16
   as threat, 9
   use by China and Russia, 3
   use to support front groups and highjack social movements, 8

social movements, social media and high jacking of, 8

socks, pair or heavy, 230

soft tissue injuries, in war zone, 96–109
   bandaging principles and methods, 103
   blood stoppers and packing, 101
   hypovolemic shock/hemorrhagic shock, 101–103
   securing cloth bandages, 104–106
   severe bleeding, 96–98
   tourniquet application precautions, 99
   tourniquet application procedures, 98–99
   tourniquet devices, 100

soft tissue wound treatment, 103

solar cookers, 169–170

solar plexus, as target for attack, 196

solar power storage and recharging systems, 168

space, in the twenty-first century war, 2

Space Blanket, 60–61

SpamR, 162, 233

splinting
   methods, 111–115
   principles of, 111

stance and grip, Weaver, 207–208

staple food, 161
   coffee, 161, 162, 234
   milk, powdered or condensed, 233
   rice, 158, 160, 162, 233
   salt, 160
   sugar, 159, 162, 234

State Atlas Gazetteer, 127

State Defense Forces, 17